SORTING THE PRIORITIES

AMBASSADRESS AND BEAGLE SURVIVE DIPLOMACY

SANDRA ARAGONA

ISBN:1542733405
ISBN-13:9781542733403

DEDICATION

TO HIS EXCELLENCY.

FOR CENSURING SOME OF THE FACTS BUT PERMITTING THE FICTION.

CONTENTS

ACKNOWLEDGMENTS

To Candida, fellow writer and wife of Ambassador, who once arrived at an Embassy lunch with a book of my anecdotes which she had secretly had published for me. So much more enduring than a bunch of flowers.

And to Beagle, now at rest under an oak tree next to her beloved horses.

PREFACE

Spring 2004

We were back in Rome on a home posting when the phone rang, far too early, one Saturday morning. I rolled over and tried to go back to sleep while he dealt with it discreetly in the bathroom, but he was back almost at once.

"It was the Minister."

Yes. It usually was at that hour on a weekend. No home to go to? For once?

So where is war about to break out *this* time?

Not a million miles from where I was reclining, apparently.

"It seems he remembered that you were of British origin."

Well that's a first, anyway. Acknowledging the existence of The Wife and Family was never particularly high on their list of priorities. On the other hand....

Shit. What have I done now? Or had Italy decided to reclaim Chiantishire? Or accuse us of inciting a national insurrection by putting pineapple slices on our pizza?

"He wanted to know whether we might possibly be interested in a posting to London?"

I was out of bed and halfway down the corridor before he'd even reached the question mark.

"I'll go and pack," I said and even as I uttered the words, I could hear the removal lorries revving up their diesel engines and smell the cigarette smoke and see the piles of cardboard boxes and tissue paper blocking up the corridor. Again.

But then complete euphoria set in. It was, after all, rather splendid to be posted back to my home country after all those years of being an ex-pat. It was also rather satisfying to defy all those envious folk who were spied huddled in a corner at the magnificent farewell dinner given by the British Ambassador to Rome on the eve of our departure - folk who, I was later to learn, were bitchily discussing the demerits of sending, for the first time in the history of Italian diplomacy, an English wife to the Court of St James. "She'll go native" was the general opinion, pausing only to shoot me radiant smiles as I brushed past.

*   *   *   *

Event :Presentation of Credentials
Date :As informed by the Marshal of the Diplomatic Corps
Dress : Gentlemen: evening dress with decorations
Spouse:
Ladies :Day dress, hat and gloves

Spouse? You mean *me?* Like I exist? Like I get *invited?*

And there is even an apologetic addenda "The reason for different dress for Heads of Mission and spouses is that Heads of Mission are received in formal Audience for the presentation of their Credentials; spouses, as private citizens, are received in private Audience."

Do I care? No I do not. That will do fine by me. I'll turn up in jodhpurs and hacking jacket if you like. Just send the horse and carriage, and I'll be on the doorstep, behatted, begloved and feeling beloved.

OK, it was freezing cold and the slanting sleet was coming straight through the top one third of the carriage window, but the Queen's household had thought of everything and sent not only a rug but even a couple of hot water bottles bearing the royal coat of arms.

The Marshal of the Diplomatic Corps dismounted from his carriage and, sword gleaming, swept into the Embassy to collect us with tricorne tucked elegantly under one arm. Teetering less elegantly on uncontrollably high heels, I swept out behind him and clambered with as much grace as I could muster under the circumstances into the coach. Despite the inclement weather, half of Grosvenor Square and all of Beagle's disreputable friends and their owners were out there enjoying the sight of the gleaming carriages, the snorting horses pawing at the ground impatient to be off, the coachmen in their splendid livery and the elegant Rolls Royce which always brings up the rear on these occasions just in case. We clip-clopped away, on time to the second – no mean achievement for the Italian Ambassador whose interpretation of time is fluid to the extreme.

We clop-clipped up the Mall and through the gates to Buckingham Palace. Mistaking us for royalty, a horde of smiling Japanese tourists pressed their digital cameras to the carriage windows, clicking away furiously. I smiled my most regal smile and wished I could hear their interpretation of events and explanations of those photos once they were back in Tokyo.

"On arrival at the Palace the carriages draw up at the Grand Entrance, where you will be met by the Equerry and the Lady-in-Waiting." Paying great attention to heels and hat, I emerged somewhat in the manner of a cork from a bottle and proceeded up the stairs and along the corridors to the Bow Room.

"The Marshal will escort you through the door. Curtsey, Walk towards the Queen and curtsey. When the Audience is over, curtsey again, turn inwards and walk back towards the door. Turn inwards again, curtsey and leave the room." Four curtseys in all.

Did it! You could hardly go wrong – cocooned by centuries of court ceremony and Royal charm we swept out on a cloud and made our way back to the waiting coaches and, yesssss, they were right - I think I might go native as prophesied.

I had earned it, after all.

PART ONE

ROME

CHAPTER ONE

Rome, Summer, 1993

The noonday sun shone unhelpfully on a mess of discarded wrapping paper, straw and broken crates scattered around the entrance to the building. The trail continued across the main hall, along a corridor and in through the open door of a ground floor flat where it came up against a solid wall of stacked cartons. There was no way in and no way out. Somewhere inside this cardboard city an imprisoned radio was entertaining itself in excited Italian, thrilled to be back home. Beyond the disembodied voice, a precariously towering pile of bed linen waited to be assigned to a cupboard. A torrent of impressively evocative oaths in picturesque Roman dialect coming from the direction of the bedrooms indicated, presumably, yet another victim of the flat pack wardrobe. From the kitchen there floated the unmistakable odour of burnt coffee and melting percolator handle which seemed, fortunately, to be dissuading the mosquitoes from bringing their relatives inside to hunt for a liquid lunch.

"Has anybody seen that damn beagle?"
It was my fourth move, but the first with a puppy helping. An entirely different set of circumstances.

"No, but the removal man is complaining he's lost his little handbag."

We were both pretty stressed out, but all the same my younger daughter's replies weren't making much sense. Was she on drugs? I couldn't deal with drugs *and* a move. *Please*, Lord.

"Sorry?"

"This is Italy, remember? Men *do* handbags. Car keys, cigarettes, portable phone – their trousers are too tight to put anything in the pockets and saggy jackets aren't sexy. Anyway he's lost it, and that smacks very suspiciously of Beagle to my mind."

"Well, see if you can find where it went. Try the garden."

"The what?"

"It will be, one day." No imagination, the younger generation. Perhaps that's why they turned to drugs. No no no. Insert head in hand immediately. Go away.

"Firstly, if Beagle *has* buried bag and phone out in that jungle, your chances of ever finding them again are pretty low: secondly, if we do find phone and fags, even less work will get done, so if you ask me, she just did everyone a favour."

Good logic. We may just be in time to save her. On the other hand, it won't get the bloody handbag back.

"Please, Alex. Before we get sued by the removers for chewing their lines of communication. Seek. Please. I'll start cooking some lunch to distract them while you're hunting. I'm starving and exhausted and we've hardly made any progress at all this morning. Why isn't your father ever around on these occasions? Why does he invariably have a Mega International Crisis every time we move house, so that much to his eternal regret, he cannot possibly leave the office until the last sock and shirt are correctly positioned in their respective drawers? Alex, where am I going to put all this stuff? Have you *seen* what's out in the hall waiting to get in?"

I tripped over a pile of boxes and swore softly but undiplomatically.

"Not to mention what's still on the lorry – I just popped out to have a look. If I were you, I'd stick it straight back on the van and put it all into storage until your next posting abroad where you might possibly *need* two dozen asparagus tweezers and vases for three foot six hollyhocks."

"That's another thing. Alex – where *is* that lorry? Don't tell me they managed to get it down this glorified alleyway?"

"Of course they didn't. It's parked up on the main road, and they are more or less bringing your precious possessions down by mule. Anorexic mule, at that. And the mutterings amongst your friendly Italian removal men as overheard on my way past were to the effect that it'll cost yer.

They reckon everyone else in this street must have brought their furniture in first and then built their apartments around it. It *is* rather narrow, even by Roman standards. Oh, and the lorry in question, you'll be pleased to hear, is surrounded by a swarm of police and men from the Ministry of Finance."

"*Now* what?"

"As far as I could make out, there seems to be a great deal of excitement over a certain motor scooter mixed up with all the furniture. They don't like the look of its documents."

How dare they! My Saviour! My Scooter! The only possible way of getting from A to B in Rome without ingesting tranquillisers on an hourly basis.

"There's absolutely nothing wrong with its documents except that they're in Japanese, which I concede might just be beyond the scope of your average Roman cop. Tell you what, if you can persuade someone to roll it carefully down the hill, I will personally volunteer to go and buy pizza."

"Mmm. It's a bit more complicated than that. You see, until it has passed its road test, its little wheels aren't allowed to touch hallowed Roman soil."

Splendid.

"And where do we have to take it, pray, for this entertaining ceremony?"

"San Giovanni."

"SAN GIOVANNI? You practically need a passport to get to San Giovanni. It's right the other side of town! How the hell am I supposed to get it over there – Hertz Rent a Stork?"

"Probably. I'll go for the pizza – anything else we need?"

I sat down on a packing case as if to consider, but the obvious solution was already dancing before my eyes.

"Yes – a bottle of something not-necessarily-vintage. I feel I'm going to need it."

"If you promise not to make it a habit like the rest of all the Dip. Wives, I will."

I raised my eyes to the newly painted ceiling.

"Of course I won't promise any such thing. Don't be so cheeky. It already *is* a habit. But if it bothers you,

I'll promise to give it up completely just as soon as this move is over."

"What, and have you going all righteous and virtuous like when you gave up smoking? No thanks – I couldn't go through that again. Keep *some* vices at least."

"If you insist. Make that two bottles, then. We'll need one for tonight."

"No we won't: Papa's going to take us out to a restaurant. He says he'll need to unwind after his very stressful day back at the Foreign Office."

CHAPTER TWO

Rome, September 10th

Dear Mother   Here we are back in Rome. Not counting various evictions from bed-sitters during my student days, this was my fourth. Back, like I said, in Rome, we are experiencing the forgotten delights of living in an apartment underneath a family of insomniacs and I am looking for a job. Whilst I appreciate that at my advanced age and with my rusted qualifications, this will not be an easy task, the alternative is too gross to contemplate. Awaiting another foreign posting surrounded by a bunch of Italian housewives debating the best way to make tomato sauce or tiramisu, lose weight or select an aubergine, is not my idea of carping the diem. Sitting in an office pretending to be hyperactive must surely be less demanding.

Watch this space.

Love,   Sarah

Within a week I had found a job. The first day in an office after eight years of being an unemployed diplomatic wife was a revelation. I staggered into the flat under the weight of a raw ham which a grateful patient had thoughtfully presented to one of the doctors for whom I was now working. Eight years of easy living, albeit in places like Nigeria, and suddenly one was expected to become maid, cook, gardener, and wage-earner overnight. And butcher. None too efficiently, I applied myself to the task of removing the bone from the ham, wishing I had taken instruction in basic anatomy from the doctor in question before accepting the gift so eagerly.

Half an hour later, I was still struggling. It had been a bad day all round. A large part of it had been spent trying to conceal the fact that I was computer, fax and dictaphone illiterate and now it appeared that my culinary skills were rubbish too. The phone rang as I was debating whether I had time to nip out and buy an electric slicer which might just turn the mass of dead flesh before me into something edible.

"What's for dinner?"

"Giorgio, I'm not hearing this. I just spent an agonising day trying to fight my way back into the job market, cranking up what's left of the memory after overfilling it with worthless information (mostly names and titles) for the past eight years, and when I succeed in snatching employment from under the noses of a dozen dolly birds half my age and eminently more qualified than I could ever be, he asks me what's for dinner? Not: "Darling, I've been worrying about you all day, how did it go?" Just what's for bloody dinner. Perks is what's for dinner. Porky perks, to be precise, but that'll be beyond your command of my native tongue. Hallo? HALLO?"

"One momento, please. Your 'usband was called away to speak to the Secretary General on ze ozzer line. I put you on 'old."

Like 'ell you will, I thought, slamming the phone down and returning to the 'am. Come back Dieudonné, our aptly named God-given Beninois cook who had worked for us in Lagos, who could throttle a chicken with his bare hands and turn it into a fricassee in twenty minutes flat. Who on one occasion, admittedly, had appeared at table with blood stains all down his beautiful white uniform, having just separated two of his wives who were intent upon killing each other between courses. Who could squash giant cockroaches with his bare feet but would roll the whites of his eyes, freeze rigid and face Mecca in a thunderstorm. Who came to us soon after I had arrived in Africa, shaking, eyes tightly shut, muttering that whilst he personally had seen nothing, if I would kindly take a walk to the end of the garden where the edge of the lagoon lapped gently against the coarse grass.... and when I had obliged, and seen the bloated greying body which the tide had just washed up, had eventually been persuaded to take a pole and push it gently beyond the next bend in the creek where it would become someone else's responsibility. All this with his eyes still tightly closed so that he could tell the authorities in all honesty that he had seen nothing should they haul him in for questioning.

"You see, you guilty," he had explained. It was as simple as that.

At least the dreaded move was now over – going back to living in a tiny Roman flat after those residences abroad was always a culture shock of the first order. Most of the furniture we had painstakingly acquired in order to fill them had gone straight into storage, as Alex had suggested.

The very unfashionable street where we now lived on the outskirts of Rome had achieved notoriety in the seventies for having harboured a well-known politician, Aldo Moro, during the time he had been kidnapped by the Red Brigades. It had continued to sink into a steady decline and was now a haven to prostitutes, transsexuals, illegal immigrants living six to a room on shift systems, to drug addicts, pushers and sundry other shady characters, all of whom kept the most peculiar hours. I could only hope that no burglar in his right mind would dare to exert his paltry trade amongst this collection of cut-throats. Even by Roman standards it was an art to get a car up or down and required such high precision manoeuvring that Giorgio's driver had been instructed to take a couple of dummy runs to see if he could manage it without lopping off all the wing mirrors from the parked cars to left and right.

The ham had been persuaded to lie in petal formation on a serving dish and was being surrounded by slices of ripe melon just as our elder daughter Francesca arrived, exhausted after a day of earning herself pocket money from a temporary job at one of the Arab Embassies.

"Hallo there. How was your day?"

"Pretty foul. Yours?"

"Complete migraine. First day back at work after eight years absence tends to take a toll. People don't use pens and paper any more, have you noticed? This dead pig didn't help much either. Frankie, how *do* you operate a fax machine and a word processor and a dictaphone with foot pedals and things?"

"You don't: the secret is to delegate. You have to have a real secretary to help you, and then you do the intellectual stuff like translating documents or standing around looking decorative in three languages. What's for dinner? I'm supposed to be going to the cinema at nine – can I eat before you lot? Do you know what my Ambassador said today when I got into work? He said 'Who the hell is this Giacomini person with a name like yours who is refusing to grant me audience at the Foreign Office? He thinks he is Allah, or what?' I nearly died. If he ever finds out Papa practically *is* God in the F.O. he'll sack me on the spot."

"Not if you play your cards right, he won't. I wonder what an audience with Himself is worth on the open market? Nice little pre-Christmas bonus would go down a treat. Now tell me, please: how do I learn to operate a computer in twenty-four hours? I think I'm going to have a senior moment of epic proportions. I'm too OLD to learn all this technical stuff. I mean, there are days when the washing machine defeats me."

"Of course you can do it – have you got any dishy doctors to work for?"

"One macho Italian breathing down the phone wanting to know what's for dinner is about as much as I can handle at the moment. So be nice to me – my ego is feeling particularly vulnerable this evening. As if the threat of all this user-unfriendly machinery hovering over my head wasn't enough, I was Put On Hold by your Father's secretary. Whilst in Full Flow.

I'll bet where you've just come from that would justify a dollop of I divorce you, I divorce you, I divorce you, and all over bar who gets custody of the beagle."

"Well that would be a no contest, at any rate. You know Papa can't stand anything that gets mud on its feet and doesn't wash its paws before eating. Which reminds me, where *is* Alex?"

"Your little sister stayed on at school to use the library books for a project she is researching. Global warming in Tashkent or something."

"And you swallowed that? God Almighty, you are in a bad way. I wonder which of her spotty classmates is researching with her. Still, they can't get up to much under the beady eyes of those nuns, I suppose. When I was her age, though, you'd have been up at the school gates with a crowbar and a chastity belt."

"And a fat lot of good it did either of us, if I may make so bold. Who are you going to the cinema with, if I dare ask?"

"Usual bunch. No need for crowbars. The phone's ringing, I'll get it."

"If it's your father, tell him I left a tapioca pudding in the oven just before running away with my Indian guru. I'm getting into a bath, if you need to borrow anything."

A bath. Hot transparent water. It still seemed like a miracle. In Nigeria even Ambassadors used to go visiting around aperitif time with a bar of soap and a towel under one arm, trying to find a fortunate friend who could offer them a shower. Our house had boasted three magnificent bathrooms all equipped with superb Italian ceramic tiles and state of the art Jacuzzis. Yet every drop of water had to be purchased at vast expense from lorry drivers who would slurp the stuff out of the gutters and sell it back to us at exorbitant prices. On a good day it was the colour of cold tea. On bad days it defied description.

A face appeared around the door, cutting through the memories.

"He says 'whatta issa thissa tapioca?' and he doesn't want to eat any Indian goo. Also he wishes you to know that he is leaving the office NOW. Shall I unroll the red carpet down Via Gradoli or will you? You know, this flat wouldn't be so bad if we each had a separate bathroom – why don't you re-design it in your free time? On your new office computer? Are you going to be much longer in here? I need to wash my hair before I go out."

Skulking beneath the bubbles, I wondered whether to laugh or cry, and upon emerging, opted instead for a very large glass of vino bianco. Chilled.

CHAPTER THREE

As if moving house, starting a new job, administering to the needs of a demanding husband, helping the girls to settle in, picking up old friendships and trying to make new ones were not enough to occupy my time, there were several official events to attend in honour of visiting Ministers and their delegations, and the usual dinner parties in honour of any old excuse whatsoever. One such joyous event – to congratulate some newly appointed Italian Ambassador – took place in a rather elegant Sardinian restaurant in the heart of Rome's chic residential area – the Parioli. The restaurant was, in fact, filled with the local Pariolina fauna – the male of the species instantly recognisable by the portable phone clamped to his ear, the female by her consequent air of ennui and by the long dyed blonde hair straggling over the shoulders of her mink coat. Custom decreed that the long hair was only cut shorter when the wearer was well into her seventies, and the mink was abandoned with regret around mid-June.

I made my way over to the table reserved for the new Ambassador, found my place, and began to listen to the Sardinian waiter holding forth in great detail about the freshness of his fish and the versatility of his chef. The choosing of the menu is always an interminable process in Italy, and on this occasion was not helped by the inevitable prima donna amongst the guests describing, in some detail, her allergy to fish. I thought back almost with longing to my boarding school days where one ate what was on one's plate with no comment – indeed to comment on the food at all was considered the height of bad manners. Eventually the conversation turned to more important matters, and slowly I began to understand that the newly appointed Ambassador had been chosen for his obvious willingness to take care of the private commercial interests of Someone in the Government. No one seemed the least embarrassed by this revelation: on the contrary, the special relationship with the Minister in question appeared to be a source of pride. Fortunately the fish was excellent. Two other guests at the table spent the evening congratulating each other at nauseous length over their Andy Warhol minutes of fame when they had once succeeded in persuading no less a personage than Chancellor Kohl himself to change a semi-colon during the pre-Maastricht discussions.

The obsequious waiter began extolling the virtues of Sardinian cheeses. So far as I could follow this panegyric, it seemed that the quality of the product was evaluated according to the density of the worm colonies inhabiting it at the time of consumption. Your true connoisseur would chase the little beasts across the tablecloth and endeavour to scoop them back on to his cracker before they escaped amongst the toothpicks. But I concede that something might possibly have got lost in translation as a result of the man's thick Sardinian accent.

I made a mental note to check it with Giorgio later that evening. Meanwhile my neighbours to left and right were continuing a debate in which both had participated on a recent television show. This immediately ruined my chances of asking either of them who the hell they were. One does not ask a Television Personality, one of whom, I perceived, was being addressed as "Excellency" by all present, what he did for a living. I would just have to bluff it out with my customary uncontroversial conversation and hope for the best. I only wished I could think of a way to make him understand that whilst I had no desire to endanger my husband's chances for promotion, the encroaching leg was not welcome, Excellent or not. I flashed him a bright smile to show it was nothing personal and applied my attention to the cheese, watching very closely for the least sign of movement.

*   *   *   *

"Giorgio?"

"Uh!"

"Did you enjoy that dinner?"

"Excellent fish; very fresh. They have it sent across from Sardinia every morning."

"That's not what I meant. I want to know whether you liked those people, whether you could bear to be stranded on a desert island with them. Whether you are happy at the prospect of spending the rest of your life with people like that. Whether you consider them as intelligent as they consider themselves.

Whether you don't sometimes wake in the middle of the night and wish you'd become a brain surgeon or a missionary to a leper colony or something. Do you ever?"

"Of course not. Fish is awful in leper colonies. Not fresh at all. Very dangerous."

I realised the conversation was doomed to failure, and that in any case intelligence, in his view, was exclusively the expression of an opinion in total agreement with his own. Preferably at full volume. Anybody expressing a contrary opinion was automatically classified as a cretin.

"So you never have even a niggling little doubt that diplomacy is at best a hollow superficial pastime and at worst downright corrupt?"

"What? I'm shocked!"

"Not enough to put the newspaper down, I notice. I thought you were paid to read it in the office?"

"I can't imagine where you get your information."

"Certainly not from you, dear. I never see you long enough to get a complete sentence out of you."

"If you made the effort to talk to me in your wonderful Italian at such a late hour, you might have more success. I'm too tired to speak a foreign language at this time of night."

That was how we had met, of course. I was pretending to know enough Italian to translate some projects which had been submitted for the prospective bridge (or tunnel – they still hadn't decided which option to back in those days) between Messina and the mainland. It was love at first sight – anything seemed a better option than spending the rest of my days reading about elliptical thingummies, trusses, polyurethane resin, and two span partly submerged whatsits. Even marrying a diplomat. I was out of my linguistic depth and floundering, but nobody noticed. On the contrary, they thought I was highly talented. So did Giorgio when he found out how much they were paying me. Money for fibre-glass jam. I went right off seismic problems and static or dynamic experimentations, though, for a bit. So did the rest of the country, presumably, for, forty years later, they still haven't succeeded in building the famous bridge.

"And how do you suppose I've been feeling all evening between Sardinian waiters and aspiring T.V. Personalities of the Year? I didn't notice any of your compatriots giving me a break at the end of a long day."

"We've been through all this before. As the wife of an Italian diplomat, you represent my country. Impeccably. But in the Italian language. Please."

"Vai al diavolo. And another thing. Why don't you speak English with a vowel at the end of each word like your daughters pretend you do? I might even remember to speak Italian to you if you did."

"Mamma mia – whata lengtha I 'ave to go to for piece of quiet."

"Peace and quiet. Was it true about the worms?"

"Very gooda cheese. Very gooda fish. Come-a closer. Tomorrow what you cooka me?"

With a sigh, I resigned myself to the fact that there would only ever be two ways to a man's heart. And one of those would always be through the stomach.

Luckily for my self-esteem, there was Michael.

We had met at a dinner given by the British Ambassador for some Italian Eurocrat. I had been placed between a boring but important Italian politician on my right and Michael on my left. By the end of the first course, I had more or less exhausted my limited knowledge of the merits and demerits of a two party system in any future government of my adopted country, and noted with relief that the politician in question had been duly snared by our hostess on his right.

"Turn with the fish," I muttered out of the left side of my mouth.

"Pardon?" He squinted surreptitiously at the place card, noting the name "Giacomini" and thinking he must have misheard.

"Turn with the fish. Like they taught us at boarding school. Impolite to commandeer or be commandeered at table for more than one course. Got to change sides every now and then. Like the Italians in the war."

Damn. I'll get lynched.

"Pretend you didn't hear that last bit."

He concentrated on his plate for a second, frowning slightly.

"Shouldn't be allowed, respectable Brits spouting all these foreign languages. I thought you were Italian the way you were chattering on all through the soup. I'd prepared my Bella Italia routine. Now I'll have to rethink my whole plan of attack. Also, as you've just made abundantly clear, I've only got to the end of this salmon and chip to make my indelible mark before you swivel off again."

"Most people do. Most non-Italians, that is. But I can do you both verses of God Save the Queen on a good day, and quote the twenty-third psalm from start to finish. If you're not careful. So there's your proof. Italians never read the Bible – they reckon they don't need to. Just having the Pope so close at hand gives them this special relationship with God."

Mind you, I thought, Miss Peabody, terrifying headmistress of the boarding school where I had passed my formative years, had claimed a special relationship with God, too. And look where that had got her. Ended her days living in so-called sin in St. Leonards on Sea with that other old bat the History Mistress, so I'd been told. The school had proclaimed itself to be an Anglican establishment for the educating of young ladies, and the laying on of guilt was one of its more successful achievements. One of the fastest routes to hell, I remembered as I reluctantly turned away from my English neighbour and back to the politician, had been to leave a gap in the conversation at table. Controversial subjects were taboo – not that we knew of any, given that newspapers, television and radio were forbidden, and contact with the outside world was minimal. On Sundays we talked about the sermon – exclusively.

On Saturdays, it was the school's performance in the weekly lacrosse match. Tuesdays we were only permitted to speak French. Privately we thanked the Lord in our prayers for the ever-changing English weather.

"They say," I confided to the politician on my right who aspired to be something important in the next government, and whose anxiety whilst he awaited The Call was rendering him virtually monosyllabic, "they say it's going to be an unusually cold winter."

As the speeches wound to a close with the usual applause and raised glasses, I dragged myself back to the present and became aware of a melting pool of ice cream on my plate.

"Why do they do that, do you suppose?"

Michael waited.

"I mean, serve an elaborate dessert which some poor sod has most probably been slaving over for the best part of a day, and then hammer away at the Stuart Crystal for attention so that we all have to down tools and pretend the last thing on earth we wanted to do was to actually eat the bloody stuff. By the time they've finished telling each other how wonderful they are, you need a straw." I pushed the pool around my plate unenthusiastically and reflected I had just broken two of Miss Peabody's golden rules in one sentence: talking about the food and using bad language. I glanced up at him, but he was grinning with delight.

"You did it," he said, with evident relief. "Turned, I mean. I wasn't sure you'd make it."

There was a moment of unease as people looked anxiously up and down the table hoping to see ashtrays but finding none. The politician lit up regardless, perfectly happy to flick his ash into the melting ice cream if and when that should prove necessary. Gradually, packets of cigarettes appeared as the die-hards recognised fellow spirits and the waiters began distributing minute silver receptacles designed to limit the damage to one cigarette per sinner. The British Ambassadress shot a look at her husband as if to seek forgiveness for being so politically incorrect, but he was deep in conversation with Mrs. Italian Politician, whose excessive verbosity more than compensated for her husband's preoccupied taciturnity.

Edging away from the smoke, I faked an asthmatic wheeze and half turned my back on the man who was to become the Minister of Something Important that very night. He didn't even notice, of course, but Michael raised an eyebrow.

"Unless I'm very much mistaken," he remarked to the ceiling, "Body language was not on your boarding school's curriculum." He had absolutely beautiful hands, I thought incongruously. And a voice that came from the depths of some dark cave and had the effect of twanging every nerve in the body. I pushed my champagne glass away and vowed to stick to mineral water for the rest of the evening.

"Listen," I said sweetly, "I have sung for my supper in two languages throughout this meal. I have sung for my adopted country throughout courses one and three in the face of considerable opposition. Now I am entitled to breathe the air of my choosing, and the air of my choosing," I added, as a scraping of chairs signalled a move towards the lounge for coffee, "is over in that far corner by the open window, preferably unaccompanied by anyone with a cigarette or a tendency to add superfluous vowels to the end of each word."

The Italian got his Ministry and feigned not to recognise me next time we met, whereas Michael – well, Michael turned out to be an enigma. Little did we know it at the time but he was to play a bigger part than anyone could have imagined in our lives.

CHAPTER FOUR

Rome, October 7th

Dear Mother,

Life in Via Gradoli has been considerably quieter since a bunch of the illegals spent last Sunday night knifing each other all down the street. Dead bodies were carted off around 2.30 a.m. according to the next morning's papers, or roughly around the time Giorgio got out of bed to go to the bathroom and refused to call the cops despite my muffled exhortations issuing from beneath the bedclothes. Said it was just the ethnics having a party and I was showing racial intolerance. Some party – seems they got into a fight about who had territorial rights over which set of traffic lights: you may remember that you cannot stop at a red light in Rome without being coerced into either having your windscreen washed or buying cigarette lighters and paper handkerchiefs you didn't want in the first place. Those as were still alive at the end of the "party" were hiked off to prison, and the decibel level has been considerably more acceptable ever since.

Just off for a couple of days in the country.

Call you next week. Love, Sarah

Exhausted by the move, the new job and generally re-adapting to life back in Italy, we had decided to escape to Tuscany for the weekend. Giorgio was just back from a mission with his Foreign Minister and in need of a break, the girls were old enough to look after themselves and with any luck the dog might get enough exercise chasing rabbits to keep her quiet through till Tuesday.

So, stuffing a recalcitrant beagle into the back of the car, we set off to visit some English friends, Julia and Anthony, who had retired some years back to a picturesque village in "Chiantishire" and who, like so many of their compatriots living nearby, had learnt not one word of the Italian language in all the time they had been living there. The fact that this little deficiency inevitably added ten percent to all their bills in and around the village of Greve, (or "Gravy" as they insisted upon calling it), worried them not at all. Sipping wine on the open loggia of the converted farmhouse, we feasted our eyes on the scene below: the rolling Tuscan hills, the neat rows of vineyards, the dramatic dark green of the cypress trees mingling with the lighter green of the umbrella pines. Before leaving for our last posting, we had spent a memorable weekend here helping to pick and tread the grapes together with a houseful of English friends who had come over especially for the occasion. Arriving from Rome on that occasion, it was already clear just which of the invited guests had any intention of making themselves useful, and which had only flown over for some dedicated imbibing under the early autumn sun. Some of Anthony's cronies from his Oxford days had already set up a makeshift bar under an olive tree, and were busy tasting a random selection from earlier harvestings. Passing them on my way to procure the necessary basket and scissors, I had overheard snatches from a quasi-serious conversation as they sniffed and sipped the rough red Chianti wines.

"No nose, old chap, no nose at all. That's the trouble with these amateurs. Fellow like Anthony comes out here, thinks he'll retire gracefully, do a bit of gardening, dabble on the stock exchange. Julia sees herself stuffing lavender bags and cooking fragrant legs of lamb in home-grown rosemary – you know how it is. Next thing you know, she's writing a book on Tuscan cooking full of garishly coloured photos of the sort of food no self-respecting pub would even dream of serving, and he's squashing olives and grapes and thinks he's Signor Bloody Antinori. Nothing wrong with the stuff, mind you, and please don't think I'm being unappreciative of our host's generosity, but I just hate to think what it's doing to the lining of my stomach."

"Don't be ridiculous, Charles, your stomach hasn't had a lining for at least twenty years. Wouldn't be room for one, for a start. Try a little of this bottle, instead. I think you might find it rather amusing."

There was a moment of silence as they swirled and slurped and settled back in their deck chairs to contemplate the cloudless blue sky before pronouncing judgement.

"More than amusing, I'd say. Hilarious, old boy, perfectly hilarious. By the way – where are the ladies?"

"In the pool, most of them. Some are doing the straw Panama bit amongst the vines. You don't think we should go and make a gesture, do you? Snip the odd grape, that sort of thing? I do believe that's what one was invited for, come to think of it."

"Nonsense. Old Anthony's got all these herds of willing peasants out there to do it for him. It's just an excuse for a jolly booze up, this grape harvesting business, you know. Now don't go and show your ignorance by offering to help. They'll think it's your first time around. Also you have to tread the horrible gunk afterwards, so it's better to be pissed rigid for that little caper. Pretty disgusting, all things considered. Makes you wish you'd never touched the stuff. Too late by then, of course."

"*Must* you, Charles? I do believe this one has a hint of corn plaster in the bouquet. Perhaps I'll have a lie-down until lunchtime."

Treading the grapes with a bunch of my compatriots had admittedly been somewhat revolting. Before the treading, the men had been largely resplendent in those short grey nylon ankle socks so beloved of the British male. Over these, in deference to Being Abroad under the Italian sun, they wore the infamous open sandal, displaying as always, the requisite amount of white hairy leg betwixt sock top and trouser bottom. The women were equally attractive though without the socks and (mostly) slightly less hairy. Eventual removal of footwear did nothing to enhance the situation. After everyone had partaken of an excellent lunch unlikely to have been served, as Charles had so astutely commented, in any English pub, they had all proceeded in unruly fashion to the old barn. Here vast tubs of freshly picked grapes awaited the onslaught. A token plastic basin of water was provided for everyone to rinse their feet, but by this stage nobody was over-concerned about stuffy British manias for hygiene. They trod, with somewhat uncertain gait, until the cool grapes became warmer and warmer as they squelched up between their toes and over their ankles. The comments as they pounded up and down in the tubs were memorable.

"It all gets sterilised, you know, as soon as the fermentation process begins."

"Bit of toe-nail dirt never did any harm to an honest little Chianti. Adds flavour."

"Chateau de Pied de Charles – can't beat it."

"I don't think I want to come back next year to drink this little lot – Amanda's got the most horrendous verruca."

"Do you suppose I should have removed my nail varnish?"

"It's terribly therapeutic, you know. Cures Athlete's Foot instantly."

The chances of our being offered the verruca vintage this year were thus pretty high.

Anthony was pottering around the gravel drive as we drove up and greeted us with enthusiasm.

"Good show. Right on time. Fantastic year for the grapes. Come and see. Gloves and scissors await."

We followed him down the path towards the vineyard as he kept up a constant stream of social and vinicultural chatter.

" Half a dozen diehards got here last night and have been at it since dawn.

Consume as much as they snip, of course, but that's all part of the fun. Some of the buggers only show up for the bean-feast afterwards anyway. Chap here from the Embassy trying to claim immunity for being left-handed. Says he can't manage our clippers. Now that's one I haven't heard before. Top marks for originality, I reckon. I sent him orff to do some press ups."

He stopped dead in his tracks as a thought struck him.

"I say, you don't want a game of tennis either of you, by any chance?"

Giorgio shook his head vigorously. No, he most definitely did not want a game of tennis which would keep him tied to a court for at least an hour with no excuse to read the morning papers. In amongst the vines, he reckoned he could get away with pleading a back ache or a telephone call after about twenty minutes of showing willing.

Anthony turned and looked me up and down as if considering whether it was worth ruining his reputation as impeccable host to partner a fit left-handed sportsman with a mere supporting member of the diplomatic cast. He weighed up the pros and cons.

"How about you, Sarah? Julia can lend you some gear. Fancy giving him a game or two?"

"Giving" he'd said. As in "on a plate." On the other hand, a bit of exercise before the gastronomic onslaught might not be such a bad idea and if the competition was just a diplomat having difficulty with his D.J. buttons because of a middle aged paunch brought on by an excess of eating and drinking...

"Well..."

"Right. Julia's in the kitchen. Get her to lend you some togs. Splendid. Keep him from under the feet of the ladies, too. Positive liability. When in Rome, I suppose. Clearly been here too long. What size shoes do you take?"

I told him.

"Not a problem. Grass court. You can play in bare feet. Just sluice them off a bit before you start treading the grapes."

Ten minutes later I was heading for the tennis courts where, from a distance, I could already see the outline of someone jogging half-heartedly around the perimeter whilst simultaneously conducting an animated conversation on his mobile phone. No paunch as far as I could see and clearly a strong respiratory system. I began to have doubts. The prospect of a gentle snipping of grape followed by a slightly more vigorous imbibing of Vin de Verrue suddenly seemed rather attractive. Without so much as turning around or breaking his rhythm, my unknown opponent called back over one shoulder.

"God, you're late. I could have had an extra hour in bed this morning. What kept you?"

I was nonplussed.

"Michael? Did you know we were coming, then?"

"Of course I did. Checked the guest list before I accepted. Where are your shoes? You can't walk along Tuscan lanes barefoot."

"I thought I was supposed to be performing a public service keeping you off the ladies' backs by playing tennis with you."

"What on this court? No way. Might be all right for a round of mini golf. Go and get some shoes on and we'll clear off till lunchtime. Nobody will know."

I took one look at his calf muscles and decided that a country walk was most probably the lesser of the two evils. Also I could hear Beagle in the distance trying to claw her way out of the car to the detriment of any remaining leather upholstery. I obeyed orders and went back for hound and shoes.

Beagle had a glorious time playing her Dog of the Manor role, putting the family cat in its rightful place up the nearest tree, then disappearing off into the surrounding countryside in hot pursuit of imaginary game. Bearing in mind that cats and dogs are believed to have only seven lives in Italy – and who could dispute those statistics, seeing the way the inhabitants drive – this latter activity was not encouraged. We took her for a delightful walk through the country lanes, returning somewhat late for lunch and in need of some serious grooming, for Tuscan mud has a very high clay content and after heavy rain becomes decidedly non-Teflon in nature. Whilst it is thus ideal for the growing of the grape and the rose, it has to be said that the impression on the unsuspecting city-dweller is that he is ploughing through a field of porridge.
We contrived, innocently, to sit next to each other.

"Michael – are you really left-handed?"
"Ambidextrous. Best of both worlds. Keep it to yourself, though."

Right. I think I will.

Ten minutes of watching the others tread the grapes was quite enough for Giorgio and he soon suggested going for a walk instead and of course, always eager to please, I said I thought that was a lovely idea. As the mud clung ever more heavily to hound and husband, I could sense the first storm clouds of revolt gathering. Amidst dark mutterings, we eventually scraped ourselves off to the best of our ability and drove into Florence to nourish the soul and, later, the body.

CHAPTER FIVE

The daughters had frequented French Lycées all over the world. Swear words and endearments were always in French. Their friends were multilingual and multi-ethnic and the conversations around the Club swimming pool at weekends invariably vacillated between at least three languages at any given time. One of the best aspects of being back in Rome was, in fact, the Foreign Ministry Club. Situated on the banks of the river Tiber, it was an oasis of peace within the otherwise chaotic city. It boasted tennis courts, a gymnasium, a large swimming pool, rowing facilities, and manicured lawns upon which to lounge, study, work or just gossip. In addition it had two restaurants which in themselves epitomised the dual nature of the establishment. One was a more formal affair with waiter service, where retired Ambassadors and their wives gathered to reminisce over the good old days when you could still get the staff, and when it was permissible to coerce junior members of the Embassy into carrying out domestic tasks whenever necessary. The other was a self-service counter. It was here that my tennis-playing friends and I preferred to grab a rapid bite before dashing off for a quick game in our respective lunch-hours. It was here that I was joined by my younger daughter one Saturday morning.

"Why are you lurking in this corner? I couldn't find you anywhere. Thought for a minute you must be in the restaurant proper with all the wrinklies."

"Alex, do you mind not using that particular expression? I don't know at what age one qualifies for wrinkly status, but I have a strong suspicion I'm fast approaching it. I am lurking, as you put it, in an endeavour to commit a minimum of this computer handbook to memory (hollow wrinkly laughter) before Monday morning. How old *are* wrinklies, anyhow?"

"Don't worry: it's not so much the age as the attitude. You know, the little suits, brooches on the lapel, designer scarf round the neck, reading glasses on a chain. All that. Plus the boring conversation. 'Should one go to Cortina this summer? Its become so crowded, don't you think?' Or the cost of Filipinos, or their last bridge party. They're relics, for goodness sake."

I pushed my glasses deep into my handbag and reflectively tried to un-powder my nose.

"Just because my friends charge into the self-service, grab a sandwich and run out again so you think we are all leading full and rewarding lives, doesn't necessarily mean our brain cells aren't withering at a rate of knots too. I don't suppose our conversation would be any more edifying to your generation's ears were you to stop and listen to it."

"I have done, and it is. Last time I honoured you with my presence, there were three of you analysing the Pope's recent encyclical, someone else was tearing the latest piece of bureaucratic lunacy to shreds, and your lawyer friend was sitting over there in a corner going 'SELL! SELL! SELL!' into her cell phone as if the whole market was about to come crashing through the Clubhouse roof into her minestrone. Not a sound of anyone exchanging recipes for pasta al forno."

"So how would *you* know what they talk about in the restaurant? You've never even set foot in the place, to the best of my knowledge."

"Have, too. I was meaning to tell you. I took Riccardo in there for lunch that time you were in Tuscany. I put it on your account – you don't mind, do you?"

"Riccardo *who*?"

"MUMMY! That's just about the wrinkliest thing anyone could ask. How do I know what his surname is? My generation, as you call us, doesn't use surnames. But since you're obviously dying to know, yes, he used a knife and fork, and no, he doesn't have earrings, tattoos or a pony tail. Plus he is Caucasian and wore a tie. You have to in there – did you know? That nice waiter with the crinkly hair lent him one. And all you could hear were these relics talking about Grand Slams and Winter Breaks."

"And what, I wonder, were you two discussing? No, let me guess. Global warming in Tashkent, I'll bet. Some project, that. Or have you progressed to sheep farming in Outer Mongolia this week?"

"Very droll. You might possibly be saved from premature wrinkliness by your Breetish sense of 'umour. Which reminds me: can I go to Geneva with Nathalie for New Year's?"

"*Why* does it remind you? Where, if it's not too wrinkly a question, is our friend Riccardo spending New Year?"

"Under a clapped-out Fiat, probably, at his Dad's garage. He works jolly hard when he's not researching the Dalai Tala basins. You should see his fingernails. Old frizzy locks couldn't take his eyes off them: it seems there's no product on the market which can get rid of the grease."

"ALEX! Tell me you didn't take a motor mechanic into that restaurant with all those harpies adjusting their lorgnettes at you?"

"OK I didn't. But can I go to Geneva with Nathalie? Her Father is an Ambassador, Maman chérie, as I'm sure you know already. Did you ever think about taking up Bridge, by the way? The time might just have come."

Brat. Upon discreet enquiry, it transpired that the chances of the said Riccardo ever having been near a clapped-out Fiat, let alone underneath one, were highly unlikely, given that his Father owned a bank rather than a garage, and that the boy himself was followed around by a bodyguard for the major part of his waking hours.

CHAPTER SIX

Rome, January 5th

Dear Mother,

The family has now returned from their New Year celebrations. Francesca went to Vienna and came back highly enthusiastic. Alex went to Geneva and came back highly enthusiastic. Dog went to kennels and came back thoroughly unenthusiastic having caught kennel cough and small wonder since, as far as I could see, the establishment in question was heated by glow worms if at all. She is finally off the intravenous drips and injections which, with the usual Italian mania for needles, I had to learn to administer, and is now partaking of antibiotics orally. Equally, she is back to eating any old rubbish as opposed to chickens roasted on the spit with a garnish of mixed steamed vegetables. Yesterday she tried out her first bark, which rather surprised her since it came out a bit falsetto. Last but not least, Giorgio came back and caught the 'flu, so I had to contend with him under my feet in the kitchen, stirring things which didn't need stirring, whilst I was trying to create an elegant little sauce for a dinner party. He is now recovered and has returned to annoying the secretaries instead, which is a great improvement, all things considered.

I could have done without all this, of course, whilst

preparing for the visit of my mother-in-law, in whose honour I have been cleaning and scrubbing during my hard earned lunch hours ever since I returned. Though I don't know why I bother, since she travels with a Calabrian crone who is her companion/lady-in-waiting/general dogsbody and slave, and who, once she has finished installing her cardboard suitcase, jars of tomato purée and live hens, is supposed to lend a hand. House pride strikes at even the most intellectual of hearts, obviously.

More soon when, no doubt, I shall need to take refuge in letter writing as a means of avoiding the making of interminable conversation.

Love, Sarah

For the past forty years my mother-in-law had lived the life of a professional Sicilian widow, lamenting loudly and oft that she had been abandoned by God, fate, her husband and her son, and that she awaited with piety and joy her imminent demise. As the only male child of a Sicilian widow, Giorgio had been brought up with certain indisputable guidelines by which to abide. For a start, he had been sent to a Jesuit school – the nearest thing to an old boys' system Italy can produce. The Jesuits protect their own and teach discipline and respect for hierarchy. His early years and entry to University went without a hitch. Stage Two somewhat backfired upon her when he married a foreigner to protect him from his mother, who was once heard to mutter that had he at least chosen to marry a rich one, she could have protected him from his Bank Manager, too.

As time passed, we came to terms with each other, but there were some fraught moments during the early days.

Signora Giacomini talked incessantly – a habit the family found exhausting. We would all take it in turns to retire to the bathroom for respite, though this temporary refuge was constantly threatened as a result of her bidet fixation. Having noted from her infrequent trips abroad that this commodity was all too often a rarity in northern Europe, she had taken it upon herself when they were younger to forestall any potential neglect in her granddaughters' upbringing. Thus when the child finally managed to escape from her non-stop monologues and had retired behind a locked door, its peace would be shattered within two minutes by rattlings of the handle and raucous Sicilian tones inquiring as to whether Nonna might help by running the water for her bidet?

Maria, the Calabrian who accompanied her on her rare travels outside Sicily, was a distantly related, penniless spinster. Thinking to gain indulgences in heaven by performing an act of human charity, Signora Giacomini had taken Maria under her roof when it was clear that the latter's chances of ever finding a husband were finally extinct, and she used her mercilessly as cheap labour, confidante and fellow wailer when the occasion required. Good news not being of prime interest in the circles which they frequented, the wailing was in constant demand.

Signora Giacomini, or the Nobildonna as she was referred to in Sicily where exaggerated flattery is the order of the day, and where it is almost obligatory to invent a title for anyone unfortunate enough to be lacking one in their own right, had decided to pay us a visit in the New Year. The understanding was that we would then drive her back down to Sicily in order to see the other relatives who for some time had been making disapproving noises regarding the family's long absence from Sicilian shores. Brought up to be a realist in such matters, Giorgio had already calculated that given his relatives' need to compete with each other's generosity, this would hopefully solve the problem of everyone's spring wardrobe.

Maria arrived with a severe case of sciatica brought on by sleeping in extreme discomfort on the overnight train from Messina. To this she rapidly added the symptoms of a bad cold, and was persuaded to take to her bed for the first three days of their visit. Nonna sadly slipped on the bathroom floor soon after her arrival, and though apparently in no pain, had to be taken to the hospital for a couple of stitches in the middle of the night. I found myself playing cook and nursemaid as well as wage earner, wife and mother, and took to rising at 6 am in order to prepare lunch and dinner in advance for both family and invalids. The girls rallied round splendidly by dissuading their grandmother from wandering into the kitchen whilst I was slotting the prepared dishes into the unheard-of microwave. Already the arrival of the freezer in Sicily had created the biggest upheaval since the historic earthquake and the older generation of the Giacomini family was quite definitely unprepared for the concept of micro-waving pre-cooked pasta.

The trick was to sprinkle everything with lots of fresh parsley and slide it rapidly onto a beautiful serving dish, preferably one of the family heirlooms, which would then provide a subject for conversation well into the main course. I survived the week with difficulty, not helped by Giorgio's doubtless well-meaning assurances that the food served was ALL freshly home-made, including the tagliatelle, and that his wife would be delighted to provide Maria with her personal recipes just as soon as Maria was feeling fit enough to commit them to memory. The girls did not help by asking apparently innocent questions throughout each meal.

"Mummy, will you make your Soufflé Rothschild tomorrow?"

"No, the home-made lasagne, *please*! And some of those little bread rolls with the nuts I'll buy the fresh yeast for you on my way home from school, if you like."

The prospect of leaving for Sicily finally came as a welcome relief.

The drive down was fairly uneventful, except for a drama of mammoth proportions somewhere south of Naples when Giorgio realised he had left his mobile phone back in Rome. Nonna went into a major O Mamma Mia! Dio Santo! Siamo Rovinati! Che Disgrazia! routine with much renting of raiment and pulling of hair, which lasted for a good thirty kilometres until we conspired to reassure her that it was actually in everybody's interest to have a quiet weekend uninterrupted by annoying calls from the office. She subsequently kept up a flow of subliminal chatter all down the Autostrada del Sole until we reached Reggio Calabria.   Maria clutched at her rosary, not daring to lower her concentration lest an accident result from a single moment of inattention. Giorgio's contribution was the occasional grunt. After an hour or so, I claimed to be suffering from carsickness, took a pill and slid into a half-sleep interrupted by frequent stops for petrol, cups of coffee, lavatories and lunch. Each time we piled back into the car, I watched with fascination while the ceremony of the sign of the cross was renewed and wondered fleetingly whether I dare suggest that buckling up the despised seat belt would perhaps be more appropriate for warding off the evil eye. Upon arriving at Reggio Calabria, the need to take the ferryboat, thereby placing herself in the hands of someone other than her trusted Giorgio, sent Mamma into a frenzy of crossing, finger kissing, and frantic incantations to the deity and His Mother. That we eventually arrived safely was considered a miracle she had achieved single-handedly. With a little help from Maria, whom she had the grace to congratulate for her contribution in having selected the correct saint for the specific situation and for having said her prayers with the required devotion.

The aunts, as prophesied, insisted on buying clothes for everyone, (almost everyone: Giorgio opted for a new tennis racquet instead,) and in accordance with what had become the custom at some stage in every holiday, we made a last minute dash to the shops to purchase another suitcase. By the time this and a bulky selection of local produce had been stashed into the car, we bore a strong resemblance to a family of returning immigrants rather than that of a high ranking Civil Servant heading back to advise his Minister on urgent matters of Foreign Policy.

I was reflecting aloud on this matter just as the car hiccupped to a halt in the middle of the Calabrian mountains, with the result that I was immediately accused of having brought about the misfortune personally with my loose talk.   Fingers were extended and certain parts of the anatomy surreptitiously touched to protect them from a similar fate, (hiccupping to halts), whilst Giorgio disappeared under the bonnet to search, ostentatiously, for the cause of the trouble.

"What do you think he's looking for?"

"The engine, probably."

"At least he's got the right end for once. Do you think he knows what he's doing?"

"He's not *doing* anything, thank goodness. Just looking and saving macho face. In a minute he'll appear at the window and tell us it's the petrol supply."

"How do you know?"

"Been there already. Bet you both a couple of glossy mags from the next service station."

"Since when did you read glossies?"

"All right: if I win, you do the early morning Beagle run tomorrow."

"You're on. Shh! He's coming."

It appeared that the trouble was a fault in the petrol supply. Poor Giorgio had to hitchhike to the nearest mechanic in a truck driven rather erratically by a garlic-breathing shepherd accompanied by sixty-odd sheep. Pausing briefly to remove his tie (and wallet) before embarking, he headed off into the sunset leaving the rest of the family stranded in the heart of 'ndrangheta land without so much as a jewel between us to barter should the need arise.

"If they want a slice of ear, do you mind offering yours? - I'd hate never to wear earrings ever again."

"Don't be silly: they only slice ears when the family refuses to pay the ransom – oh, I see what you mean."

"Wouldn't you believe it? The one time in his life that stupid phone could have been useful. Where did he leave it, anyway?"

"In the bathroom, apparently. Seems it was the only place he could phone in peace without Nonna interrupting, so he nipped in there at midnight to call New York and forgot it in the basin."

"Best place for it in normal circumstances. Do you think he'll be long? I'm starving."

Giorgio finally returned some two hours later with a mechanic who proceeded to fuss around the car and request innumerable tools all of which were hidden under mountains of home-cured salamis, bottles of tomato purée, crates of lemons and the odd ceramic from Taormina which we had acquired over the weekend. During the course of the upheaval a couple of bottles of tomato sauce were smashed over the highway, occasioning horrified reactions from the occupants of passing cars convinced a dead body had only just been removed from the scene and that the group of survivors were acting most indecorously given the circumstances. Giorgio stopped pretending to demonstrate enlightened interest in the proceedings and pulled out a newspaper. After another hour or so it began to rain, slowly but very steadily, and a series of picturesque Calabrian oaths which would have sent Maria scuttling for her rosary, floated back from beneath the bonnet.

Eventually the mechanic straightened up and pronounced us cured. Giorgio lowered his newspaper and gingerly tried the ignition expecting at worst, an explosion, and at best, total silence from the engine. Miraculously the car started, and we headed north once more.

A general strike was called near Positano with a majority decision being taken to stop for a real Neopolitan pizza and to ditch all preceding good intentions of getting back to Rome at anything like a respectable hour.

CHAPTER SEVEN

"Hola!"

"Manuela! Where the hell have you been? I've been calling you for months!"

"Argentina. I went to Buenos Aires to see the family and sort of got stuck. Then a cousin was getting married, and then my parents were celebrating their fiftieth wedding anniversary, and after that it was Christmas and New Year, so what with one thing and another, I only just got back. How are you all?"

"Fine. Surviving – just. Fifty years! That's a lifetime!"

"I know. Do you think any of us will get that far?"

"Some of us might, but I don't rate your chances very highly, the way you carry on. What did you bring off the plane this time?"

"Ah, funny you should mention that. You see they upgraded me at the last minute to Magnificat, or whatever it's called these days. You do get a better class of pick-up in First, I have to admit. Stefano, his name was. Rather appetising."

I shuddered in anticipation.

"Not again! I don't think I want to know. I happen to be enormously fond of that long-suffering husband of yours. Where is he, by the way? Can you manage lunch? We could go to the Club so you can drive everyone wild with your suntan."

"Good idea. He's in Durban – shall I bring Stefano?"

"Not if he's anything like the last one, no.

All that jewellery and long hair curling over the shoulders had the wrinklies hyperventilating for a week."

"That's *their* problem – they shouldn't be so xenophobic. Argentines *wear* long hair and jewellery. Which reminds me: I went to the Malvinas whilst I was back home, so I thought of you."

"Falklands, Manu. Falklands. And well you might have – we didn't speak to each other for a month during that little episode. Our own personal Diplomatic Incident. How were Her Majesty's Sheep?"

"Blooming. Speaking of Dip. Incidents, perhaps lunch at the Club isn't such a good idea after all. I've been away so long I can't remember who all the important people are any more. I'm sure to get them mixed up – you know what I'm like. They should have a prize for the gaffe of the year, I might just win something, for once in my life."

She had a point. Somehow we brought out the worst in each other.

"You'd have some pretty stiff competition. Do you remember that time we grabbed a passing waiter at a Ministerial cocktail party and asked him where they were hiding all the Fizz? Only it was the Director General of Political Affairs dolled up in a D.J. on his way to some far more important party en smoking. Not amused, he wasn't."

"Don't remind me. Then there was that time you held forth about how absolutely brilliant the U.S. President's spokesman was. You waxed very eloquent, I remember. His sense of timing, political expertise, human warmth, impromptu sense of humour, ability to defuse the tensest of situations.

Not, you added, unable to let a good thing go, like our useless specimen who only got the job because Daddy knew someone in the Government."

"How was I to know I was sitting next to his Italian counterpart? He doesn't speak to me whenever we meet, these days. Which is often, because wherever there is free booze and a plethora of journalists, you can be sure to find him. Me too, unfortunately."

"How come we still haven't ruined our husbands' careers despite such total dedication, do you suppose?"

"Because we're foreigners. People expect us to be vague and eccentric. It reassures them when we live up to their idea of us. Also, it gives them something to talk about. The day after you or I hit a cocktail party, the phone lines fairly buzz with activity. How's the weight?"

"Terrible, but I started this great new diet this morning."

Of course. Monday. You always knew which day of the week it was by Manuela walking into the Club and demanding bean shoots or five hard-boiled eggs or a glass of hot water and a lemon. There had been the potato diet, where you ate as many plain boiled potatoes as you liked until they came out of your ears, but nothing else. There had been the Mainly Milk diet (obtained from her milkman), and the Liquids Only diet, which she had never managed to survive beyond teatime. On each occasion she had thrown herself into the search for a newer slimmer image with unlimited enthusiasm and undiminished hope, only to lose heart around Day Five when the initial weight loss of half a kilo per 24 hours had dwindled to a mere ten grams.

Manuela weighing herself was a sight not to be missed. Off came the clothes, the jewellery, the hair band, even the make- up, in a desperate endeavour to drop another point on the scales. Manuela weighing the food for her latest diet was a unique experience, too. 100 grams of fruit? It was blatantly obvious in her opinion that bananas should be weighed without their peel, cherries without their stones, and grapes without their pips. Carrots should be scraped first. Spinach, on the other hand was to be stripped of the stalk but left unwashed and uncooked. Elementary.

I prepared myself to listen to the latest miracle diet.

"Amaze me."

"Well, you separate the protein from the dairy products...."

"Manu, you've DONE that one. I'll never forget it. We ate in kosher restaurants for weeks. I used to go home and pig out on sausages without telling you."

"You didn't – did you really? You bitch. And you lost three kilos, I distinctly remember."

"I can't help it. I burn more. So what is this all about?"

It had to be the best one yet. Tailor made for Manuela. She was allowed eggs and grilled vegetables for breakfast and then she starved and rested until lunchtime.

"Rest? – you've only just got up, for goodness sake."

"South American women have to rest more than you lot – we tire more easily. It's the climate. Also, that's how we keep our skin looking so young."

"Yeah, that and all those plastic surgeons. You know very well you guys get tucks here and snips there like the rest of us go to the hairdresser's. Some of us. Present company excepted. Then what?" Then, it transpired, came the best bit. You were allowed one reward meal daily, during the course of which you could eat anything your heart desired and as much of it as your stomach could hold, but within the space of one hour only. The logic here was that after this shock treatment, the body started producing industrial quantities of insulin and independently combusted in preparation for the next onslaught. Which never took place. Because you went to bed on a glass of herbal tea.

"Poor old body. You don't half let it in for some heavy disappointments. Build it up to fever pitch and then leave it trembling in anticipation all night long."

"Rubbish. It has other things to think about. You must meet Stefano. I know, let's go to the beach and have spaghetti with clams, instead. I'll pick you up from your office around one o'clock."

But it rained. Bad weather always brings back my childhood fears that the sun might just forget to shine ever again or, if it did, would choose to do it on a day when I had an examination. Or was in bed with bronchitis. Or would in some way be prevented from giving it my undivided attention. On this occasion it rained, as it does frequently in Rome, with a violence equal to that of any of the tropical storms we had experienced in Nigeria. The first time the rains began in Lagos, I was unprepared for the speed and the devastation. Within ten minutes the water had swept right across the scullery, through the kitchen and into the dining room. At this point the steward had managed to catch the tide and turn it with a broom before it attacked the sitting room carpet. Upstairs the corridor was awash as the water poured through the ill-fitting windows. Even Giorgio had donned shorts and rubber sandals, native-style, and got going with a mop and bucket. The next morning the road leading to the Italian Embassy was impassable, and it was one of my great disappointments in life that I had not witnessed the procession of diplomats abandoning their cars, rolling up their trousers, removing their shoes, and wading through the muddy waters to reach their smart air-conditioned offices.

In Rome the rain started during the night and kept me awake crashing down onto a tin tray that one of my neighbours had thoughtfully left out on his terrace. By morning the city was waterlogged and black lowering skies signalled it was set to stay the week. The phone rang.

"Hello?

"Just wanted to tell you not to forget the total sun block."

"Shall we relocate to that place on the Via Flaminia where they have a roaring log fire? The 'Casale,' or 'Casalone' or 'Casalino'. Something like that."

"One o'clock Argentine time."

"Meaning two-thirty?"

"No. Meaning don't go all narky and Anglo-Saxon on me just because I get there at 1.03 having run into a fatal accident involving a twenty car pile-up on the motorway. I know you and your British punctuality."

"Manu, you only live a couple of hundred yards away from that restaurant – you could walk there in ten minutes and burn off some calories in anticipation of the meal to come whilst you were about it."

"I couldn't do anything of the sort – my mind and body have to be in a state of perfect repose to prepare for the onslaught of all that food. I couldn't possibly insult them with exercise."

"Well don't be late, because some of us have to be back in the office being pro-active by 2.30."

"Being *what?*"

"An expression which one such as yourself would consider the equivalent of a four-letter word. I'll see you later."

*   *   *   *

"So tell me more about Stefano."

We were sitting at a corner table, surrounded by the debris from the antipasto, a plate of spaghetti alla carbonara, a grilled veal chop, a dish of roast potatoes swimming in oil and rosemary and a mixed salad. Manuela was signalling furiously to one of the waiters.

"Classic. The three wise monkeys. No-one can avoid eye contact that assiduously. If he doesn't bring me my dessert within the next four minutes, I'm not allowed to eat it. My hour is up. WAITER!!"

A towering pyramid of profiteroles filled with fresh cream and dripping with hot chocolate sauce appeared by magic, and with an agonised look at her watch, Manuela set to work.

Over coffee, she deigned to turn her attention finally to the unanswered question.

"Tallish – not by your English bean-pole standards, but taller than me."

Manuela was five foot two. As a result, she always maintained that her basic problem was not an excess of weight at all, it was merely a lack of height.

"Good looking – at least *I* think so. Difficult to tell when you're squinting sideways at each other."

"Come on! How long is that flight – twelve hours? Don't tell me you didn't have time to check him out thoroughly in all that time. You're losing your touch. Technically you even slept with the guy."

"Sarah! You shock me! And me the mother of two sons! Oh yes, that was another problem. He must be younger than I am, so to be on the safe side, I lopped ten years off the kids' ages. Took them out of university and stuck them back into school – wouldn't they be furious if they found out?"

"And, excuse me for being curious, but I don't suppose you even considered mentioning that poor husband of yours? Or did you lop something off him, too, while you were about it? Where did you say he was?"

"Durban. Totting up lots of lovely Frequent Flyer miles to send me back home again. It's the secret of our successful marriage. That and my well-known frugality."

I choked over my coffee.

"Your what? You can't even walk past a designer label without leaving a little something on account. Not to mention your compulsion to buy the entire range of the World's Most Expensive Face Creams. Are you still using them?"

"Of course I am – can't you see? But I decant them into Nivea pots now that we're back in Rome to make him think I'm economising."

"Beats me how you pay for the stupid things, or are you being allowed a credit card these days?"

"Good lord no! But I am allowed a chequebook, though only for paying food bills and the car insurance. Nothing else. He goes through the stubs each weekend."

"So how do you manage?"

"I start from the back and work forwards. He only looks at the ones in the front of the book. If I want to buy something illicit, I sign a cheque at the back."

"How long do you think you can keep that up?"

"Hopefully until he's gathered enough free Flying Hours to send me back to Daddy to live in the style to which I desire to be accustomed. Shouldn't you be getting back to your grotty little office?"

*　　*　　*　　*

There were no patients booked in for that afternoon but the phone was ringing furiously in my grotty little office when I finally made it back after our extended lunch. I amazed myself by answering it quite brilliantly. Wine does that for me, I find. After a mere twenty minutes I had cured a sore throat, advised on cystitis, and calmed a manic-depressive. I was just settling down to make a cup of coffee and write a couple of letters when the swing door swung violently open and a huge bouquet of flowers entered. Presumably there was somebody behind it because even I could perceive that it was being propelled by a pair of legs. The face was, as yet, invisible, but the voice was unmistakable.

"I really wanted to see a doctor," it said, " but I was given to understand there were none in the surgery this afternoon. So it occurred to me you might be feeling lonely and unloved. So here I am. Any chance of a cup of tea? Or a quick glance at a medical dictionary? I think I might be developing a liver after all this funny foreign food and drink."

He put the flowers down and started wandering around, absent-mindedly lowering the blinds. Perfect. I am about to be imprisoned by a raving maniac in a doctor's surgery bristling with hypodermic syringes and lethal drugs with just a bunch of roses as consolation. I picked up the phone and dialled a number but nothing happened. In desperation I began holding an imaginary conversation with somebody. Anybody.

"Hi. It's me, Sarah. How soon can you get here?" Inconceivably his attention had suddenly been caught by one of the gardening magazines in the waiting room. Instead of pouncing with a loaded hypodermic, he was engrossed in an article about greenfly. I sobered up and started to feel rather less vulnerable. It was only Michael, after all, paying compliments to the ladies in his usual manner. And lowering the blinds keeps the heat out.

Except that it was raining. And cold.

"Five minutes will be fine. Thank you. The patient will wait."

The patient, in fact, had not the least intention of going anywhere. Settling himself deeper into an armchair, he finished the article on greenfly and moved on to the best way to transform manure into mulch. I made him some tea and considered the option of adding a drop or three of Valium but he was so engrossed in the horse droppings I decided it was unnecessary. I dealt with a couple of dozen more phone calls, only one of which, (the one concerning the advisability of using yoghurt as a local application), fascinated him sufficiently for him to lift a quizzical eye from his gardening hints. Eventually he pottered over to my desk and began trying to read the patients' charts over my shoulder.

"That quack's taking his time. I could be dead by now. Perhaps you should have pressed the connect button after you dialled the number."

He yawned and checked his watch.

"Right. It's almost aperitivo time. No wonder I'm getting lethargic. Come on – close this place up and let's find a glass of real medicine somewhere."

The rain was still pouring down and it was beginning to feel a long time since lunch. Surely nobody in their right minds would want to see a doctor urgently on a day like this? And having realised that he was really not that interested in committing an act of indecency, I was beginning to feel almost offended by his complete indifference. Flowers or no flowers. Greenfly and mulch, indeed. I wasn't that old. Or perhaps the examining couch was just too narrow for his liking. I recorded a soothing message on the answering machine, locked up and arm in arm we snuggled under an umbrella up to the nearest bar.

CHAPTER EIGHT

Francesca was groping around the kitchen in search of coffee as I was preparing to leave the flat.

"Salut Maman. Are you lunching at the Club?"

"If I survive my morning's ordeal, yes."

"Now what?"

"Hospital visiting."

"Not again. Who's the unlucky victim this time?"

"Barbara. Went in for a scrape and woke up with a total hysterectomy. Wretched surgeons. Same genes as hairdressers." I ran my hand through what was left of my hair.

"Yes that *was* rather unfortunate. What happened?"

"I was hot and one of my less tactful friends intimated one should not continue to wear one's hair in a pony tail in one's mid-fifties: *that's* what happened. In her opinion, when one reaches a Certain Time of Life and Imminent Ambassadress-ship looms, one should assume one's capillary responsibilities. Apart from which, I couldn't see the ball when serving. As always it looked fine after it had been forced round a red-hot brush and lacquered to immobility prior to leaving the establishment. And also, I was brought up to say yes, very nice, thank you. Five minutes on the back of a horse and I looked like Genghis Khan meeting Attila the Hun."

"It'll grow. Meet you for lunch – give my love to Barbara."

The Regina Coeli prison sits at the foot of the Gianicolo hill on the banks of the River Tiber. In the evenings and at weekends, relatives of the inmates would gather at the top of the hill to shout messages to those incarcerated within. The acoustics were far superior to those of the Terme di Caracalla where the outdoor summer opera season took place. Almost next door to the prison was the Santo Spirito Hospital, parts of which dated from Roman times. One of the original inmates, to all appearances, was shuffling up and down the pavement outside in his carpet slippers. A hard-faced nun instructed me to go to Room 116, Department of Obstetrics, where an even harder-faced nun looked disapprovingly at her watch and informed me that visitors would not be admitted for another forty minutes. There was nowhere to sit or even lean, so I wandered off to look for the bar and queued up with a long line of pyjama clad men and women, some pushing intra-venous drips, others clutching X-rays and blood reports, all eager to describe symptoms and experiences in shameless detail. Occasionally the arrival of a member of the medical staff, his white gown definitely not advertising a famous washing powder, would cause a reverent hush to fall upon the assembled company. The waves of dressing gowns would part to allow these eminent personages to be served immediately.

Wandering back to the ward, I noticed the dreaded nun was deep in conversation at the far end of the corridor and took the opportunity to slip into Room 116 unnoticed. Barbara was staring at the ceiling with a glazed look in her eyes.

"Hey, come off your cloud – it's me. Bearing grape. How are you feeling?"

"Terrible. Get me out of here before I die of malnutrition. Why is it automatically assumed you left your teeth at home when you cross a hospital threshold? If I see another meatball, chicken galantine, fish pie or puréed ANYTHING..... How did you get in? I thought I had another forty minutes of spiritual contemplation to get through before I could see anything human."

"Slipped past the gorgon when she wasn't looking. Being a lapsed Prot. helps: you don't have to stop and worry about those aeons in purgatory you might be notching up. When do they let you out?"

"Well *you* try and find out. I can't get a word of sense out of any of them. That ruddy nun won't even let the doctor near me, so I've no one to ask. I'll go crazy if I have to stay here much longer. Couldn't you spring me, somehow?"

"I suppose I could always go next door and ask for an escape kit. Where's Luciano? Couldn't he get his hide over here and pull some strings? Or is he too busy looking after the children? "

"Not him. On a business trip to Milan, isn't he? Mother-in-law's holding the fort. Another prime reason for getting back home as soon as possible. They'll be spoiled rotten by the time I get there."

"Are you attached to any tubes anywhere? Fever? Antibiotics? No nasty infections? Stitches?"

"Nothing I can't rip out with my own teeth once I'm safely home. I'm fit as a fiddle. Just get me out of here before I start screaming for intravenous Valium."

"OK, I'll see what I can do. You weren't planning on

coming back for any reason in the near future, were you?"

By her reply, it appeared fairly certain that this was not and never would be a probability, though it took a while to express it fully and to her complete satisfaction.

"Wow! You look better already. Got some colour in those cheeks now. Where are your clothes, or did they take them away and seal them in a large brown envelope?"

"Inside that cockroach-infested cupboard at my last inspection."

"Right. Get dressed and stick anything you don't want to bequeath to the gorgon into that plastic carrier. I'd have brought you a Gucci bag if I'd known. The Italians treat you with far more respect if your carrier bags come from somewhere prestigious. Wait here – I'll be back in a minute."

I strode back out through the walking wounded.

By the time I returned, triumphantly waving a piece of paper, Barbara was dressed and stuffing unwanted camomile teabags down the back of her bedside table.

"Sign here."

"What does it say?"

"Roughly translated that they hope you will rot in hell after succumbing to septicaemia. Also that Dr. Worzel Gummidge never wishes to set sight on your genitalia ever again. That shouldn't keep you awake at nights, though. Now we just have to deal with the dreaded nun. Count to fifty and then stroll with authority straight up the corridor and out of the front entrance while I promise her an audience with the Pope. The car's parked fifty yards up on the left, take the keys and keep your head down. And feel free to peel all the parking fines off it whilst you're waiting."

I staggered into the Club for a late lunch muttering under my breath about nuns in general and Italian hospitals in particular.

"How did it go?"

"I sprang her. Took her back home to mother-in-law and kids which will probably finish her off and burst the remaining stitches. Who was I to demur? Any of you layabouts want a game of tennis?"

CHAPTER NINE

"Pronto, Francesca?"

"Si – ciao Papa! What's new?"

"Niente – la Mamma?"

"Went to play tennis with someone from Taiwan – the Ambo, I think."

"Who taught you your Political History, cara? We don't have relations with Taiwan, therefore there is no Ambassador."

"Well Mummy's having tennistic relations with someone, so you'd better tell her to get her alibi straight next time. Did you need her for something vital, or just to enquire what's for dinner?"

"Why isn't she in the surgery?"

"It seems the sun was shining and all the patients started feeling better, so they decided to go home early. All right for some – here am I slaving away for my Statistics exam. What did you want her for, in case she should make contact?"

"To warn her there's a dinner tonight – you know how long it takes her to plan what to wear these days. I thought if she was told long enough in advance it might avoid some of the hysteria. Tell her to give me a ring when she gets back."

"Ask, as we say in English."

"Sorry?"

"Forget it – hold on, I think she just came in. Want some advice?"

"What?"

"Have her call you back after she's taken a hot shower. Looks like the Taiwan experience left her exhausted. That and half a hundredweight of shopping in a burst carrier bag which can't have helped."

I was, as my daughter had rightly observed, desperate for hot water and two minutes with my feet up before tackling the boring task of ripping the tough outer leaves off a pile of artichokes and stuffing them with mint, garlic and breadcrumbs. The news that Giorgio was waiting for me to call him in the office filled me with trepidation. Had I forgotten another engagement, and was he at this very moment standing outside some foreign Embassy waiting in vain for me to arrive in my finery? It seemed not.

"Who is this Taiwan character you were playing tennis with?"

"Taiwan? I played with a monocular pilot from Air One!"

Well, it was partly true. Mixed doubles, actually, with Michael being the other man, but who's counting?

" You have *such* unreliable sources. We decided it was as good a way as any to show how well the other eye had adapted. The insurance company was out there videoing the best bits to prove his monocularity didn't stop him from beating me 6-1, 6-0. I nearly died. I'm only used to playing with the geriatrics: we never do more than a gentle one set and a bit interspersed with lots of gossip and then straight to the bar. What's up?"

He broke the news, and although I attempted to modify the hysteria, I cannot say, in all honesty, that it was a huge success.

"Am I allowed to ask where? By whom? In aid of what? Dress code? Other guests likely to be present? Boring little details like these? It's just that it might help me to decide between the inevitable little black uniform or the thigh length boots with fishnet stockings and Vivienne Westwood corset."

"*Please*! Half the government will be there, you have to be on your best behaviour. Oh, and we leave for Russia on Tuesday – just a couple of days. Wives were an option, so I signed you up."

He was right about half the government being at the dinner party. Surveying the assembled company, I could only hope for the future of the country that the other half were better. A minister to my left was decrying the dishonesty of the press who had quoted him as having made some highly disparaging remarks about a fellow politician.

"It's completely outrageous to infer that I said anything of the sort. These journalists just write anything that comes into their heads – 'at best inept and at worst dishonest,' indeed. The man's a very close personal friend of mine. We were at university together. Admittedly he finished a couple of years after I did, but a lot of people take a bit longer to qualify. It took him a while to decide what he wanted to do in life afterwards, I recall, but eventually he set up some kind of a business and made a load of money, no one quite understood how, but that's by the way. He's certainly no more corrupt or inept than a host of others I could mention. Not intentionally, at least. You could perhaps argue he might have done better in another sector, that I grant you. Cultural affairs for a man who never read a book or set foot in an art gallery to the best of my knowledge wasn't perhaps the wisest choice, but they had to give some Portfolios to the right of centre parties to keep them happy or they wouldn't have played ball. I don't say he's a genius, but there are probably worse than him in politics if you look hard enough."

I reminded myself that I was on my best behaviour, nodded understandingly and murmured something helpful about the fickleness of the average journalist. My neighbour to the right had arrived very late to demonstrate his importance, claiming to have been delayed by a phone call from the Prime Minister just as he was leaving home. A thoroughly jolly evening.

Returning well after midnight, I began to throw warm clothes into a suitcase for our departure to Russia, praying that the accompanying delegation would not comprise any of those who had been present at the dinner.

Rome, March 19th

Dear Mother,

Here I am again back from doing the accompanying spouse bit to Moscow and St. Petersburg. The night before our departure found me crawling on my stomach through the false ceiling above which I keep my unseasonable clothes, in search of furry boots and earmuffs. I hazard the suggestion that Scott might never have made it to the Antarctic if he'd been cursed with my storage system. I subsequently spent most of the flight studying a Russian phrase book so I could graciously accept more caviar if offered.

Moscow was edifying, in the sense that it taught me to realise that's *not* the post I wish to be sent to, no matter how prestigious. Most of the people I met were verging on alcoholism if not verged, making my poor consumption of the odd glass of vino or three seem very paltry by comparison. Our hostess fell off the arm of her own sofa twice during the course of a fairly important gathering and, becoming maudlin, had to be encouraged toward her bedchamber before the festivities were over. The men went off to Siberia to open a kindergarten which the Italian Government was most generously donating to the Russian population, and rejoined us twenty-four hours later with varying degrees of lost voices and sore throats as a result of having slept in under-heated quarters. Our Defence Minister had the best room yet still had to write his reports by candlelight and sleep with his overcoat on. Back in Rome, I shed the winter coat and spent another morning rooting around amongst the cardboard cartons looking for summer wear. Repacked the suitcases and left for the next trip which involved a stop-over in Oman – astounding ultra-modern architecture in the middle of complete desert, luxury hotels, pools and tremendous planting of trees and shrubs in an effort to change the climate and make it rain. Each bush is watered individually through snaky hoses with desalinated water. Pity they don't know about my hidden powers – I could be saving them a fortune. I only have to put on a pair of gardening gloves and down it comes in sheets. By this stage I had had enough and sent Giorgio off to Tokyo for the next trip wife-free.

In the interest of persuading you to come and visit us, I have, of course, omitted to answer your letter in which you worry about murderous Mafiosi and unclean drinking water and such, but should you seriously be awaiting news on these subjects, I have to say that no, we were not planning any earthquakes in the near future, but could lay on the odd thunderstorm if you should particularly feel the need. Or perhaps something a little more spectacular were you to inadvertently plug your hairdryer into the wrong socket.

Awaiting news,

Sarah

I sealed up the letter and tried Manuela's number. I hadn't heard from her since our lunch together and was beginning to suspect she was not answering her phone. Not a good sign. I decided I would leave it for a few more days and then go round and hammer on her door. And whilst I was waiting, perhaps that layabout Michael might like to inspect my photos of St Petersburg over a leisurely dinner, since Giorgio was presumably dallying with geishas by now.

But I had calculated without the accompanying journalists, all of whom were his staunch drinking companions. He had heard about my calling off the trip to Tokyo and was already outside my door with a bottle of Bollinger, a single orchid and an invitation to the latest "in" Night Club. So much for my staying behind in Rome to relax.

CHAPTER TEN

Rome, April 2nd

Dear Mother,

Let me keep you up to date with my trivia.

This week we have been looking after a couple of hamsters – Coca and Cola – who belong to a child from Alex's school. We thought we were doing rather well keeping them from the maws of Beagle and confining the smell by locking them in the kitchen and leaving all the doors and windows open, until one day I came back to find one of them lying on its proverbial back with proverbial feet in the air. Rigor very mortis had set in at least four hours previously, and a quick consensus of opinion favoured rushing out to replace it forthwith before the owner returned from her holiday. We thought that we might wait until after dinner to bury it (or even touch it – bleargh!) and in the meantime, just on the off chance, I squirted some of our best cognac down its throat with a syringe. This treatment seemed to give it the jerks, though some disbelievers present said it was but the twitch of the hand (reluctantly) holding it. Be that as it may, I wrapped it in a clean duster and stuck it on a radiator to warm it up, and forgot about it until it fell off and, what with one therapy and another, came back to life again. It spent the rest of the evening falling drunkenly off its Ferris wheel. The word up at the convent the next morning was that a miracle had occurred, and Saint Cola is currently awaiting canonisation, though strictly between you and me, I have since been told that hamsters go into a kind of hibernation when they get too cold (open kitchen doors don't help), and that there is a strong possibility my actions may cause it to have dreadful traumas for the rest of its hopefully long life.

As if this were not enough, Alex has just been presented with a pair of goldfish which no-surname Riccardo apparently won at a fair. Practising his shooting skills for when his bodyguards have their day off, no doubt. And I am not even mentioning the horse which some colleague of Giorgio's has just bequeathed me prior to leaving en poste for Dublin. I suppose it would have been rather coals to Newcastle to take it, but as a result, my lunch hours and weekends are becoming so energetic I look forward to Monday mornings when I can slump down behind the office computer for a rest.

More soon,

With love, Sarah

I headed for the stables.

In preparation for the morning's excursion, the riders were buckling up various bits of leather designed to keep both themselves and their horses from coming asunder for the next couple of hours.

The General, as usual, was already present and correct: saddled, be-hatted, girth tightened to within an inch of equine asphyxiation, eye conspicuously on watch as he mentally assigned fatigues to any latecomers. Retired from the service some years previously, he took it upon himself to maintain certain standards. All leather items to be polished and oiled daily. Rubber boots will most definitely not to be tolerated no matter how vile the mud and puddles. Stirrups to shine until they dazzle or, in his case, until they reflected his moustaches. Crash caps to be worn at all times. Excuses evoking Her Britannic Majesty's preference for headscarves to be treated with a republican disdain. Protestations regarding the temperature inside a hard hat whilst galloping across the Roman countryside in the middle of August to be simply ignored. He himself wore a blue velvet one with ventilation slits in the crown through which he doused his head liberally with a bottle of ice-cold water carried specifically for that purpose. He also wore a prawn in one ear, or Bluetooth as one was supposed to call it, in case he was called upon to direct some unforeseen manoeuvres whilst wasting his precious time with us amateurs.

The Tuscan shot into the car park in a cloud of dust, scattering stray mongrels, cats and pigeons, slammed his silver Mercedes into the nearest space and headed for the changing room at the double, cutting a last couple of deals on his mobile phone whilst clawing at belt and buttons. By the time he had wrenched open the door of his locker he had only to wrestle himself into a pair of jodhpurs and pull on some boots. Nobody ever discovered what it was the Tuscan did for a living, but during normal working hours he was to be found astride an ex-racehorse he had acquired from Newmarket and most of his dealings were conducted from the saddle. From time to time his companions were required to freeze or ride up onto the grass verge so that whoever was calling couldn't hear the tell-tale sound of hooves which would have destroyed the image he liked to create of working a twenty-four hour day out of a high-tech office somewhere in the heart of the city.

The General sighed heavily. Four minutes late already. Spud bashing or latrines today. Sloppy lot.

The Neapolitan drove in gently trying not to raise the dust. No point wasting an expensive car wash. Muttering oaths fit to shock the most hardened ostler, he took care to avoid eye contact with the General whose early starts were the reason he had been obliged to drag himself out at dawn, thereby losing half a night's sleep. The effects of the grappa to which he was notoriously partial tended not to wear off until mid-morning and given the option, he preferred to be grumpy and monosyllabic until lunchtime. Early Starts did not qualify as Sport in his opinion. Left to his own physical preferences (which, needless to say, were dictated by low blood pressure rather than high alcohol intake), he would have heaved himself into the saddle at a far more human hour. Two o'clock, for example, in lieu of lunch which he considered a waste of time.
Then there was Fernando on his French thoroughbred. Fernando and his mount had between them once been the Italian national champions of Endurance, a cross-country marathon where rider and horse run a gauntlet of veterinary surgeons who pop out from behind trees at intervals to measure the horse's heartbeat and sweat levels.

At last we were off. Beagle by this time had already downed half a bucket of pony nuts, terrorised the stable cats, toyed with the odd Jack Russell and was ready to follow us in search of further prey. With complete disregard for danger, she nipped in and out of the horses' hooves, sometimes leading the hunt, sometimes bringing up the rear if a particularly succulent fox poo caught her imagination. Occasionally she was batted out of the way by an ironclad hoof belonging to the Endurance champ who was not going to risk losing his stride and possibly his reputation because of some pesky hound footling around under his feet.

A brisk trot through a shady wooded section, a gentle canter up and over the crest of an unploughed field soon sorted the field into its customary pattern. The General was out in front on "Accolade" convinced, as ever, that its rightful place should be in a circus and therefore having no intention of keeping all four hooves on the ground simultaneously. Restrained swearwords – for our General was a reformed character now: a pillar of strength to others at his local branch of Alcoholics Anonymous and a devout member of the congregation at his local church – began to fly. Behind him, a close second, in fact far too close a second, came the no longer taciturn Neapolitan. Apparently there were circumstances here beyond his control, if one were to judge by the far less restrained comments issuing from his lips. "No (expletive deleted) brakes", would describe the situation adequately, it seemed. There being no crime worse than overtaking the Master, or in this case the General, he heaved furiously but ineffectually at his horse's mouth and when this proved unproductive, had no alternative other than to turn the beast in a half circle into a ploughed field, the crime of incurring the wrath of the local farmer being a soft option compared to that of overtaking a Superior Officer.

The Tuscan, his phone clamped to one ear, was endeavouring to yank his horse's nose up from ground level and kick it out of a series of bucks with which it liked to disrupt its owner's wheelings and dealings.

Fernando at this stage was just a dot on the horizon, for his mount, champion though he may once have been, now preferred to warm up gently by striding resolutely backwards for the first ten minutes. How fortunate this horse did not belong to the Neapolitan: they would never have made it through the stable door each morning.

Once out in the open country, the main business of the day would begin. Conversation, as the art would usually be understood, was out of the question due to the disparity in speed, the increasing distances between the riders and their various individual preoccupations. But it would take more than such minor trifles as these to impede the flow of exchanged insults which soon echoed across the fields. Being, with the notable exception of myself, all Italians, it was politics first and foremost. Fernando was an outright fascist and proud of it, though from an equestrian perspective the joke was on him, for his horse steadfastly refused to lead on its right foot at the canter and was thus nicknamed Lefty by all and sundry. A good gallop across an unploughed field would usually be punctuated by the General's imprecations against the Communist swine who were destroying the landscape (council houses on the far horizon), Fernando's colourful comments about the European Union in general and rotting set-aside crops in particular, the Tuscan's phone ringing unattended in the depths of a hidden pocket and the Neapolitan's oaths as his horse tripped and took a sharp nose-dive over some unforeseen obstacle, catapulting him violently into a muddy ditch.

A few lengths behind, the Endurance team had finally warmed up and, with whoops of joy, Fernando would succeed in convincing his "Ferrari" to overtake the General's "Fiat."

Triumph was short lived, however, for the Ferrari, champion though it may have been in its heyday, was getting a little long in its remaining tooth, and on the uphill stretch reverted to a gentle, undulating canter which not even the clouds of dust and drumming hooves of the Tuscan and the resuscitated Neapolitan thundering up from behind could persuade it to abandon as it fell back into fourth place, leading nicely with the left foreleg. The Neapolitan, by now thoroughly awake and sobered, decided to put his newly circulating adrenaline to good use by jumping over any relatively inanimate object within sight. Tree trunks, ditches, dead branches, dead porcupines, live but otherwise preoccupied beagles – whatever. He was just coming up to face a tricky little puddle cum double twiglet combination when Beagle caught a whiff of rabbit in the air and was off over the horizon howling in delight and fury, doing a steady 50kph with a following wind. Perking up considerably, the horses seemed to think this was a pretty good idea too and proceeded to set off at a flat out gallop hoping to be in at the kill, though in military terms the manoeuvre resembled a rout more than a triumphal charge, because for some reason they all decided to take a different route. It was an undisciplined unit and the despair of the General that eventually regrouped back at the stables some half hour later, to find Beagle sunning herself innocently in a patch of manure, chewing pensively on a couple of horse droppings.

CHAPTER ELEVEN

I was trying Manu's number for the hundredth time when Alex appeared for breakfast looking harassed, turned down the volume of the Hallelujah chorus with which I liked to begin my day, and poured herself a giant glass of orange juice with a pained expression.

"So what's eating you, apart from adolescence?"

"Can't stand classical music before breakfast. After last night, not before lunch or supper, either. Had a rough evening, if you must know."

"Yes I noticed you were back early. What happened?"

"Riccardo had tickets for this awful concert – John Sebastian Bludi Bach and his Bludi Goldberg Variations – all thirty of them! I nearly died. Are you aware that the Bach family sat around amusing each other by writing those things during the long winter evenings? Having FUN doing it. I mean picture to yourself, if you will, Mr. and Mrs. Bach and all the little Bachlets sitting in front of the fire going "O goody, I just did a Quodlibet with a couple of minor fifths – who wants to hear it?" When they could have been doing crosswords or playing charades or watching Eastenders like any other normal person – oh no, they have to bore the pants off future generations by writing inversions in B flat major. "

"You didn't enjoy, I gather."

"ENJOY? Do you know there are two folk songs in the middle of all that interminable plinking, one of which goes: 'Mother dear, if you'd fed me more meat and less cabbage, I might have stayed around longer, but an excess of greens made me leave home.' Whatever kind of a spiritual experience do you call that? People like that need a television. What's for lunch?"

"Spinach and grilled hamster. Can I have my Handel back, now, please? I have to prepare myself spiritually for a fight with a computer, which means either an equine dose of intravenous tranquilliser or "I Know That My Redeemer Liveth" at full volume."

Alex downed her orange juice and headed for the front door. The strains of Michael Jackson's latest masterpiece floated back as she plugged herself none too hermetically into her Walkman for the journey to school. No sooner was she out of the door than the phone rang and another Michael's voice was vibrating in my ears and demanding attention as I tried ineffectually to persuade Beagle to relinquish one end of the duster and let me tidy up the bedrooms.

"Sarah, where the devil do you disappear to these days? I ring you two days running trying to fix a game of tennis during the lunch hour and all I get is the office answering machine. Much as it would amuse me to leave you clinically explicit details of an imaginary nature for your boss to find during your absence, I refrained from even leaving a message. For the which you may express your undying gratitude and accept an invitation to lunch instead. Today."

I explained about the horse and how Beagle and I liked to nip out for a quick gallop occasionally instead of being Ladies that Lunch every day of the week but promised to arrange a mixed doubles at the earliest opportunity before rushing off to the office to deal with some correspondence –to be strictly honest, most of it mine.

Rome, June 5th

Dear Mother,

As I know you must be awaiting this letter with baited breath to hear the latest in our zoo saga, I will keep you in suspense no longer. Coca and Cola were duly returned to their rightful owner in roughly the state in which they had been delivered, give or take a tendency towards alcoholism, and a family-sized sigh of relief was heaved by all upon their departure. As you will recall, they had been joined latterly by a couple of goldfish, the which are only ever sold in pairs in Italy due to a conviction that singly they pine away for lack of company. This is obviously a ploy to push fishy sales up by 100%, since one of ours promptly killed off its mate whilst I was out at work one morning. Coming back home in my lunch hour I was greeted by a dead fish lying on one side with its fins in the air (c.f. recent hamster experience). Tossing up whether to feed it to the local cat or give it a proper burial under the lemon tree, I opted for the latter, given that Alex attends a convent, and so we held a moving bilingual ceremony albeit some forty-eight hours later because I had forgotten to tell them of its demise and neither of them noticed. The deceased was somewhat the worse for wear due to Beagle's penchant for seafood, but we pretended it had been necessary to perform an autopsy. The fish, by the way, had eventually been dubbed 'Campari' and 'Soda', and should you be wondering about the use of the past tense there, it is because the survivor kicked the bucket this very evening as I staggered in after fighting the Romans and their traffic off and on from 8 a.m. till 9 p.m., and after a day like I've had today, I confess he's going out with the garbage.

I am currently counting the days until we leave for Corsica – the thought of four weeks sunbathing, swimming and clambering up and down goat tracks in disreputable attire seems just too good to be true. No high heels or uncomfortable clothes, no stultifying conversation, no make-up, no television: just read, walk, swim, sleep in the sun, and transcendentally meditate.

Back at the Foreign Office, rumours are abounding that Giacomini could possibly be in line for a nice little job not a million miles from the very heart of Europe, and we are all crossing our fingers and paws that something is in the offing. Maintaining a gastronome husband, two daughters and a Beagle in a reasonable state of repair requires a minimum of financial resources, and the miserable pittance meted out to home-based diplomats, with or without dependents, does not permit over-indulgence.

Love, Sarah

"Hola!"

"Oh *at last!* I mean don't bother to stay in contact, or anything. Just tip up out of the blue, renew an age-old acquaintance as if we'd only left each other the day before yesterday and then disappear without trace for another six months. Why the hell don't you invest in an answering machine, just for starters? Where on *earth* have you been?"

"Nowhere, I was in deep depression and not answering the phone, mostly."

"Manuela, don't you dare do that. What in heaven's name are friends for, if you can't spread a little depression over us too? Why should *you* keep it all? And on my off days, what am *I* supposed to do if you're not there to mop me up? Where's the legal wedded?"

"Colombia, losing a lot of money by not smuggling certain substances. Been there for the past ten days. Before that he was in Delhi losing a lot of money not bringing me back suitcases full of semi-precious stones I had a ready market for. Useless man."

"What happened to Adonis?"

"The Roman Candle."

"Sorry?"

"I nicknamed him the Roman Candle. You know, those firework things. All fizz and not much bang, unless you get particularly lucky. In any case, not worth what they cost you one way or the other. Not to mention that should you wish to compete with your average little Italian female number who is just desperate unless she has a male companion of any description by her side, you have to spend the rest of the evening telling him how unique he is. I'm off tomorrow. Just rang to say good-bye. Boredom factor went over the danger level. Alarm bells started clanging. Terminal Disillusion set in. Plus I've run out of money and husby isn't being over-forthcoming. Time for Daddy to inject a little something into my account and wardrobe."

"You put on weight again, didn't you?"

"That has absolutely nothing to do with it. But what do you expect with all this pasta? A week or so of Argentine beef, and I'll be transparent. I can't take all these carbohydrates."

"What are you doing tonight? Come and eat with me, and I'll drive you to the airport tomorrow."

"Yeah, good idea. There's that place near the Via del Corso where you can get a real Neapolitan pizza with a two-foot high dough base – not the thin biscuit thing they usually serve in Rome. Can you get there by eightish? I go into a perilous decline if I have to eat any later these days."

"Be there. Promise."

The pizza was enormous and oozed like a Dali watch over the edge of the plate. At a rough estimate, Manuela had put on about four kilos but still looked fantastic and had the waiters tying themselves in knots to serve her within minutes.

I tried to tell her so.

"Maybe you should just live with your weight after all. At least you'll never get wrinkles like the rest of us, and the men seem to love it. Shall I ask for an extra napkin to cover all that cleavage, or don't you mind the ogling?"

" 'Course I don't – it's what cleavages are for, not that you'd know anything about it. And the ogling restores my self-confidence which took a severe beating from the Roman candle."

"Pissed off with a little Italian number?"

"Something like that. Shouldn't we be having some bowls of health-giving mixed salad on the side with this? Then we could justify having a rum baba afterwards – it's a Neapolitan speciality."

"Oh my God, you'll kill me – have you seen the size of those things? They're like giant suppositories for dinosaurs. The pizzas are surreal enough without having to lie awake thinking about those all night."

"You need serious analysis, you do. That or a lover. Come back with me tomorrow, I'll fix you up before you're even off the plane."

"Manu, I keep trying to explain to you, I'm a well balanced, happily married housewife with a cosy little part-time job which allows me time off to play tennis and ride horses and...."

"YOU are totally, but totally deluding yourself, my dear. And as for all that crap about your sheltered childhood I was getting on the phone this morning, you can feed it to the dicky birds. I've seen you stretching those rubber grips over the handle of your tennis racquet, and for someone who swears she was a virgin the day she married and went on the pill the night before the wedding and only came off it to have two kids, you slide them up and over with remarkable professionalism.
WAITER!"

Either the rum baba or the suspicion of what I might possibly be missing, kept me awake most of the night. At seven in the morning I picked up a radiant Manuela in full fighting make-up and drove her out to the airport for the flight to Argentina. Crawling back along the ring road in second gear, I hit the early morning rush hour and cursed solidly in accurate Roman dialect for forty minutes trying to get into the office on time. I began to wonder whether perhaps Manu was right after all, and maybe I was wasting my time at this precious stage of my life. Then I began to think it was just pre-holiday exhaustion setting in, and my first action upon reaching the surgery was to contact a travel agency and make some bookings for the ferry to Corsica. A large dollop of fresh air and sparkling sea with a dash of mountain would surely work its perennial magic. And any other delusions to which Manuela so indelicately referred could just wait until the autumn.

CHAPTER TWELVE

Loading the car was a nightmare.

"Why do we take all this stuff each year? One tee shirt and half a bikini is all we ever use, yet each time we leave we are loaded up to the roof, no room to stretch the legs and the dog has to sleep on the tennis racquets. What's in all those bags, anyway?"

I really couldn't remember, if I was being honest. I slammed the doors and drove off towards the Via Aurelia.

"Just a few essentials I picked up on sale throughout the winter months. I thought I'd been rather restrained this time."

"In the sense that you left the golf clubs and saddle at home, perhaps, but I fail to see the need to transport two crates of inferior Italian plonk to the island of vineyards. The natives will bomb you before you even get off the ferry."

"It's a gift for Monsieur Orsini for letting me ride his horses free of charge throughout the summer."

"Free of charge? *He* should be paying *you*. You can't even catch them half the time and in any case nobody else in their right mind would go near them. You get more exercise chasing them around the maquis with a rotting halter and a bunch of carrots than they ever get for the rest of the year. When you do manage to grab one, you end up water-skiing half way across the island attached to the rotting halter by an old rope. It's more of a

suicide trip than a sport."

"I always hope that the heat of the Corsican sun will sap their energy. Just look at the colour of those fields!"

Nature had been busily imitating Art most spectacularly ever since we had left Rome. Vast expanses of newly harvested corn in perfect Van Gogh texture and tonality had given way to fields of scarlet poppies and blue cornflowers striving to outdo Monet in the early morning light. And now these in turn had given way to rows and rows of golden sunflower faces bowing towards the sun. An orange tractor was ploughing massive sun-baked clods to our left, a dainty yellow parasol perched precariously over the head of its sun-baked driver. Oleander bushes swayed in unison away from the passing cars – a riot of colour marching determinedly onwards down the central reservation all the way to the sea.

"It hasn't rained for months, how on earth do those bushes survive?"

"Beats me. Mine shrivel up in despair unless I hose them down daily."

"That's not lack of water, it's excess of Beagle pee."

"Which reminds me – did anyone think to let it out before we left?"

"Nope. Could be why it's pawing at the bars instead of quietly chewing the luggage?"

"Nah, that's just Mummy's driving. She has that effect on most people when she hits a motorway. Let's stop at the next service station, though, and we can all use the facilities. Also I want a Hoha Hola."

"A *what?*"

"A Coca Cola – only in this part of Italy the locals pronounce the "c" as an "h". Hoha Hola. Hon una hannuccia horta."

"Go on."

"Con una cannuccia. With a straw. Corta. A short straw."

"Someone get her and the dog a drink and then to a bathroom or we'll have no peace for the rest of the journey."

Restored, and with the inevitable renewed supply of cassettes, chewing gum, and magazines from the Autostrada supermarket, we resumed our drive to Livorno and the ferry. Having terrified the life out of two cats and a Yorkshire terrier during the brief visit to the service station, then delightedly wolfing down a hardly-touched hamburger and bun someone had abandoned in mid-forecourt, Beagle settled into her customary occupation of chewing gently on the tennis racquets, and everyone relaxed. Sunflowers gave way to umbrella pines and cypress trees as we drove further up the coast. In keeping with tradition, we caught the ferry only because it was running half an hour late, and proceeded to fall asleep as soon as we had fed the remains of the insipid lunch provided on board to the dog.

Spring had been particularly wet that year, so Corsica was fresh and green and smelt even more than usual of wild herbs. We drove across the Cap Corse, gazing up at the mountains and stopped to walk through a shady forest whilst Beagle gambolled in and out of the trees snuffling for wild boar, running for her life in the opposite direction the minute she imagined a scent. We drank from sparkling streams and rock pools, immersing ourselves in the water when we were too hot from the climb. Later we drove on to the coast and parked on a deserted beach for a late swim.

"Are there any traffic lights at all on this island?"

"I think there's one in Bastia, maybe a couple in Ajaccio. Are you getting withdrawal symptoms?"

"Nope. In fact I'm taking my shoes off NOW and that's it till the end of the holiday. You have been warned."

"You can get your own tetanus jab when you cut your feet, too. My close association with all things medical ended the moment I closed the door of the surgery. I'll buy you some of those sexy rubber flip flops if you want to feel footloose."

"Oh, yuk! Don't you dare. The epitome of everything un cool."

"Alex, I love it when you launch into sophisticated English, but the accent is on the 'i', not the tome."

"Then you should hear how my English teacher pronounces it – she compensates for all the words she forgets to aspirate like 'orse' and 'ound' by calling it a 'happy tome'."

"When I think what that school costs ...."

"Hey, I just had a great idea. Why don't you chuck the surgery next September and come and teach us English instead? At least you *are* English."

"What? A roomful of thirty-odd things like you giving me hell all day long? You must be joking! That's why I send you to school in the first place so I don't have to put up with you till nightfall. Might curtail Riccardo's extra-curriculum activities, though."

"Very funny. By the way, he's arriving the day after tomorrow – is that all right?"

"Oh perfect! Just so long as he doesn't expect a bed or anything like that."

"Of course he doesn't. There are only five of them, and they have a couple of tents so I said they could stick them up on that patch of waste land you like to think of as a garden. Story of your life, what with that back yard in Rome too."

"Splendid. I'll go and buy five spades ready for them. Can they cook?"

"Mumm-ee. This is a holiday!"

"How odd, that's what I'd thought. Just tell me that there are no vegetarians, no eating disorders, no allergies and no plaster casts among them, and I'll provide anything you want."

"What's plaster casts got to do with it?"

"They don't go with sandy beaches. You need knitting needles to scratch inside them and plastic bags to cover them for swimming, and I am not giving showers to spotty adolescents with bits of their anatomy wrapped up in cling film to keep the water out. You were obviously too young to remember, but we had a particularly bad summer some years back when a friend of your sister's fell out of a tree. Plaster of Paris in the heat of the Corsican summer is not something I would wish on my worst enemy."

Heading finally for the house, we paused for a plate of thickly sliced charcuterie with bowls of tiny black olives and a carafe of rough rosé. It was going to be a good holiday, regardless.

Corsica, July 6th

Dear Mother,

Alex has no less than five cronies from school camping in and around the house, so I spend my time stuffing them with baguettes at lunchtime and with vast quantities of pasta in the evenings. When the wind drops we light the barbecue and grill huge mounds of sausages with piles of spuds nestling in the charcoal and great bowls of salad for the dieters amongst them.

Beagle has so far refrained from chasing goats and sheep and donkeys, all of which activities are always somewhat detrimental to village relationships. Next door's Alsatian half decapitated a chicken last year and they spent the best part of the night agonising whether to pretend they knew nothing about it, or to stick it back where it came from. In the end they acted innocent and had it for dinner the next evening.

Apart from which, we seem to be mouse-free and locust free this year, and my local village handyman has, with his usual technical expertise, fixed the annoying leak which dripped ice cold water onto one's back every time anyone sat on the loo: he simply hung a rusty pail over the dodgy pipe that was responsible. Always an avid reader of Homes and Gardens, I went immediately to the local hardware shop and purchased a colour co-ordinated bucket to match the bathroom tiles, and we have been sitting comfortably ever since.

Upon which erudite note, I will leave you in order to contemplate the sunset.

Love, Sarah

P.S. There is a travelling circus in the next village. You'd think this bunch would have grown out of circuses by now, wouldn't you?

We now possess another goldfish.

CHAPTER THIRTEEN

The return to civilisation was painful. For a start everyone's feet seemed to have grown, and none of our shoes would fit. Wearing correct clothes as opposed to throwing a pair of shorts over a bikini seemed a waste of time, especially since Rome was even hotter that Corsica. Getting up early in the morning to go to work or school was a daily tragedy. Eventually, though it took a while, we all slipped slowly and reluctantly back into our respective routines and a semblance of order re-entered our lives.

Until the phone rang one day whilst I was in the surgery.

"Sarah I've got news – you'd better sit down."

"Darling I'm in the office – that's the only place I ever do sit down. Only make it quick because I've got a bad case of suppurating boils waiting to be lanced in the next room."

"Don't tell me they let you loose with a scalpel in that place now? You don't even have any proper medical training."

"I know, but I do a nice line in hand holding and undemanding prattle, as if you'd never noticed, and am considered invaluable on the psychological front. In several languages. I've also just rushed a suspect dollop of HIV infected blood up to the Lab bearing the pseudonym of Giovanni Rossi – I believe that's the equivalent of Joe Bloggs. I had to hide in a cupboard until the suspected infected had left because it was one of your rather more important colleagues. Scared rigid, he was. And don't think you can get me to divulge the name, because my lips are professionally sealed. When I think I helped remove an ingrown toe-nail from his foot last week, too...."

"Sarah! Do you wear gloves, at least?"

"Of course I do. What was the news?"

"What news?"

"Yours. That's why you rang me."

"Well, it's a rumour more than actual news. Who was that colleague who might be infected? I think you should tell me so I can at least avoid using his toothbrush and girlfriends and things."

"Nothing doing. Keep away from anything secretarial, is my advice, just in case. What's the rumour?"

"Movements. People running up and down corridors, waiting in line to see the Minister. There's a musical chairs of Ambassadorial postings going on, as far as I can make out."

"What's it all got to do with us? We've only just got here. I only just finished unpacking. I've only just started to get on top of this job. Alex only just started to settle into school and make new friends. Francesca only just started a highly stressful course at Rome University. Beagle only just started to realise that a Roman dog's bark is worse than its bite. And you cannot pack a goldfish."

"Sarah ...."

"And there are fifteen people in the waiting room listening to every word. Why do you always do this when I'm at work? a) I don't want to know. And b) if I have to know, it can wait till I get home. And c) just tell me it's not true before our friend with the boil has to come and hold *my* hand instead."

"You're right, there's probably nothing to it. We'll talk tonight. Mind you scrub your hands before coming home. And don't forget the gloves."

Great! The boil was particularly nasty and bled all over the surgery floor, a sprained ankle turned out to be fractured in two places, necessitating immediate transportation to the nearest hospital, an Irish journalist turned up for a repeat prescription completely drunk and had to be hustled out of the back entrance before he could insult two nuns awaiting pap tests, and three small children from somewhere south of the Zambesi had to be forcibly restrained from shredding the magazines in the waiting room and playing wedding confetti with all the bits.

And Michael, I noted when I finally had time to check my silenced cell phone, had rung fourteen times.

What else? I wondered, letting myself into the flat after a hair-raising slalom on the scooter up the Via Cassia, at least a couple of hundred yards of which was only negotiable by using the pavement. There seemed to be a lot of noise coming from the kitchen and as I slammed the front door behind me, a loud pop sent Beagle scuttling for cover. Giorgio, Francesca and Alex suddenly emerged grinning broadly with an overflowing champagne bottle and tray of glasses. Whatever it was, it was done and they were all looking pretty pleased about it. With a feeling of impending doom, I realised another era was over having hardly begun: roots to pull up, newly rediscovered friends to lose all over again, an unknown city to find my way around. More new faces, names, titles, occupations, nationalities would come swarming through my front door. No more holding people's hands as the needle goes in, or talking them through a panic attack over the phone. Time to move on. Well, if it was a cause for celebration, let's hear the worst.

"Where and when? In that order please, and without the background notes and who nearly got what and why they didn't and why they asked you instead although you're still only a Minister and not a full Ambassador yet until your next promotion whenever that might be."

"Come on Mummy, this is so exciting. I can have the whole flat to myself, now. No more fighting over bathrooms."

"Mummy, can you imagine? Nathalie's father just this very minute got posted to Brussels too – we can start school together. And Papa says the Residence is mega - he says I can throw parties for hundreds of people whenever I want."

I sat down heavily on a kitchen stool and tried to think. Brussels.

"I didn't know you were an Eurocrat?"

"Nato. Multilateral." He grinned mischievously. "No third world countries to invite to your Ladies Teas."

"Fallacy N°1: you're the one with the third world phobia. Down in Messina you're just too close to it all. Some of my best friends at university were of extremely interesting hues. Fallacy N°2: I don't give Ladies Teas."

"Bet you will, so, after a week in Brussels. Did you go to bed with any of the hues?"

"Alex, please. Go and do some homework and let me talk to your father in peace for a minute. I need to know how and why and what the hell *for* my life is being suddenly disrupted all over again. If he's as good a diplomat as his bosses obviously think him to be, perhaps he'll be able to persuade me that it's far more worthwhile to arrange flowers and dinner parties for people who are mostly trying to lose weight to start with than to reassure a terrified patient about to undergo chemotherapy or have triple by-pass surgery."

It was at this juncture that I suddenly remembered poor terrified Giovanni Rossi, and escaping from the general euphoria, put through a call to the Laboratory to check on the results of his HIV test. It was negative. I took it as a good omen, and in gratitude, swore to try to think positively about the future. Returning to the kitchen, I glanced up at the goldfish and, despite its usual expression of gormless disbelief, fancied it winked at me.

PART TWO

BRUSSELS

CHAPTER ONE

September 5th, 1996

Dear Mother,

Packing nearly finished - fifth move coming up. It certainly concentrates the mind and the possessions: just the thought of crating up all the back numbers of The Economist and Horse and Hound and having to unpack them upon arrival sends me running for the recycling bins. Alex is being sent off on a military flight to Brussels on Monday so that she can start school on Day One, as opposed to Day Fourteen and Three-Quarters, which is when I hope to arrive, by highly overloaded car with Beagle and the latest goldfish. Incidentally, how do you stop a goldfish sloshing around when transporting it halfway across Europe in its bowl? This is a detail I am going to have to work on sometime between now and Day Thirteen. Goldfish's owner is currently having to be forcibly restrained from packing into her suitcase the entire contents of her bedroom, right down to the china cat collection and about eight pairs of policemen's boots which are apparently the latest thing in footwear for trendies. We explained that military aircraft do have weight limits and that taxis are not allowed within miles of military airports, so she'd better be mobile upon arrival, but I fear she is not convinced. She will stay with her beloved Nathalie, whose father has just been appointed

Ambassador to the Swiss Embassy, until I get there. The Swiss Foreign Ministry, you note, take into consideration such minor details as dispatching an Ambassador to a new post in time for his children to start the school year punctually. Must be all those cuckoo clocks.

I took time out from my last few days in the office to go into town this morning. I met up with my English friend Patricia and we pottered around looking for the sort of clothes Ambassadresses are supposed to wear, trying everything on, buying nothing and generally making thorough nuisances of ourselves. Italian sales girls terrify the pair of us, though Patricia is more hardened to it - had her nerves shot to pieces when they were posted to Baghdad during the Iran/Iraq war, and has rightly acquired a sense of proportion with regard to mere shop assistants. Afterwards we headed towards the Club for lunch and met up with Francesca who was also there, taking rowing lessons down on the river. The sudden enthusiasm is linked, I suspect, to the latest boyfriend who wishes to lure her into a double skiff (I can't think of anywhere safer as far as my daughter's honour is concerned - have you seen how those things rock? you only have to blink and you're overboard.) The most important part of the instruction, by the way, is the exhortation to keep your mouth closed and stop breathing if you do happen to capsize. The floating turds in the Tiber are, by all accounts, heading for the Guinness Book of Records. Much to her disgust, we are moving her out of the flat during our absence and into a rather foreboding Institute run by the Sisters of Mercy. She is already chafing at the bit at the thought of compulsory mass twice weekly and curfew from 10.30 p.m. I have a strong foreboding we may have to rethink this one after a while.

If I don't get round to writing again before we leave - forgive. Next news will be from Belgium.

Love, Sarah

In the end, the drive to Brussels was fish-free. A friend of Alex's had begged to be allowed to keep it as a souvenir. Beagle was a different story: she spent most of the journey hurling herself against the bars designed to keep her securely out of the way in the back of the car every time I shifted into overdrive. By the end of the trip, however, she had mastered the art of peeing on hard shoulders and drinking out of paper cups, and was showing a marked preference for classical music over Bob Dylan whom she accompanied with uninterrupted howling in the manner of wolves to the moon.

I eventually arrived at the Residence to be greeted by a bevy of Filipinos in their best starched uniforms, all vying for the privilege of taking my coat and belongings, offering me coffee, tea, gin and tonic or a hot bath, showing me around the house and, most especially, avoiding dog-contact. I took advantage of most of these offers, and eventually subsided thankfully into freshly laundered sheets to prepare myself for the impending onslaught of getting to know the house, the staff, the town, the wives of our colleagues, those of all the other Ambassadors, finding out where best to purchase food, drink and flowers in bulk, to hire waiters, glasses, tables and chairs. The removers had left Rome the day before with our personal possessions and were due to turn up the following morning. I had agreed to collect Alex in the afternoon after school, and Giorgio was to arrive three days later at the airport in pomp and glory with full military honours from the various attachés resplendent in their ceremonial uniforms. And, hopefully, with all his socks and shirts already unpacked and neatly stored in their new cupboards.

The house fell silent. Beagle for once in her life had no complaints about the size of the kitchen she had been allocated as sleeping quarters, and was prowling contentedly before collapsing onto her folding bed and favourite blanket. The staff had retired to their rooms where they would no doubt dissect me, my belongings, my clothes and the dog for another hour at least. Outside, an owl hooted and a gentle breeze rustled through the branches. With a sigh of contentment, I thought I could probably learn to live without the Roman habit of friends and neighbours shouting to each other across three balconies, thumping their car horns as a signal they were waiting outside even at three in the morning, or just listening to their television sets at full volume with all the windows open on a summer's evening. I fell asleep and dreamt, for some reason, that the driver of the removal lorry had got so drunk he had driven off the road into a canal, and that all the crates of Italian wine we had so carefully purchased prior to departure were slowly but surely floating off towards Holland.

I needn't have worried about the flowers or the crates of wine. The former started arriving the next morning sharp at 9.30, together with a series of little cards which were presented to me on a silver salver by the smiling Filipino-in-chief, Erlinda. Most of the names were unknown, apart from the wives of Giorgio's colleagues, and as feared, I spent half the morning ringing up the social secretary in panic asking a) who was this person? and b) how on earth did one pronounce their name? In the midst of which the removers arrived, were duly fortified with coffee having spent only a minimum of the night asleep in their lorry in a motorway service station, and had to be shown where to unload and unwrap and hang and install. The crates of wine seemed to have multiplied during the trip, and now occupied an unbelievable amount of space. Soon they had filled all the main hall where I stood with the lists of my goods and chattels in one hand and a portable phone in the other. It occurred to me that once again Giorgio would arrive when it was all over and would thus continue in his conviction that it was the removers who did everything and that I was highly privileged to be able to move house in this uncomplicated, stress-free fashion. Luckily Erlinda had been through all this before and brought me, at hourly intervals, unsolicited cups of coffee which I was too embarrassed not to accept, By noon my heart was pounding so wildly with the excess of caffeine I needed nailing to the ground.

* * * *

At lunchtime, I shared a bowl of spaghetti with the staff and the men before shooing them out into the garden to smoke their inevitable cigarettes and slumping down amongst the empty packing cases for a quiet moment of despair whilst I thought no-one was watching. This was always the worst stage. Another new life to get started and total chaos as far as the eye could see, phones ringing with unknown people graciously welcoming you to Brussels, and the ever-present risk that some well-meaning person would turn up personally to offer help and assistance and catch you without make-up, in jeans and wholly cashmere-free sweater. I alternated between the lists and the telephone until, with something resembling relief, I realised it was time to collect my younger daughter from the school I had not even seen and was not even sure how to reach.

* * * *

Well, very cosmopolitan, I thought, as the usual motley crowd fought its way out of the French Lycée. Same the world over - elbows to the fore, survival of the fittest, brownie points for getting to the head of any queue. It had its useful side, I had to admit - in any situation where I felt my British upbringing was holding me back, I would send in the girls. Their first strike capabilities in airports, supermarkets, at bus stops, in banks and cinemas were unequalled. They also had no problems whatsoever about conserving the space they considered due to them on public transport. Whereas

I would invariably give a groping hand the benefit of the doubt rather than Create a Scene, my darling daughters preferred to spontaneously inform the entire bus as to what was going on under that raincoat, and the famous policemen's boots had on more than one occasion inflicted considerable local damage.

Alex was in great form. She had managed to manoeuvre herself into the same class as Nathalie, and the two were loudly united in their loathing of the History teacher ("seven solid pages to learn off by heart INCLUDING THE COMMAS. I mean, what a waste of time...") the English teacher ("you'll never believe how she pronounces "thoroughly" - well of COURSE I didn't correct her, I'm not THAT stupid") and the food ("dis-guss-ting.")

"And do you know what? They had the NERVE to ask us to fill in questionnaires on our first day asking the most intimate details about our private lives, like what our fathers and mothers did for a living and how many half brothers and sisters lived with us and the number of bathrooms in the house. You get put down for sessions with the school shrink if you have to share a loo with more than four people. I said you were a hairdresser - I hope you don't mind? and that my Father was unemployed. If they give me a grant can I use it for riding lessons? Nathalie said she came from a broken home and was being brought up by gypsies and lived in a caravan with satellite T.V. that was parked in a lay-by just outside Waterloo. Can we stop by the Godiva shop and buy some truffles before I STARVE to death? No, Mummy, you can keep your raw carrots for the horses, I need serious calories to feed my brain cells right now. Did my china cat collection arrive safely? Nathalie is collecting beer cans, which take up far more space, so you can consider yourself the lucky one. Can she sleep over with us this weekend - pleeeze? We want to go down town together and drink fruity beer in this great place called the Morte Subite - Sudden Death - isn't that a fantastic name for a bar? Of course it's non-alcoholic, what do you take us for? Anyway you have to be about fifty before you're allowed to drink anything other than milk in Switzerland. It's to protect the cows, or something. How's the doggle? When does Papa arrive?"

She kept it up all the way back to the house, having, after all, very little in the way of opposition from her mother who was far too busy concentrating on giving precedence to anything at all which approached from her right, be it animal, vegetable or mineral. I was also striving to remember the need to check my driving mirror and use the indicators. Old Roman habits died hard.

Brussels, September 20th

Dear Frankie,

I was so glad to hear that the initial impact with the nuns was no worse than you had feared, and that you feel you may be able to survive for another couple of months without turning into a total bigot.

It is so good for the character to be able to adapt to changing circumstances, as your Father, a product of a Jesuit education, will tell you ad nauseam if he hasn't already done so.

Speaking of which or whom, he has adapted so well to being driven around by a chauffeur six days of the week, that Sundays have become something of a nightmare, automobilistically speaking. It seems to me that even the Belgians dive for cover when he appears behind the wheel, though he maintains this is merely my over-active imagination. This said, a scene occurred last weekend that I wouldn't have missed for worlds. As he was ill-advisedly backing the car out of the driveway, I heard the most almighty scrunch, and Guess Who had driven the Alfa straight over three (full) dustbins (plastic) lined up on the kerb awaiting the lorry (due any second.) And no amount of reversing could dislodge them from the undercarriage where they lay, squashed hopelessly out of regulation shape, and regurgitating all manner of unsanitary rubbish over the normally sterile Belgian thoroughfare. I had to absent myself for a while until I could stop laughing, but upon returning found Erlinda getting the blame for not knowing how to remove the spare wheel and reach the jack (as if he'd have known how to use it!) So I watched them fool around for a while bashing things with hammers, (from which we learned that in the event of a puncture there's not a hope in hell of getting that spare wheel out,) and then jumped into the car and did something rather clever with a reverse gear and a bit of a wiggle and drove it to freedom in insufferable triumph.

We are finally straight after the move and have started giving dinner parties on matching plates. As I write this, a gaggle of generals are gathered below for a working lunch, due to be served at one o'clock sharp to enable them to be back at their desks by 3.15. At 12.10 cook looked up in surprise as I hove into the kitchen where she was sharpening the odd knife, and confessed she thought they weren't coming until tonight. I am now wondering how to let myself down from an upstairs window so I can get into the kitchen unseen by the guests and rescue the sorbet which she will most definitely have omitted to remove from the freezer, and which will otherwise need to be served with a pneumatic drill. After which I shall head very rapidly to the woods for an outsize dollop of fresh air, and endeavour to walk off some of those dreaded chocolates people keep giving me.

Enclosed is a cheque in lieu of luncheon vouchers so that you can occasionally opt out of the boiled chicken and carrots at weekends. Or cheer yourself up with a shopping spree.

Miss you something rotten. Come over soon. XXXX Maman

CHAPTER TWO

The trouble with the countryside, I thought, as I pounded through the woods, was that it was not always compatible with being married to an Ambassador. All that mud, for a start, and the risk of treading in undesirable substances, and getting back home with blackberry stains and scratches and armfuls of colour-uncoordinated wild flowers. I could feel the disapproval emanating from the staff each time I returned from one of my trips: their contracts, I was given to understand, did not extend to the arranging of twenty different varieties of weed in formal vases, nor to the removal of afore-mentioned substances from disgracefully non-designer footwear. Nor, indeed, to the transforming of a bag of sickly blackberries into something worthy of gracing His Excellency's table.

Not that H.E. was given to eating dessert, at the best of times. Far too concerned about the dreaded possibility that his girth might one day burst the waistband of his bespoke dinner jacket, and thus cause endless personal sorrow to the exceedingly obsequious tailor who had staked his reputation upon it all those years ago.

Regretfully I turned back towards Brussels, whistling, none too competently, for the dog to follow. Beagle's strong point was not obedience, and the whistle didn't get too much practice in and around the diplomatic circles I had to frequent, so between one thing and another, it was the customary reckless drive back home, trail of mud to the bathroom and realisation that once again I had no time to wash the wind out of my hair before Cocktails, somewhere or other, at 7.30 p.m. Oh well, thank God for the hair band and a pair of earrings.

Himself was being Unamused. He had had a trying day. Someone back at the Ministry was jockeying for power (again) and the usual bunch of morons were poised to grab all the best positions. As if that were not sufficient, the new Second Secretary had arrived wearing the most appalling tie and had already revealed himself to be incapable of writing a grammatically correct sentence. Furthermore, he suspected, could not spell, and had to zip everything he wrote through the computer spell check before presenting it to his Ambassador for signature. This computer literacy alone rendered him suspicious in the eyes of his chief, who belonged to a generation which considered even the carrying of a pen to be undignified behaviour. Moreover he had been brought up to judge the importance of a mission by the number of administrative staff it could squeeze out of the Foreign Ministry, and was thus highly antagonistic towards any attempt to have them replaced by machinery.

In my opinion, most of this chagrin could have been relieved by a stiff G and T, but in the light of the waistline consideration, all it got was a dousing in mineral water which did nothing to diminish its irksomeness. I forced myself to concentrate on his recital of the day's problems, which had now progressed to the difficulties involved in replacing a cipher clerk, acquiring a new flag for the car, and obtaining a meeting with Someone of Political Importance in the Government. I started, as always, to feel guilty about my carefree afternoon in the woods and vowed to spend tomorrow bossing the Filipinos around, getting the silver cleaned properly and re-arranging the flowers as an act of contrition.

*　　*　　*　　*

The evening's gathering was one of those classic diplomatic affairs where the waiters brought around trays of undrinkable vin de table and Campari sodas the colour of cough mixture. The token glass of inferior fizz, I noted, was as usual placed strategically at the back of the tray, so that one had to go against all one's careful upbringing to reach over for it.　After all those years in the game I could manage that and hook a canapé without so much as a pause in mid-anecdote, though this evening I had got off to a bad start mistaking a well-known Belgian Princess for the wife of the new Dutch Ambassador. The standard "Oh how nice to meet you - when did you arrive?" was in consequence met with a rather surly "My family has, you should know, been here for fifteen generations."

Quelle horreur, thought Mme. la Princesse as she peered short-sightedly at what was surely a stray leaf in that badly cut hair?　Patting her own lacquered helmet, she moved off through the crowd in search of some blue blood where she would feel on safer ground. You just could not tell with the diplomatic corps, these days. Some of them, she had been told, even dressed from the second-hand shops. A slight shudder passed through fifteen generations of classic bone structure at the thought of one of her own garments turning up where she least expected it.

Fortified by the bubbles, albeit inferior, I circulated.

The French Ambassador sailed in looking harassed. Rumours along Quai d'Orsay corridors had it that his days were numbered, and that a vacancy was about to be presented to him as an offer not to be refused. A prendre où à laisser, quoi. Should the rumours prove to be well founded, he would have to come up rather quickly with a face-saving explanation as to why only he amongst his colleagues could be relied upon to fulfil this extremely delicate mission and his farewell cocktail was liable to be more like a wake since, by all accounts, he didn't want to go to Bogotà at all, much less at such short notice, poor bastard. The hardest of all to convince would, as usual, be his wife, at his side this evening looking like the fairy off the Christmas tree in a designer frock clearly purchased when she had been two sizes slimmer. As I approached to pay my respects, she was busily canvassing contributions towards a cookery book she was compiling in aid of the enfants handicappés and succeeded in coercing me into providing her with a new recipe for pasta. The bubbles were, on second thoughts, not such a good idea, leading one to make rash promises one would surely regret upon the morrow. I made a mental note to put some of the younger Embassy wives on to the task. Delegate, that was the answer: pull rank, damn it. Give them something to do instead of scouring the local markets for atrocities with which to adorn their over decorated apartments.

Himself, I noted in passing, was busily holding forth to the representative of one of those new countries in Eastern Europe whose name I couldn't begin to pronounce even were I to remember it. I caught his eye and raised an eyebrow, but these days neither the eyebrow technique nor even a solid kick under the table seemed to achieve the desired effect. I recalled better times when our respective thresholds of boredom had been more attuned. At one particularly deadly party we had conspired wordlessly to escape through the garden, though had been caught in the act by our hostess who had herself been feeling the need for a little fresh air spiced with a slug of neat gin straight from the bottle.

Side-stepping something very garlicky who was apparently intent upon reminding me where we had last met, I suddenly found myself face to face with, of all people, Michael.

"Sarah!" Positively beaming.

"Michael! What in the name of...?"

"Didn't you know? Didn't Giorgio tell you? I've been posted to Nato. Been here a couple of weeks already. God am I glad to see you, you're just what I needed. I was starting to talk in infinitives with all these...."

I kicked his ankle. You did have to keep him on a tight rein, I remembered. He could be quite outrageous when he was bored.

He turned to introduce me to his companion.

"Sarah darling, may I introduce you to Mr. Akumbe from Nigeria? And Oxford," he added, for good measure.

"Mr. Akumbe," I said happily, "I am so pleased to meet you. We were posted to your country for four years when my husband and I were younger, and we loved every minute of it. Except perhaps for the amoeba," I added thoughtfully. "Did you know, they used to let me play polo there, Michael? And once a week we would ride along the beach and jump the dead bodies for fun. Never on Saturdays, though; that was Public Execution day. Too many people: the horses used to get overexcited."

"Mr. Akumbe and I have just been having a fascinating conversation," said Michael rapidly, "about the superior versatility of the yam over the common potato." He fixed a point some ten centimetres over the top of my head in order to avoid further eye contact, and let me get on with it.

I rose to the challenge.

"Mr. Akumbe, I know exactly the person you should meet. The French Ambassadress is preparing an international cookery book to sell in aid of charity, and she desperately needs original ideas like how to be versatile with a yam." At my side, I could feel Michael's gaze lower incredulously, and very firmly I ordered him to find me a glass of fizz "from ANYWHERE" while I went and introduced my new friend to Mme. Sancerre.

ncorking a bottle.

e set and match to
y... ...t little item?"

"N... ...re you aware I've
bee... ...r twenty bloody
minu... ...oody piri? ME,
that g... ...ast an Indian
restau... ...British diet of
scrambl... ...you eaten?"

"Sort of... ...vol-au-vents
stopped n... ...ist as well,
probably. Y...

"No. Had... ...mething
unidentifiabl... ...uple of
things on stick... ...tually.
Shall we go on...

"Willingly, if yo... ...that
obviously import... ...Try
signalling "oysters... ..."

"Alternatively, Sara... ...k
out quietly and have... ...f
fathomless brown ey...
insistently in my dire...
flippancy shuddered to...
all about? Help! Slowly...
canapés hovering at my...
awaiting my decision. This...
British, for heaven's sake...

"We could not do anything...
know it, Michael. One foot...
couple of dozen under-emplo...
yours and ours would stop...
comments about the guests an...

manner of pornographic situations. Amongst which an innocent meal in a restaurant would not even be given a passing reference."

He took my glass and placed it on a nearby table.

"Oh well, just an idea." He waved the canapés away with a frown as I glanced at my watch.

"Right, that man is going to be surgically removed from this party if I have to create an International Incident to achieve it. Can I borrow your mobile phone a minute? I need to go to the loo."

"Forgive me, I don't see the...."

"You will. Meet you outside."

Left alone, Michael sighed and looked around for an animated group to latch on to, and had just decided that his best bet was probably a bunch of journalists in the far corner, seemingly well past both their deadlines and their alcohol limit, when he noticed the Italian Ambassador reaching none too discreetly for his cell phone. Minutes later, we all met out on the front steps as if by coincidence, having made our respective farewells with a maximum of effusion and a minimum of sincerity. I gave him back his phone and, as we waited for our cars to arrive, we arranged to follow each other to the nearest Italian restaurant.

Brussels, November 20th

Dear Mother,

Thank you for your letter and customary newspaper

cuttings extolling the virtues of Plenty of Fresh Air and No Booze, and the dangers of Walking Alone in the Woods and not having a regular Mammography. My whole life could be monitored through your clippings had I kept them all. Always Boil the Water South of the Channel; Mixed Marriages and the Effect of all that Foreign Food on the Gastro-Intestinal Tract; Mothers-in-law: How to Deal With; the dangers of the pill and of mixing horse riding with having babies... etc..

I enjoyed, too, your entertaining experiences with slugs, and will endeavour to bear in mind the properties of beer should the necessity arise in my daily stroll around the garden. I know you will be fascinated to learn that scientists are still debating the question of whether a snail was originally a slug forced to grow a shell for reasons of survival, or whether it started off with a shell and lost it for lack of calcium. So keep on taking the tablets, dear, (or jelly cubes, was it this week?) You never know.

Last week I was pounding through the woods with the fauns and bunnies, this week we are covered in snow. The Belgians have immediately donned cross-country skis even to do their shopping, and the ponds have been taken over by skaters. I spent hours shovelling the stuff from the driveway so we could get the car out of the garage, and then the automatic gates froze, imprisoning us all for three and a half days until they came to fix the motor. Also we apparently had a pipe full of frozen shit which put most of the bathrooms out of action. Sir was frantic. We sent out an emergency call to the faithful Iglesias, plumber, decorator, mechanic, and proud owner of all the stray cats that have turned up in our garden and after whose welfare I assiduously refrain from enquiring, since I strongly suspect him of turning them into Paella. The good news is that we are now shitless, though it involved poor Iglesias standing outside in Arctic temperatures trying to thaw the endangered pipe with a glorified hairdryer, and succeeding only in burning out the hairdryer whilst shrivelling half the pipe and having to reconstruct it with lashings of concrete - a substance of which your Mediterranean worker is particularly fond.

The girls are fine - Francesca is, by all accounts, losing half a kilo a day back in Rome at the Institute where she is staying. Why is student accommodation invariably in the hands of flagellating nuns in Italy? Giorgio made the mistake of thinking she was giving him the good news of her new slim-line figure, and proceeded to get an earful of how that was NOT the point, and how she couldn't exist on boiled dandelions for much longer. The heart almost bled there for half a minute, so we finally decided that she is perfectly old enough to survive on her own, and will try to evict the non-paying tenant who is now living rent-free in our little flat in Rome, and re-install her there instead.

Well, Cook is waiting for me to show her how to make a mushroom risotto as opposed to rice pudding with cèpes, so I will go and pretend to be efficient.

Love from us all, and do continue to keep us posted with the latest scientific discoveries courtesy of your eminently entertaining tabloids. I wouldn't miss those gems of wisdom for worlds.

Love, Sarah

CHAPTER THREE

"Ma'am? You awake ma'am? Phone is ringing, ma'am!"

"Yes, how funny you should have noticed, Erlinda. It does seem to be ringing. For some time now, too. Perhaps you could answer it. That's probably what one should do in the circumstances."

I turned over and stuck my head under the pillow. Mornings aren't my best time of the day.

"Ma'am, you want I answer it, ma'am?"

"Erlinda, I can't think of anything I'd like more. You do that."

" 'Scuse me, ma'am. I answer phone now."

Too late, of course. But the chances of whoever it was giving up were so remote that I felt justified in relaxing back into a semi-slumber for the ensuing brief respite. I drifted into a delightful daydream in which I was pottering round some remote farmhouse in a track suit and old sneakers with a selection of stray cats, dogs and village disreputables for company. The phone was ringing.

"Please ma'am, phone for you, I bring."

Pre-programmed to hand her employers whatever they might need on a silver tray, Erlinda finally made her triumphant entrance into the bedroom five minutes later with the portable phone lying in splendour on a dinner plate covered with a freshly starched linen napkin. Monday mornings were silver cleaning mornings. This had hampered her severely in her search for the necessary tray, and she hoped her employer would be content with a Herrend dinner plate instead. Her employer probably would have been satisfied with just that, had the damn phone still contained a damn caller, she gave her to understand. As it was, the damn caller, unaware that he or she was being offered the privilege of speaking from amidst a flurry of butterflies hand-painted by Hungarian artisans and from within a cocoon of Flanders linen, had rung off, the Philistine. I tried to sink back into my daydream and thus put off the dreaded moment of getting to grips with the day's problems, but the knowledge that the cook was awaiting orders for lunch and dinner, that the gardener would only sit and drink all our tea in the kitchen until I arrived to chivvy him into activity, and that the wife of the Danish Ambassador was due to pay her respects over coffee eventually forced me reluctantly out of bed and into the shower. I was well into the second shampoo and the third verse of the Hallelujah chorus when the phone rang again, and the starched napkin at least proved useful for wiping soap off the mouthpiece.

It was Michael, fresh back from an early morning jog through the woods prior to taking up his customary position behind the Times crossword puzzle.

"I suppose you're still lying unkempt beneath the sheets whilst some of us have already filled our lungs to capacity with ozone and frost and leaf mould? Wakey Wakey, old thing, I have an almighty proposition to make and it will need your maximum concentration. Has that Concita person filled you up with coffee yet? Because if not, ring for it forthwith. I don't have time to explain all this twice over, I've got a very tricky 15 across which threatens to occupy the better part of my morning here."

I grabbed a towel.

"I don't know about lying unkempt, but there's shampoo all over the cushions, wet footprints on the Italian Government's carpet, a budding career in the New York Met. brought to an untimely end before it even got off the ground, and Concita alias Erlinda can't bring coffee because the trays are being cleaned. You'll just have to be content with brain cells batting on two cylinders. What the hell do you want at this uncivilised hour, anyway? No, go on, amaze me. You saw the first swallow in the woods this morning? or heard the first cuckoo? or tripped over a carnivorous snowdrop? Or broke your record for croissant eating before breakfast? Or was Karla himself waiting by your dead letter box hollow tree type thing when you panted up through the morning mist? Are you ringing to tell me you just got jabbed in the ankle by a Soviet umbrella, and are about to be winched off the top of the Atomium by men in balaclavas? Because it had better be good, my friend. I do not fall about laughing at the idea of being hauled out of my shower just to furnish suggestions for a possible solution to 15 across."

"Sarah, you know I get Uncommonly Upset when you make your spy jokes. Someone might just be hooked into this phone listening and think you had an undisclosed source, and it could jeopardise my famously impeccable reputation. And you might like to know I've solved 15 across whilst I was waiting for you to finish blathering: "picaresque." Ha! Wait till my Ambassador gets in, that'll impress him. Might even get me an extension of tour of duty. Or a posting to Rome - did I tell you I'm learning Italian? Little things like Making Oneself Vital with the Crossword can do a lot to enhance a chap's career. Shit. Now I've forgotten what I rang you for, and its time for morning prayers."

"Morning *what*?"

"Staff meeting. Obligatory. All ranks including tea ladies. Every Monday morning. Sorry - I'll call you back as soon as it's over."

Resuming my preparations, I fell to wondering precisely what Michael did achieve in the course of his day's work. He seemed to have an extraordinary amount of time left over for physical excercise and chatting on the phone or having leisurely lunches with his various contacts. When he finally rang back, having remembered what he had called for in the first place, it was to invite us both for a week's skiing in the French Alps.

"Chap's lent me this chalet. One of those God awful custom-built ski resorts. Hideous architecturally and dreadfully un-chic, but you can practically jump out of the window with your skis on and straight into the lifts. No humping of cumbersome equipment or waiting around for elusive sleighs that have been booked out solid at the start of the season by the glitterati. Thought it might be fun if you're both free - we can get Giorgio mellowed with the vin d'épices, and kit him out in those skinny legging things and shoot him off cross-country while you and I hit the glaciers. How about it?"

"Michael, whilst I now freely admit that this proposition of yours was worth digging me out of the shower for, there is one very basic but very important fallacy here. It involves the hilarious notion that anyone at all could get me onto a glacier, or, come to think of it, anything hairier than a blue run. And preferably pale blue at that. I do not ski with the professionals. I ski with the kiddie ski school in the mornings, and get talked gently up and down the slopes by preferably gorgeous instructors. I then stop for a liquid lunch and ski divinely down anything in my path under the influence for most of the afternoon. If I'm not sunbathing. Which I do with total dedication. We'd love to come, or I would, but I have an awful feeling Giorgio can't possibly take a week off. I'll talk to him about it this evening, but you know how indispensable he likes to think he is. When were you planning on leaving?"

"Week after next. Plan B. Just a sec. 'Incredibly long Dutch kipper.' What the hell kind of twisted minds do these people have - any ideas on that one?"

"No! In fact my intellectual capacities at this hour in the morning are at a notoriously low ebb. It's all to do with the blood pressure, you understand. Nothing personal, but we were discussing an interesting proposition here, and if we could just conclude before I catch something life-threatening from hot shower interruptus, I would be highly gratified..."

"Rip Van Winkle. You want my autograph? How many chaps do you know can solve the Times crossword that fast, before elevenses, whilst carrying on a sophisticated conversation with a beautiful woman under her shower?"

"I WAS under the shower, ess aitch aye tea: I am now trying none too successfully to apply some make-up. Plan B, you were saying, until you rudely interrupted yourself?"

"Was I? Yes, yes, of course. Here's what we do ...... Oh ho ho ho, how about this, then? 'Decorator hanging around a low joint' - Anklet. No, forgive me, I'm being poco serioso, here. What we do, is, you guys come up for a long weekend and join me there. By train, or something. Public transport, you know the sort of thing. Tickets, platforms, all that. And I come and collect you at the station all sweetness and light with a candlelit dinner pre-booked at the local boozer, and you hit the slopes first thing the next morning and the one after that, and even the one after that, and he's back in the office by, say, Tuesday with no one the wiser. They'll just think he took an extra long lunch. See?"

"In the interest of our undying friendship, I am willing to give it a try. Where do I find you this evening?"

"At the Volkaersbeke's, God help me. Aren't you invited?"

"No idea. Erlinda can't bring the day's programme up because the trays are being cleaned. Is that really how you pronounce their surname? How fascinating. I'll call you, or leave a message, or maybe even see you there, if we're in and invited.

Michael, I simply must finish getting ready, I've got the Danish Ambassadress coming for coffee to discuss Charitable Objectives."

"How extremely unwise of you, especially with your criminally low blood pressure. You should take better care of your health - I can see I'll have to intervene. Quote Booker T. Washington at her, that should do it."

"Who? What?"

"He said 'If you want to lift yourself up, lift up someone else.' It's all a question of motivation, see? By the way, the chalet comes with all the trimmings including Chateau de Plonk equipped cellar. Look I can't chat to you all morning, I've got a report to write - Oh Lor', triple groan: 'School that equips one to break new ground' - Harrow. That is pathetic . 'Bye, speak to you later."

Right, I thought. And a facility for quotation covers the absence of original thought. Quote Peter Winsey. But like all good repartee, I'd already put the phone down and it was too late. I had to admit that he had a point concerning the Dane. The lady in question was very earnest, very boring, very bad for my blood pressure. The only positive feature was the rather good coffee served on an impeccably gleaming silver salver by an impeccably gleaming Erlinda. The conversation, as feared, turned to the annual charity bazaar. The Scandinavians, I was given to understand, were achieving great heights with their homemade lampshades and biscuits, and were striving to a woman to beat last year's record. The Italian wives must be activated before it was too late.

By the time the coffee had been cleared away it was almost one o'clock. I just managed to check the table settings for the monthly NATO Ambassadors' luncheon before the first guests started to arrive. Since these monthly meetings were Men Only occasions, I nipped out of the back door and headed for the stables. A couple of hours cantering through the woods and jumping the odd tree trunk, I reckoned, might just prepare me mentally for dinner at the Volkaersbeke's château, to which I had just learned I was privileged to have been invited that evening.

In White Tie with Decorations. Blaspheming steadily under his breath, Giorgio was standing in the bathroom trying to achieve a respectable bow in mirror image. Shoelaces he had mastered, despite his mother's reluctance to impart this skill in his youth. The more he was obliged to depend upon her, she had felt instinctively, the less he would be inclined to fly the nest and leave her (horrors) or, (worse) set up with some Dreadful Woman or, (unthinkable) Foreigner. Tying his own shoelaces had been a major step on the path to independence and freedom from maternal suffocation. Changing light bulbs, cleaning shoes, inserting cuff links, taking out the rubbish, were still un-acquired arts, and liable to remain so, given that he had passed straight from his mother's excessive solicitudes to his wife's Anglo-Saxon practicality and thence to the Concitas' paid capabilities. Resplendent in décolleté and satin sling-backs, not a trace of horse or beagle hair on the black Armani classic, I whipped the offending tie into submission and broached the subject of a weekend break in the French Alps with undeniably superb timing. By the time we arrived at the château, we had only to order the tickets.

Brussels, 26th November

Dear Frankie,

Having just received my latest phone bill, which I was lucky enough to have delivered to me before your father got hold of it, I thought I had better substitute typewriter for telephone. Sir will most certainly have to be scraped off the ceiling if he catches sight of it, and I have decided that next time you have to be talked through pre-examination nerves, I shall just hop on a plane, which should effect a saving of at least 80% in real economic terms.

Last night we were privileged to be invited to dinner at the Volkaersbeke's château and to this end were driven through the fog and murk for an hour and a half in all our sartorial splendour. The guests were predictable, (that Brit. Mil. attaché was there taking the piss out of everyone and everything, so I wasn't entirely on my best behaviour), the food was mediocre, the temperature within was about half a split degree above freezing, and a dodgy canapé did something unspeakable to my stomach a little before midnight, so all things considered we were relieved your father doesn't shoot, which at least got us out of being invited back for a long weekend to wreak havoc on the pheasant. We snuggled home in our heated limo and furs, picked up a group of your sister's multi-coloured cronies from a party on the way, spread out a selection of mattresses and blankets on the Embassy carpets, and let them all sleep it off until about midday this morning, there being no school today. The diversity of the crew that appeared demanding breakfast around that hour startled even the usually unfazed Filipinos - the ruling element of the Belgian Congo does tend to have a very large and very sociable family, most of whom seem to be in Alex's class at the French Lycée, and a considerable number of whom were most content to swap their four poster beds for our sleeping bags on the floor last night.

Next weekend we are off skiing for a couple of days - no don't laugh, I am absolutely capable of staying upright if I concentrate hard enough, and the exercise is just what your father needs to break up a long and inactive winter. When I get back we'll start some radical work on that flat and try to get you free from the clutches of the nuns before it's too late.

So don't panic. Exams are not the end of the world, and you just have to learn to take them in your stride. If you ask me, you aren't praying hard enough.

Lots and lots of love, and I'll call you very soon. Maman

We left for the mountains by train as foreseen, and were met at the station by a tanned and snow-capped military attaché dying to drag us up to the glaciers even before we had unpacked. Giorgio went off to the cross country runs each morning whilst I struggled with the finer points of the parallel turn, helped up by Michael every time I fell over my feet. In the interest of keeping up his Italian, he amused himself by practising his extensive collection of swear words - invaluable whenever some snow-boarding cherub came careering towards us - before progressing to a repertoire of rousing excerpts from sundry operas which he would sing fortissimo as he slalomed down the slopes. It was, all in all, a very jolly though entirely platonic weekend. Manuela would have despaired.

Brussels, December 3rd

Dear Mother,

We had a few days in the mountains to take advantage of the snow, and acquired impressive tans and the odd muscle. Stayed in a rather odd chalet with a somewhat effete decor, but since it belonged to a friend of a close friend and was thus gratis, my Scottish blood turned a blind eye with no trouble at all. Achieved some very impressive skiing, despite my customary problem remembering my original Swiss instructor's admonitions about the "body wight" going on the "downvarts", not the "upvarts", ski across the "sloop." After a bit I remembered it was mostly just a question of getting positively pickled and reaching with the "pool" and going "HUP" and keeping your eyes closed wherever possible. Came back on the ski-train with Sir effing and blinding because I hadn't managed to get first class tickets, not that it makes much difference to my mind, being that in any case you are just as cramped, hot and impregnated with everyone else's odours whether it's a first class slot or a second. By his reckoning, the allotted space would have been larger by a centimetre and a half, which he maintained would have made all the difference to his getting a modicum of sleep or none at all. Also there just might have been one of those dinky little gadgets to stick his opened bottle of mineral water into for the night, thus avoiding having it spill over his trousers somewhere between the German and French borders. Then, of course, the train was so long that our carriage didn't make it to the platform upon arrival, so there was some rather undignified lugging of suitcases which, by this time, had multiplied themselves a smidgen, what with the sopping wet ski gear and all, some of us having been dragged off the slopes at the very last minute, you understand... Then we crawled into this taxi which was straight out of a junk yard, with a driver smelling of the Moroccan spice markets, and all the stuffing coming out of the seams, and His Excellency cursing for not having detailed his chauffeur to be on call, whilst the rest of us were feeling very silly in maxi mink coats.

We lurched into Brussels which was looking all grey and horrid in the dirty snow, and it took an excellent lunch at his favourite restaurant to restore anything like good humour.

Looking forward to having you for Christmas here, this year - Erlinda has been detailed to prepare and freeze mountains of food before disappearing into the folds of her extended Filipino family for a week, so if I play my cards right we can zap things into the microwave from December 22nd through until you leave on the 29th. And feel free to bring a selection of Fortnum's Mince Pies, Brandy Butter and ready-to-inject chestnut stuffing, none of which, I fear, feature in her repertoire.

See you very soon, Sarah

*   *   *   *

One of the Approved Activities for diplomatic wives languishing in forgotten lands is fund raising: in fact Charitable Works have long been the saving of many a desperate housewife teetering on the verge of alcoholism or the necessity of taking a lover. All the more so when condemned to a three year posting in Ouagadougou. Once acquired, it is a feel-good habit that is hard to break, and by the time the wife of your average third secretary attains the dizzy heights of Ambassadress, she is unstoppable.

"Carissima!"
When I was younger and got called "carissima" by my Ambassadress, I thought, I used to throw a silent fit and *swear* I'd never do it to anyone else. It's as

good as saying "I can't remember your name but I need you to do me a favour." During our first posting to Vienna, the favour frequently involved spreading canapés for anything up to five hundred people for the National Day celebrations, the Ambassador in question being reluctant to employ a large enough staff to take care of these details. On more than one occasion the wives had physically transported vast numbers of hired chairs from the lorry to the ballroom and arranged them around innumerable tables in preparation for an evening's dinner dance. We were later given to understand that to have been invited to partake in this communal effort was a privilege. That particular Chief of Mission used to love organising balls and concerts and fancy dress parties. Diminutive in stature, (approximately five foot nothing in his socks), he nevertheless considered himself a ladies' man, and kept a garçonnière down town which he liked to think nobody knew about. Certain members of his staff currying for favour were, it was rumoured, happy to furnish this abode with female companions whenever necessary, and gain themselves an extra mark in the end of year reports as recompense. He loved giving masked balls, for he fancied himself terribly in epaulettes and braid and at one such occasion, he strutted around looking like a mini Napoleon inviting all the Austrian princesses to dance the polka whilst he leered up at their cleavages. He judged the success or failure of his parties solely according to the hour at which the last guest left the Embassy. Members of his staff were therefore detailed to prevent the departure of said guests for as long as possible and would be Cinderellas were hauled back by their ears and persuaded to take another turn on the dance floor by ageing Minister Counsellors eager for promotion. Sadly his wife spoke no German and finding the long winter afternoons increasingly tedious while her husband was away hunting the boar or the filly, she hit upon the brilliant notion of convening the Embassy wives to keep her company with sewing-bee sessions. This too was a privilege awarded for good behaviour, and not to be invited was considered a Slight of the Highest Order. Memorably one of the wives once turned up resplendent in Chanel suit and earrings, designer bag and shoes and astounded everyone by producing, not an elegant piece of petit-point, but her husband's old socks to darn. No one ever understood if the tongue was in the cheek, but the lady was not invited the following week, and after her husband had been discovered slumbering peacefully behind the heavy brocade curtains at 3 a.m. during one of the famous balls, they were transferred soon afterwards to a hardship post.

"Renata, carissima! How *are* you? I haven't seen you for ages. You must come over for coffee some morning when you have a moment, but I know how busy you are and I do hate to impose on your free time."

Steady now, Sarah, or she'll take you at your word. I took a deep breath and started to explain about the Nato bazaar and how there would have to be a concerted effort to get a stall full of saleable objects gathered together in order not to disgrace the Italian Embassy's hitherto unsullied image. Wives with talent were to produce whatever they were good at: that year's crop were heavily into picture framing, book-binding and dried flower arranging, it seemed. Those without talent were to go around the Italian firms and beg. Anything would do, from silk scarves to packets of pasta and bottles of Chianti. See to it, was basically the underlying message, whilst I get on with the more important things in life like walking the dog. Or meeting up with Military Attachés.

"Well, can I leave that with you, then? Oh, and see if someone can come up with something original to throw over pasta while you are about it. I've got the French Ambassadress breathing down my neck. Says at this rate they'll be re-posted before she can get to the printers. Let me know how you get on, won't you?"

I had no doubt on that score. Erlinda must be programmed to say I was "out" or "receiving company" three times out of every four. Luckily Renata revelled in this sort of activity and she would boss the junior wives around mercilessly. I would begin to think about my own contribution to the stall just as soon as I had made a couple more phone calls.

"Michael?"

"Amore, I was thinking of you this very moment - pure telepathy."

"Hmm, well don't pick up the phone to call me, or anything strenuous like that, will you? What are you up to? How about some tennis this afternoon?"

" I'm far too scared to call you. That Sicilian husband of yours terrifies the life out of me. Luparas make me nervous. Must be the result of a childhood trauma."

"Don't be ridiculous, Michael, You'd never been south of Brighton until you were twenty - you told me so yourself. I need some exercise - want a game?"

"I can't think of anything I'd like better, amore mio. What's my prize if I beat you? - can I choose it as my Christmas present?"

Bugger, now what have I let myself in for?

I lost hopelessly, of course. As we were returning from the courts and heading for a drink at the bar, he suddenly stopped and said, "You know, Sarah, you and I have a very, very special relationship." Now what the hell does that mean? I wondered, but it was too late to ask as, out of the corner of my eye I perceived the slow but certain approach of the Italian Ambassador. Dictating last minute memos to his secretary, he approached from the other side of the bar, and when I turned round to warn him, I discovered Michael was already half way to the changing rooms.

CHAPTER FOUR

"Holà!"

"Manu! Where are you? It must be the middle of the night in Argentina - what are you doing calling at this hour?"

"I'm at the airport trying to shake off some boring Brit. who's been insisting on carrying my computer case ever since I got off the plane."

"Computer case - since when were you computer literate? Or was it an investment on Paolo's part to cut down your phone bills? Which airport?"

"Brussels. And I'm not - I use it to keep my face creams in. No way I'll entrust that collection to baggage handlers. Anyway, it helps get you upgraded when you're travelling and attracts a better class of pick up. All white-collar stuff these days. God you Brits can be tough going, though. This one keeps asking me leading questions about how I download, or something. I thought he was just being vulgar so I encouraged him at first. Can you come and rescue me? I'm at Zaventem. Can I stay for a few days?"

Driving out to the airport, I fell to wondering just which catastrophe in her chequered existence had brought my friend to seek refuge in Belgium just before Christmas. I had a sudden nightmare flash of the looming scenario at breakfast time involving two grandmothers demanding respectively panettone and porridge at eight a.m., two daughters needing litres of black coffee, Manuela begging for Bloody Marys, Giorgio requiring fresh fruit salad and decaffeinated tea and Michael calling at half-hourly intervals with unhelpful suggestions. Nor, regarding the latter, was I any too keen on introducing Manu with her killer technique into what might still prove to be a delicately evolving relationship.

Manuela was a picture. Enveloped in furs, she waved royally as I drew up to the Arrivals forecourt. A distinguished young man not a day over thirty handed her into the front seat and immediately withdrew to a waiting taxi.

"Did you want me to offer him a lift into town? You didn't seem too keen on the phone."

"I'm not. My life is complicated enough already. Sarah, darling, could I possibly stay over Christmas? Paolo has thrown me out and I can't bear all this festivity going on around me whilst I'm all alone."

"Of course you can. You can help keep the grandmothers and daughters from getting at each other's throats. It'll be perfect therapy for you. Dare I ask what position he caught you in?"

"Supine. Flagrant. Well, semi-supine - you know. Those dentists' chairs don't go the whole way." She brightened for a minute. "Dentist did, though. Stupid receptionist walked in on us and told his wife who immediately...oh well! Never mind. He wasn't really my type."

"Who, Paolo or your dentist?"

"Dentist, stupid. I'm devastated about Paolo. What should I do? He'll have to forgive me eventually, won't he? By the way, it seems there's a truly great dietician in Brussels who still prescribes all those forbidden pills that let you eat like a horse whilst losing ten kilos a day. I thought I might check him out while I'm here. Sarah, you are sure you don't mind, aren't you? I realise it's an awful imposition, but I didn't know who else to turn to. I'm destitute, and I couldn't spend Christmas under a bridge, could I?"

"Of course you couldn't. It'll be lovely having you around. You're not seriously destitute, are you? Where's Daddy in all this saga?"

"Took Paolo's side - can you imagine? My own father, who taught me the very meaning of the word adultery. Bastards the lot of them. I'm not having anything more to do with the species for the rest of my days. You shall hereby be witness to my New Year's Resolutions. Sod all men. Cultivate your girl friends. And your figure. Just in case. Do you think you could drive a little more slowly - those radar things keep flashing at us and I'll have to touch up my make up if I'm to be photographed every two minutes."

Christmas was memorable. The girls were in fine fettle, thrilled with all their presents and tormenting the grandmothers mercilessly.

"Alex, I've run out of weed - could you roll me some of yours?"

"There's a man at the door come to collect the syringes."

"Where did you go last night, and who made that big dent in the back of the Alfa?"

"Why do you still keep all those empty fag packets in your schoolbag?"

Manuela flitted from one generation to the other with a piece of Christmas cake in one hand and a calorie-counting guide in the other.

"If I don't have any more champagne before 7 p.m., I can still allow myself two Belgian chocolates with my coffee. In any case, I'm starting a new diet on Monday."

Nonna revelled in being waited on hand and foot, wrapped herself in her Christmas presents of cashmere shawl and fur-lined slippers, and held court on the sofa each day, refusing to move an inch in case she caused a draught. Outside the snow was falling gently to the general satisfaction of everyone else.

Michael came over for drinks on Boxing Day, well diluted amongst a crowd of colleagues and friends, and was introduced to Manuela who, I noted, had spent the better part of the morning conversing earnestly on the phone. As feared, the two of them spent most of the party talking exclusively to each other. I myself hardly had time to exchange a word with him, being too busy administering to the needs of the other guests, but he managed a brotherly peck under the mistletoe and held my eyes with particular insistence whilst he toasted everyone in champagne. When they had all left, I drifted into Manuela's room to find her changing into a pair of jeans.

"That wasn't too bad, was it? How many skulls did you notch up tonight?"

"Not one, I'm a reformed character. What you see before you is a New Me. No more cleavage, just puritan collars and sensible shoes, and I'll let my teeth rot before I'll ever set foot in another dentist's chair. Paolo rang. He says he'll forgive me if I promise to concentrate solely on my cooking skills and stay within my monthly budget and swear solemnly to remain faithful for the rest of my life. So that's what I'm going to do and I'm flying back to spend New Year's Eve with him. Aren't you relieved?"

"You'll never make it. You'll die of boredom before you get off the plane. But yes, I am pleased and I do think you should make an effort. Marriages have to be worked at constantly. What did you think of Michael?"

Nobody's fool, Manu stared long and hard.

"Do not touch with barge-pole. Stay away. Commitment phobic. Professional flirt, heart breaker, probably got hurt by a woman somewhere in his varied experience and out for revenge despite appearance of tender sensitivity. Also he's British, which says it all. Impotent if not gay, if not bi. So don't say your best friend didn't warn you." I sat down hard on the bed and gaped.

"What are you talking about? He's just a good friend, and I only asked what you....."

"Keep him that way, is my advice, and don't mess up your life like I nearly did. I might need to come and stay again some day, and two of us under a bridge would be even more uncomfortable than just the one. He ain't worth it, OK? And now let's go and get some supper. I'm starving."

Two days later the girls left to accompany their maternal grandmother back home and spend New

Year's Eve in London, Nonna was put on a flight to Sicily having laid plans to return in time for her son's varicose vein operation, and Manuela swept out on a wave of French perfume designed to lure the long-suffering Paolo back into eating out of the palm of her hand. I started throwing things into suitcases in preparation for our departure for Italy the next day by car, which had seemed a good idea when we had planned it back in June. Now, with the roads iced up and visibility down to a few yards, the prospect of driving to the remote village outside Milan where some friends had invited us to celebrate New Year's Eve, seemed a little less attractive. Before leaving, I rang Michael, just as a friend, to wish him a Happy New Year in advance, but was told by a prissy secretary that he had already left for the UK.

Bastards, all of them.

Brussels, January 15th

Dear Mother,

Glad to hear you got back safely and that the UK was even colder than Brussels where the mannequin's pee has frozen by all accounts into one solid icicle, which can't be very comfortable for him.

We had a glorious week in Italy, though the journey there was somewhat fraught. The snow and ice hit us before we were even a quarter of the way through Switzerland. After two miles of crab-like crawling we worked out it would take us until Feb. 7th at that speed, so we eased off the motorway and asked at a nearby village station where one could put the car onto a train for Milan.

The story at this juncture has two versions. To be fair, the Swiss do speak a daft dialect all of their own, but I am eternally grateful that it was he who did the asking. "Zug" (train) "mit wagen" (with cars) *or* (don't miss this finesse) "carriages", notably "sleeping cars." Whatever, something got lost in the translation, and we lurched along this skating rink all the way to Zurich only to find there was no car-carrying train leaving for Milan, nor ever had been. Sleeping cars a-plenty to anywhere your fancy took you, but nothing that could deliver our car and contents safely to Milan whilst we curled up with a good book. At which point there were those of the party prepared to call it all off and go by 'plane, but the sight of all that luggage deterred. So we thought we'd try the other pass - St. Gotthard - through the Alps and see if that was any clearer. Miraculously it was, or until we reached the foot of the ascent, where signs announced that we would need chains. So we chugged back to find a garage and had them fitted in the teeth of a howling gale and snowstorm while Giorgio took advantage of the pause to go off to the bathroom. I mention this otherwise non-essential fact because it turned out to be of great importance, for whilst he was away peeing round the back of the garage, the mechanic, slotted beneath jacked up car plus luggage plus wife who wasn't getting out for anybody in that weather, was busily explaining to him (in dialect, not that it mattered, because he wasn't there in the first place,) how to take the chains off again when no longer needed. Driving a car with chains is a bit like driving a tractor - you can't go much faster than 15 mph and the noise is hideous, but they nevertheless enabled us to get up and on to that lovely little train that takes you through to the other side.

Where there wasn't so much as a snowflake.

After ten minutes of dadoumdadoumdadoum cutting up the asphalt, he thought he'd nip out and whip them off. Very amusing. There's this hook, see, as he'd have known had he been listening and not round the back of the garage having a pee...
When they didn't crumble lifelessly to the ground beneath his able touch, he thought all he had to do was drive forward a yard or so then go back and pick them up. Whereas instead, there we were, 15° below freezing lying on our stomachs with a failing pocket torch in the remotest of Swiss villages at 11 p.m. where even the cows are tucked up with their hot milk by mid-afternoon, trying to untangle knotted chains from impassive axles.
Fate revealed a guest house half a mile up the road, so we clanked towards it, plaiting the chains ever more securely into the brake cables at every turn of the wheel. The next day being Sunday, Swiss mechanics do not .... but never mind. Suffice that we did make it to Italy in time for the New Year celebrations which involved eating every five minutes, and drinking so much champagne for breakfast, lunch and supper that a good time was eventually had by all, though back in Brussels, the word "chain" is taboo in polite company.

Enough for now, except that I must warn you not to miss next week's exciting instalment in which Himself has his varicose veins stripped by a Belgian specialist so as to be fit for standing around at cocktail parties for the rest of his diplomatic life.

Love and kisses,

Sarah

Snow turned to ice. We had a visit from an old school friend of Giorgio's together with his wife and Vatican approved extensive family. The ground being too hard to ride out into the forest, I walked the dog in the garden. The path was a skating rink. Beagle took a flying leap at a crow she fancied for a mid morning snack, skidded and went splat onto her stomach, uncoordinated paws going towards all four points of the compass. The look of surprise on her face set me laughing so hard I fell over in sympathy, and we were nursing our hurt pride together when I caught sight of the Sicilians coming gingerly round the corner of the house doing the Conga. They advanced with extreme caution in single file, hands on the shoulders of the one in front to avoid sliding on the ice in the sub-freezing temperatures. Terrified of meeting with my fate as I greeted them from the middle of a snow drift, they skirted me with care and headed on into the house, where they spent the next three days putting in requests for espresso coffee, spaghetti with tomato sauce and ice cream, whilst pushing the Foie Gras and smoked salmon I had so carefully purchased for their combined gastronomic delight to the sides of their plates. Predictably,

Giorgio started working longer hours in the office, officially trying to clear his desk before his operation. It was pretty obvious to all concerned, though, that the real reason for his increasingly late return home had less to do with an excess of work and more with his irritation at the sight of his cigarette smoking, whisky and grappa imbibing compatriots. On top of everything else, Michael was being particularly assiduous calling and asking when I would finally be free for lunch again. One snowy morning I pleaded a dental appointment, coaxed the car out of the garage and down the icy drive sideways and crawled on to the main road towards the Nato Sports Club.

At first glance, the greater part of northern Europe was represented around the lunch table as I approached. One woman only amongst them - the Danish Chargé d'Affaires. One "spouse" only present: the non-legalised companion of the Swedish Ambassador - a charming if somewhat visually impaired young man in his early twenties. Michael's eyes followed me in desperation as, from his seat in the midst of this earnest gathering, he waved a greeting to my already departing form. I headed towards the indoor pool pretending I had just come for a swim. Driving warily back home in second gear, I cursed all things British and Sicilian and retired to my room feigning toothache for the rest of the afternoon. Eventually the phone rang.

"Can you ever forgive me?"

"No. Have you ever tried driving a rear suspension Alfa on sheet ice?"

"You're crazy. I should have sent you my driver."

"A great idea, then they'd really have had something to talk about. Like, not only has she slogged all the way out to the Club to have lunch with the golden bachelor, but he's even sent his driver over to fetch her. What happened? I thought we were headed for a tête-à-tête in the local bistro."

"Goddam over-conscientious Dutch, as usual. Insisted on a working lunch to refine our definitions, or some such crap. I miss you. Sarah?"

"Mmm?"

"Let's take the day off together tomorrow and drive into the country somewhere. Shall we?"

"Michael! Do you ever listen to what I tell you? I have a house full of Sicilians, my Mother-in-law arriving and Giorgio is being operated on in forty-eight hours. Wrong moment. Any other time would be great. Not tomorrow."

"I'll call you. Give my best wishes to Giorgio. Tell him it could be worse. Haemorrhoids, for example. Or prostate. Big big hug."

Virtual reality rules as far as the big hug goes, I thought, hanging up and emerging to face the Sicilians hinting at Campari sodas and olives.

CHAPTER FIVE

Brussels, February 4th

Dear Mother,

So here I am sitting in a hospital room waiting for Giorgio to emerge from the operating theatre, eating his grapes and getting high on the smell of alcohol and ether.

From time to time I toy with the graph paper in front of me, upon which I am endeavouring to redesign our flat in Rome. We have spent - (no, correction, *I* have spent, Giorgio was behind his newspaper most of the time, emerging only to complain bitterly about the exorbitant price of tiles/carpeting/wallpaper etc.) - the past week with slide rule and eraser trying to re-dimension it. Mostly it is a question of knocking down all the walls and putting them up someplace else before the main structure collapses as a result. One of the main problems is how to fit a cooker and washing machine and dryer and dishwasher and microwave and sink and cupboards and table and chairs into a space roughly the size of a wheelie bin, and as if this were not enough, I keep getting hysterical phone calls from the Roman builders who, big strapping lads as they are, maintain vociferously that 20cms to each side of a bidet is JUST NOT ENOUGH. My aim is to create a bathroom for each daughter and thus avoid daily recriminations such as "Who has been using MY soap/lipstick/body lotion, or finished the loo paper?" The things one learns along the way are priceless: were you aware, for example, that in a block of flats, everyone sits on their thrones directly over or under everyone else? Think of that, next time you are comfortably installed. And wear a hat.

Himself still not back from the operating theatre - trust him to try and upstage the liver/bowel transplant which took sixteen hours, as I recall.

Mother-in-law arrived yesterday, convinced that the Filipinos are not to be trusted with the making of gruel for the convalescent. She is, even now, driving them all to handing in their respective notices with running orders concerning the correct way to pulverise a potato until it submits to purée status. And let me make it clear that we are NOT talking mashed spud here. Your average Sicilian purea di patate should take at the very least an hour and a half to achieve if the cook has any self-esteem at all.

I shall continue this missive some other time - I hear wheels approaching.

Later....

Giorgio back home already with no ill effects except outrageous desires for gourmet meals after a hideous hospital diet of what looked like potted vomit with sultanas. Ma-in-Law so pleased with the results of her crash course in invalid feeding that she is planning to reap the benefits and have her gallstone removed while she is up for the visit. Which was probably all I needed right now.

Must go - I am being summoned to participate at the reading of the Last Will and Testament before taking her for the blood tests and ECG.

Pray for me,   Sarah

The weather continued cold and slippery, providing Giorgio's mother with the ideal excuse to stay indoors and drive the staff and family to exasperation point. Always a master of the art of attracting attention to herself, the prospect of an imminent operation at the hands of a knife-wielding foreigner was an occasion not to be passed up lightly. Tragedy in Sicily always did have a greater audience than comedy and this one was to be exploited to the full.

She would sink heavily into the sofa cushions and order the staff to serve her tea while she explained the latest amendments to her Testament. I thought wistfully of the woods outside, crunchy with the remains of the snow, the winter sunshine sparkling on the frosty leaves, but abandoned myself to the role of comforter on these occasions with as much good grace as I could muster. Gallstones, after all, were no joke.

Brussels, February 26th

Dear Mother,

Stupidly, I imagined that a dose of anaesthetic and a tube up the nose and down the throat would put the clappers on the non-stop verbal delivery which is my mother-in-law's hallmark. Which just shows how wrong you can be and should you ever need some gallstones removed, I can now vouchsafe that it is a pretty straightforward procedure, and you'll not only be back on your feet by day three, you'll be drinking champagne and going to the cinema - something she hasn't done for at least fifty years. All of which will not stop you replying with agonised groans and complaints of Greek tragedy magnitude every time a friend rings you up from Sicily for a progress report. The cynical attitude which may perchance shine through my account was evidently not perceptible to the naked eye during the days of so-called crisis, as she sent the girls out to buy me a present of my favourite body lotion the day after getting home. Well, I had been holding her hand and translating non-stop for 72 hours straight.

Delighted to see from your last letter that you have dragged the old steam typewriter back into use - the entertainment value is priceless. Pushing trillies round the supermarket vied for first prize together with your various transpot and doshwisher pluming problems. I am fervently hoping, also, that you never do succeed in finding the upper case key, as it won't be half so much fun afterwards. Many thanks, too, for sending my favourite tights. I had thought that my life would be easier without Francesca here, but now Alex has taken to filching them, and I have had to resort to keeping new pairs inside the wall safe and changing the combination at frequent intervals if I want to be sure of being decently hosed at Diplomatic Do's. This way, younger daughter has to either ask permission or equip herself with half a ton of Semtex before she can avail herself of my fifteen deniers.

Feeding the five thousand this evening - some visiting delegates are over to inspect Italy's chances of forcing a significant change in the positioning of a hyphen in the latest Euro Treatise. For their delight I am about to recycle for the third time a highly forgiving Soufflé Glacé au Grand Marnier. By stark contrast, Alex has invited half the Lycée tomorrow, so I think that will confirm us in our intention to go out to celebrate my latest birthday, (whose number I become increasingly adept at forgetting), in some liver-reducing-to-pulp restaurant with friends.

Before which, and this will amaze you, I am about to dedicate the afternoon to playing cards with Nonna, to massaging her stiff neck, and to driving her gently over the potholes to her favourite coffee bar. There is hope, as they say, for us all. In any case, she is leaving first thing tomorrow morning, restored to blooming health, and raring to be back home to recount her adventures.

Love from your born-again Samaritan, Sarah

Brussels being Brussels, it rained steadily on the morning of my birthday which I considered somehow appropriate. Abandoning plans to gallop through the woods, I headed for the covered shopping malls in search of a suitable present for the new baby produced by one of the Embassy wives who had finally given birth after what had seemed like a gestation period of about a year and a half. The blow-by-blow account of a perfectly normal pregnancy had been interminable and intolerable. I eventually chose a beautifully smocked little dress which would no doubt be dribbled upon immediately, but which would make a bella figura at its first diplomatic baby tea party. They started them off younger and younger these days. Having delivered it and paid my respects dutifully, I noticed the sky had cleared sufficiently for me to risk a quick half hour over the jumps and back in time for tea.

By the time I returned, Alex had transformed the garage into Planet Hollywood in preparation for her own party, and had to be forcibly restrained from slotting the Alfa Romeo halfway through the wall to further the illusion. The driveway gleamed already from streaks of melted candle wax which was being sprayed all over it each time the wind blew. I sank into a bath with a glass balanced precariously between the taps and the Archers grunting away in the background. It was wonderful to be able to hear Radio Four in Brussels, and The Archers was perfect for allowing me to carry on planning what to wear without necessitating any intellectual involvement on my part. Except that despite this apparent detachment, I was, for some reason, dying to find out about the latest marital rift. Alas tonight's episode was too busy concentrating on foot and mouth disease and infidelity was not even mentioned. Disappointed, I rummaged through my wardrobe searching for something amusing with which to shock the Belgian waiters and perhaps finally make that wretched British Attaché see me in a new light.

"Mummy you look terrible - you can't go out like that."

"Oh come on Alex, don't be mean - I don't want to celebrate my birthday in a stuffy old suit or one of those little black dresses. It's not that bad is it?"

"Yes. Worse. Wear a pair of jeans and your Mickey Mouse sweater if you must shock the establishment. At least you'll be warm."

"WARM? From a teenager? The last thing you girls ever take into consideration is the outside temperature. In any case, I have a teeny sneaking suspicion that Mickey Mouse may quite possibly not go down so well in your average two star Michelin restaurant. Albeit two star Michelin Thai restaurant. Anyway the sweater in question had a close encounter with an unsavoury puddle up at the stables this afternoon, and is none too nice to be near."

"Oh no, you didn't fall off on your birthday, did you?"

"Not technically, but just as I had one foot in the stirrup some mental deficient suddenly started up a mechanical drill three feet away from us. The next thing I know I'm looking up at all that grey sky and the Mickey Mouse sweater is reclining in a puddle. My thumb hurts like hell, now I think about it. Alex, you don't think I've broken it do you? People do break things on their birthdays, you know. It's all that extra subliminal stress working itself out through your self-conscious. Oh my God, tell me that's not the time? Throw me my trouser suit. I'll be back by midnight so get that bunch out of here by then and no fags and keep the noise down. And have a lovely evening. There's pizza and pasta to feed an army if you can steer them beyond the Cola and crisps."

"That's much better. Can I borrow some stockings? Please? I'll give them back, I promise."

Brussels, February 28th

Dear Frankie,

I'm typing this with a broken thumb which only goes to show that one can do just as well, if not better, with nine fingers instead of ten. One less to make mistakes with.

Had a lovely dinner last night to celebrate my don't askth birthday, and everyone was having themselves such fun, lubricated as they were, over my inability to manipulate the chopsticks in the manner in which every European citizen is supposed to be accomplished these days, when the laugh was suddenly on them as we realised that one thumb had grown to obscene proportions. Knowing I was not one of those fascinating people who swell up just at the mention of Oriental Food, (your Father, needless to say, sulked all evening at my choice of restaurant - muttered darkly that ethnic food, two star or not two star, was still ethnic food, and as such ... well you can imagine the rest), we thought it wise to head for the nearest Outpatients as soon as we'd finished the lychees. I must say that British Military Attaché was most supportive, and organised the expedition like a battle campaign, hauling orthopaedic specialists out of bed after midnight and haranguing them mercilessly until something was done. What a month - I've seen the inside of enough hospitals these past weeks to last me a lifetime. As usual in Emergency Wards the world over, it took them three hours to achieve an X-ray and diagnosis, and another hour to slap a piece of metal around the offending joint, and it was 4 a.m. before I was released into pre-dawn Brussels looking like Captain Hook. The dreaded contraption fell off during what was left of the night, and I spent most of this morning having a massive plaster cast slapped on in its place. "Got to make it solid, dear," said the orthopaedic biddy, "because I can see you're going to be silly and go riding with it despite orders." Cheeky so-and-so. Just because I'd turned up booted and spurred. To my great relief I've discovered I can slip it on and off at will should I need to scratch, so she wouldn't have got a job under a Nazi regime after all, despite her obvious aspirations.

I can't believe you are basking in winter sunshine in between your frenetic swotting for the next exam, as you protest, methinks, too much. Take my advice and don't turn up at the oral looking all bronzed and healthy: the pallid, ' burning the midnight oil on a diet of raw carrots and coffee' look is the one to go for. Let me amaze you and mention that it is raining here, and rather heavy on the mud, which doesn't bother some of us who merely wriggle into their green wellies, but doesn't amuse others of us who like to keep a fine lustre on their toe-caps. We have even had some icy cold days (well I'm sorry, but I was brainwashed into this meteorological reporting at boarding school,) when the dog had to be dragged out of her cocoon of warmth by her beagle ears, stuffed into her canary yellow polo-neck sweater (yes I know, but it was a present, and I'm somewhat embarrassed to say she likes it,) and dragged reluctantly out for a walk with frozen breath coming out of her nostrils.

The dreaded workmen seem to be progressing very slowly but surely in the Rome flat - we'll have you out of that convent yet before you become totally disillusioned by the insincerity of your average nun. I do agree that the house rule: "In by 10 p.m. or stay out all night" is asking for trouble, but since you were brought up so naicely, I am trusting you will not be following your Brazilian room mate's habits.

By the way, should they continue to insist on your attending Mass twice weekly even during exam week, I can recommend faking a bad attack of what was always referred to as continental tummy (until your mother went off and married a foreigner, that was.   After that the diagnosis was considered untactful in family circles and they all made a great effort to call it irritable bowel syndrome.)

There is a big Nato meeting in Paris next month, so Alex and I thought it might be a good opportunity to tag along and visit the odd museum whilst her father is working.

We will send you some awful corny photos.

Big bisous from Maman - kiss kiss kiss.

For some reason, Michael was not at the Paris meeting, or so my exaggeratedly disinterested enquiries led me to understand. It poured non-stop. Alex had decided to invite a friend, so I found myself queuing for exhibitions on my own whilst the two girls took themselves off to Les Halles and the Drug Stores. We met up exhausted and wet for a Croque Monsieur and compared notes. The general consensus of opinion was that the Japanese invasion of Paris was even further advanced than it was in Rome, that French rain was even wetter than the Belgian variety and that the only way to deal with a city in a downpour was to cheer oneself up by trying on bathing costumes in preparation for the summer holidays. Giorgio joined us for dinner at night, muttering something about a leak which was apparently of significant importance, and couldn't understand why the rest of us seemed to think this so funny, since he himself had been enclosed in a conference room with high security all day, and hadn't even noticed what the weather was doing outside. The girls then cleared off to the Champs Elysées and caught colds, given that, as already noted, their generation did not consider it "branché" to be seen wearing raincoats or carrying umbrellas. By midnight everyone was back at the hotel, and half an hour later we were all fast asleep. So much for Paris by night, were my last thoughts before succumbing to the combined effects of museums, shops, bistros and fighting the Metro crowds. The gentler pace of Brussels suddenly acquired renewed charm as I sank into oblivion.

When the phone started ringing, my first thoughts were Frankie! Alex! Fire! Gulf War Mark Three! What the hell time is it ANYWAY? Can that be a morning call? What is going on here? It's three in the morning for......... Wrong number - no, probably some neurotic Ambassador phoning from Washington having forgotten about the time difference - no, even more probably just not caring a fig about the time difference. But Giorgio was going Si and No into the mouthpiece and motioning for me to go back to sleep, so it was obviously just some routine Nato crisis which could only be solved by waking everyone up in the small hours before dawn.

Over breakfast of coffee and croissants, I recalled the nocturnal intermission and enquired, all sweetness and light, which effing wanker had been responsible for the interruption of my hard-earned slumbers?

But the reply was evasive. Also, room service had thoughtfully provided the majority of the Italian newspapers plus Le Monde, Le Figaro, the ruddy Enchained Duck, AND the Financial Times and Herald Tribune. Surveying the opposition, I realised that any chance of a two-way conversation was out of the question, so I crept instead along the corridor to wake up Alex and her girlfriend in order to propose a trip to the Grand Palais before a cholesterol heavy lunch in the best French tradition. I had a fleeting suspicion that if Leonardo Di Caprio had erupted into their hotel room before they were fully awake, he might just have met with a warmer welcome than I did, but this was the sort of thing to which mothers were accustomed, after all. I raised the blinds with excessive tact and diplomacy, which gained me no indulgences at all and even taught me some new expressions in that awful French slang where you have to turn the word back to front in order to decipher what the devil they are talking about. Definitely worse than talking crossword puzzle clues, I thought, wondering yet again why Michael wasn't in Paris for the meeting.

CHAPTER SIX

For some time I had been ignoring requests from Erlinda asking me to "ling back number two wife." Finally I found the courage to call Renata who, when I eventually went down to inspect the cellar, had clearly been bossing all the wives mercilessly. Such a pity it wouldn't get her husband any closer to the posting of his dreams: wifely contributions in the Italian Foreign Service never having been considered of any significant importance. It unfortunately didn't make too much difference either way whether you aged prematurely in the service of State and husband or not: statistics proved that a rather large proportion of wives were still exchanged for newer models in middle age. So far I hadn't hit that problem with Giorgio, though probably, given the state of all our hormones, I wouldn't have too long to wait. I gave her a call to say thank you and to organise a lunch for all the helpers. No sooner had I put the phone down when Giorgio called sounding frazzled saying that he wouldn't be back for lunch, and would I mind doing the Luxembourg National Day party on my own that evening because he had to go straight out to Mons for a Shape crisis meeting? Unfortunate timing, all things considered, following so closely upon my recent musings. I decided there and then that just in case the Shape in question happened to be female, I would contrive to get myself invited to dinner afterwards by Michael so at least we could keep things on an even footing. Any excuse was better than none when it came to the salving of the conscience.

I reached the Luxembourg Ambassador's residence rather late, and was afraid that Michael might already have left. A rather despondent waiter was circling the garden with a tray full of buns the size of saucers filled with raw minced beef and topped with raw egg yolk. The utter impossibility of eating such an item without the help of a knife, fork and preferably Pelican bib, was not lost upon the many guests, all of whom declined graciously and returned to balancing their drinks and peanut whilst shaking hands to left and right. I leaned up against a potted plant and proceeded to exchange staff problems with the wife of the Spanish Ambassador who had recently had all her jewellery and paintings removed whilst she was at the Opera. I was retaliating with an account of my household staff being placed under arrest in Nigeria when a diamond ring went missing (whether the police ever recovered it for their own profit I never managed to discover), when I spotted a dim figure over by the French windows making scissor movements to signify I should cut off this enthralling conversation at the first opportunity. I wandered over.

"What's with the cloak and dagger stuff, Michael? Is this the man who used to be the darling of every diplomatic hostess for his feisty anecdotes? Standing in the shadows avoiding social intercourse? Where were you all evening, or were you in the crisis meeting too? And come to think of it, why weren't you in Paris?"

"What crisis meeting? I've only just got here. Where's your charming husband? Shall we go and get some dinner, or are you still being regaled by tales of theft and dastardly doings at the Spanish

Embassy?"

"How did you know that's what we were talking about? Yes, dinner would be lovely, thank you."

"It was a safe bet - she hasn't talked about anything else for the past month, poor thing. The jewels belonged to her grandmother and one of the paintings was an Of the School Of. Someone. Old Master. Spanish. Forget now just which - did you say yes to dinner? I'm starving, I didn't get any lunch."

"No one did by all accounts - what's going on in Nato these days that's making everyone so anorexic? Not still leaking, are you?"

"Sarah I shall ignore that question, you know you should never poke fun at matters of security. One's job depends upon things like waterproofing, and it is not to be treated lightly. You, my dear, should not even know anything about it. Grab your better half and let's hoof it out of here before I succumb to severe protein deficiency."

"Can't - he's not here. Had to belt over to Shape. You're not going to withdraw that invitation, now, are you? On the grounds my un-chaperoned presence might sully your otherwise pristine reputation as a confirmed bachelor? Because I can hear a tartare de saumon calling me from that restaurant in the Sablon, and we would both of us be very disappointed not to meet over a glass of Chablis."

"What on earth is he doing in Mons? What is going on around here? Why am I always the last to know anything? I am going to have to make Representations if this sort of thing continues. Did he say why he was going to Mons?"

"Yeah - bimbos. I wasn't going to mention it, but in fact it's for bimbos. You get a better class of bimbo in Mons, apparently. Something about doing it in Flemish that really turns a chap on. They ship them in by the cartload for the American military. It's all part of the facilities, like the PX store. Tax-free too, like the booze. Come on, I need another drink." He followed, and silently we drove down to the Sablon.

Dinner was not the most joyful occasion. Michael was preoccupied with other matters, and half way through my tartare I remembered I was hosting a farewell lunch for the French Ambassadress the next day, and had forgotten to mention anything about it to the cook. Conversation was constrained. We left as soon as we could manage - service in Brussels restaurants always tending toward the leisurely - and he accompanied me back to the Residence. Straight back, no detours, eyes on the road, just a couple of good friends who had been out to dinner together. Give me a call tomorrow? I was almost relieved to get home. Sir, I perceived, was back and watching the late night news on television. I left a message for the staff to get out to the local market at dawn and purchase fish and vegetables for tomorrow's luncheon, and joined him in time for the Sports round up.

"How was Mons?"

"Awful. SACEUR is accusing us of being insecure."

"Sorry?"

"SACEUR -Supreme Allied Commander in Europe."

"Giorgio, I do *know* after all this time what SACEUR stands for. I just couldn't believe that dreadful pun. You must be overtired - shall I fix you a night-cap?"

"Yes, thank you. Would you mind bringing me a glass of mineral water? Room temperature. I rang the bell, but they've all gone to bed apparently. How were the Luxemburgers?"

"Predictable. Michael took me to the Sablon for supper afterwards, but I can't say he was on form tonight. Are you sure you won't have something a little more virile than mineral water? Whisky is considered medicinal these days, you know."

"Probably one pickled liver in the family is enough for the time being - I presume you did your share this evening, especially if you dined with Michael afterwards."

"Hardly touched a drop. He was too busy trying to pump classified information out of me, so I knew I had to keep a clear head."

"Sarah, what *are* you talking about? What classified information? Since when did you have any classified information in the first place?"

"I don't, but he doesn't know that: he thinks you tell me everything in the intimacy of our bed chamber, so from time to time I let him think you do. Then he pays me lots of lovely close attention and tells me I'm fascinating, which is so good for morale."

At least it took his mind off the news.

"Am I supposed to do a Sicilian jealousy scene here, or what? What is this you're telling me? So come to think of it, what were you two doing up in the mountains all day while I was on the cross country stretches?"

"Giorgio, I am beginning to have a sneaking feeling that our friend Michael is perhaps not a ladies' man, and if you dedicated just a tiny bit more time to studying other people as opposed to being totally immersed in your stupid career, you could have given me your invaluable male opinion on the subject. But if you're interested, that is probably why we have such fun together. Do you mean to say you spent a whole weekend in that chalet in the mountains without wondering for one minute why a chap should go in for pink satin cushions in a ski resort? Never mind, I'll get you your water. Do you get a discount from BUPA with every litre you absorb? Guaranteed extra mileage - they ought to reduce your premiums at the very least."

O.K. - that little bombshell about Michael's sexual preferences should keep the hounds at bay for a bit. Come back Manu, all is forgiven. I made a swift mental prayer for it not to be true, fetched the water, let the dog out, and prepared to retire to bed.

"Sarah, shall we have lunch together tomorrow? Someone in the office told me about a new restaurant they've opened in Woluwe, not too far from Nato H.Q. We could even play squash for half an hour first?"

"Good Lord. Are you making a Démarche? You're supposed to be dallying with secretaries at your age, not propositioning ageing menopausal wives. Annoyingly, in the interest of supporting your already brilliant career, I am giving a lunch to say goodbye to the French Ambassadress tomorrow, mainly because she needs all the cheering up she can get. Let's take a rain check, as your American friends in Mons no doubt would say, the day after tomorrow, if you've plugged your leaks and can concentrate on the ball by then. Come on, I'm going to bed. I'm exhausted. Must be a deficit of minerals through not drinking enough water."

Brussels, April 3rd

Dear Mother,

Just back from a long ride in the Forest of Soignes with my friend Monsieur le Baron, a distinguished member of the Belgian aristocracy who still, despite his advanced years, rides as if he had swallowed a broomstick and may be counted upon for an elegant turn of phrase in any situation. As we embarked upon our hack, his horse let out a series of extremely audible little fartlets - an expression of the thoroughbred's surprise and excitement at the prospect of an unexpected gallop through the woods. M. le Baron rose to the occasion with a dignified: "Excusez-moi, chère Madame, mais mon cheval a des problèmes de digestion *sonores*" - an apology which endeared him to me even when the beast in question endeavoured to kick Beagle across into Wallonia whenever she got in his way.

Francesca is finally moving out of the Institute and into the building site which is our flat in Rome. The nuns are kindly praying for both her soul and more especially, I suspect, her body as she launches into this life of debauchery. I've no doubt she will comport herself as impeccably as I did, despite my mother-in-law's accusation that we are unnatural parents, her own son, like the majority of Italian men, only having left home to get married. The chances of any of them surviving on a desert island with a copy of the Divine Comedy and six gramophone records would have to be pretty remote, all things considered.

Giorgio is hosting a wine tasting downstairs as I write, and has just sent me up a be-gloved Erlinda with choice of pink or white champagne, so I fear I must stop and concentrate upon the necessity of making yet another major decision. My life is truly one long sacrifice.

Love, Sarah

CHAPTER SEVEN

"Erlinda, is Madame home?"

"No sir, she no home."

"Did she say where she was going?"

"No sir, she no say."

"Well did she say what time she'd be back?"

"No sir, she no say."

"How was she dressed?"

"Sir?"

"What was she wearing? Did it look like she was going out for lunch?"

"No sir, no lunch. She take callots, sir"

"*Callots*? Oh of course, carrots. And stillups, right?"

"Sir?"

"Never mind. Just tell her to call me as soon as she gets back."

The woods were particularly beautiful that morning. Spring had finally arrived and the sun's warmth on my back as I trotted along the tracks made the long winter fade into a distant memory. Beagle was raising imaginary foxes at every turn, and disappeared for long spells on quests of her own. I decided to ride over to Waterloo, a couple of hours there and back if I didn't get lost on the way. Which I did, of course. Fat lot of good the dumb beagle was. Wag wag wag every time I took a wrong turn, obviously thinking 'oh goody, even longer walkies.'

Horse had lost all sense of direction ages ago, not that he'd ever had much except when within sniffing distance of a bale of hay. Took me three solid hours and by the time I got back to the stables the groom was organising a search party. The mobile phone, of course, was no use at all on occasions like this : "I'm standing under this tall tree and there's a clump of daisies to the left and a couple of logs to the right, which way to the Royal Etrier Riding Club, please?" Not to mention that I'd thoughtfully left it in the car. A compass might have been of service, though.

It was dark when I reached home and the second search party of the day was about to be initiated.

"Ma'am? Sir phoned, ma'am."

"Right, I'll just run a bath and call him back. Thank you."

"Ma'am? Please ma'am, sir call six times ma'am."

Well how nice to be missed. Obviously his crises were over in the office if he had so much time to spare. Probably wanted that game of squash.

I ran the bath and reached for the Archers, but the phone rang while I was half way out of the jodhpurs.

"Sarah where the devil have you been all day? You disappeared at noon and no one's had any idea where you were since then. What's the point of having a mobile phone if you don't take it with you? You're a walking nightmare."

"Trotting, actually. Some cantering. A little jumping - the usual. Oh and an old man opened his raincoat and flashed at me in the heart of the forest. I twirled my whip at him and he ran off. Beagle chased him for a bit but he wasn't fast enough to be amusing. Then I got lost. No other adventures, I'm afraid."

"Listen. Did you see Michael, by any chance today?"

"What in the middle of the Forêt de Soignes? Do you think we have romantic trysts in log cabins, or something? How very droll. Darling that horse is eighteen hands high: I don't know if that means anything to you as a layman, but I can tell you that once you've managed to get up on it, you think very hard about getting off it again and repeating the process. Is that the real reason you've been calling me all day? My, I am flattered. I don't think I've seen him since he took me for dinner after that party, come to think of it."

"He's disappeared."

"Giorgio don't be silly, people don't disappear. Call him on his mobile for goodness sake. You could even tell him to come up for supper - I bought all this gourmet dog food on the way home."

"No-one's seen him for three days. He hasn't been home and his phone is switched off. How was he when you last saw him?"

"Not much fun. He's probably having a fling somewhere. Have you called his batman-johnny? Try Mons. I wouldn't let it worry you too much. Doesn't his Ambo. know where he is?"

"Sir John and Lady Annabel are away on leave this week. It's the Easter Banquet or Parade, or one of those ceremonies which brings your British upper class to a grinding halt at this time of year."

"Grinding halt from what, might I ask? Look, my bath is about to flow over and down the staircase and I'm missing the Archers. Do you think we could continue this murder mystery over an early supper? I was just kidding about the dog food - cook is achieving the famous risotto."

"I'll be there in twenty minutes."

So much for bimbos: the stomach was obviously still the organ of prime importance. I lowered myself into the bath wondering where on earth Michael could be hiding. Tomorrow I would make some discreet enquiries around his favourite haunts.

I tried the Lawn Tennis Club, the Golf Club, and the Squash Club. I tried his office, his home, his mobile phone. I called his secretary, his best friend and even the chalet in France. His secretary said he'd taken a few days off and would be back next week. No, she didn't know where he'd gone, and by the sound of it couldn't much care. There were, it seemed, more important things in her life. Split ends, possibly. Nobody else had seen him or heard from him for days. I gave up and tried to fix my attention upon organising plans for the bazaar.

There was a meeting that morning of all the wives of Heads of Mission involved in the proceedings. As doyenne, the wife of the Turkish Ambassador invited us to her Residence to discuss the practical details over Belgian coffee and Turkish delight. The minutes of the meeting were taken down by her social secretary, and were conspicuously covered in icing sugar. Excusing myself finally on the pretext that I had to host a luncheon back at the Residence, I calculated that the refining of a few seemingly straightforward details had taken three solid hours. A hard core of my colleagues were all set to hammer out a hundred more insignificant details which would doubtless need re-hammering once the marquees were in place. Turkish delight was probably going to have to be replaced by soup and sandwiches before the morning was over. I felt sure they considered I was taking the event much too lightly, and were at this very minute gossiping about my early departure with disapproval. I decided I would just have to show them and, skipping lunch, spent the rest of the afternoon canvassing support from every Italian retailer in town.

On my way back home, my phone rang, and I narrowly missed a passing cyclist as I searched deep into my handbag to reach it before it stopped.

"Sarah, where have you been? Your mobile hasn't been working for days - I kept getting someone telling me you didn't exist in Flemish. How are you?"

Bullshit, Michael. Pack of lies, my phone has never been healthier. No-one else has been having any problems getting through to me, and in any case you could easily ring me at home, it wasn't that we had anything to hide. Was it? And where the hell have *you* been, that all of Brussels is out looking for you? But I heard myself saying instead:

"Oh hi! Yes, been very busy, bazaar and all that, cell phones very unreliable, aren't they? Yours was off, too - where were you? "

"Had to go to London for talks. When can I see you?"

I suggested lunch the next day, but he was non-committal, said he might have a meeting. Not with me, obviously, for although I teased him for a bit and he swore he would be in touch as soon as he could, it was a good while before we heard anything more of him.

Brussels, May 10th

Dear Frankie,

Darling I know it's not easy living on your own on a limited income in a partly furnished flat with builders covering everything in layers of dust, but do try to remember that it was you that wanted out of the convent, and that your idea of bliss was to be able to starve in peace in your own garret. And that our penniless tenant was pretty decent about relinquishing the apartment and paying a few of his bills before he left, so that even if there are unspeakable beasties crawling out of the woodwork every time it rains, it surely is nothing that a giant can of squirt can't deal with? So just keep calm, and try not to destroy any more brooms dealing with the friends and relatives of whatever it was that crept its way into your bath last weekend. You *get* beasties when you live in a garden flat.

Your sister, you will be riveted to hear, is currently getting help with her maths homework from a charming young Haitian who, as far as I can see without being too indiscreet, sports no less than three rings in his left ear. Every time your father comes in I notice he surreptitiously turns his collar up or feigns earache, so I am prepared to believe there's actually a loveable conformist hidden down there aching to be set free. He's also very good at calculus and Alex's marks are improving steadily. In return she corrects his English without too much effort on her part. Great excitement here for two minutes because the British Military Attaché went missing for a week. The amount of people who read Le Carré novels must be far greater than one imagines. I can't tell you the wild theories that were circulating. Plus there had been all these Leaks, you understand. Very bad for the image. Eventually, much to everyone's relief, or perhaps disappointment, he turned up again fresh as a daisy, having been back to the UK for Talks. Or so he says. If you ask me, he was doing a little more than talking, but when I made so bold as to insinuate, he just tutted and pretended to be shocked at my presumption. Pity, really, we could have done with a good scandal. What a milieu - chap wants to disappear discreetly to, say, have the bags under his eyes operated upon without broadcasting it to the world, and everyone automatically assumes he's the fourth man. If I ever decide to have a face-lift I'm going to throw a big "sag" party before I leave, and send everyone blow-by-blow photographs of the bruising and stitching. We once had a friend in Nigeria who was having herself a bit of a ding-dong with an Alitalia pilot. Each time he flew her off to exotic isles on complementary tickets she would tell everyone she was going back to Rome because the dog had to have an operation. The entire Italian community checked that pooch out for scars: the concern was phenomenal. Eventually she had to tell them she was doing a little trading on the side, which was at least closer to the truth, if you think about it.

I hate to have it on my conscience that reading this letter is detaining you from your books, so thinking only of your welfare, I shall make it brief. Keep up the good work and feel free to flick the odd duster from time to time: it can be most therapeutic when bogged down by economic history. Oh, and you might call Nonna once in a while - she's convinced you've stopped going to Mass and started smoking pot now that the nuns aren't breathing down your neck twenty-four hours a day. I tried to explain that you were too busy overseeing the installation of the bidets, but not even that bit of good news roused her from her premonition of doom.

Desisting NOW, as promised.

Love, (lots of it), and patient forbearing and carpe diem during the bits in between.

Maman. Kisses.

CHAPTER EIGHT

Could do with some carpe diem, myself, I thought despondently as I drove over to the Nato Tennis Club in search of some exercise to up the endorphins only to discover the courts had been taken over for the bazaar.

The marquees were going up under grey clouds and intermittent drizzle. A fair amount of multilingual swearing echoed in and around the site which, by the end of the day had turned into a mud bath. Emerging gingerly from his office, the Italian Ambassador instructed his chauffeur to drive right up on to the sidewalk, as he had learned to call it from his American counterpart. He hoped they would arrange wooden walkways at the very least between now and the opening ceremonies, otherwise he would be making his token purchases by proxy, he decided. His fears were unnecessary. A strong wind arose during the night: miraculously the marquees stayed firm, but the clouds were blown away and gave place to brilliant sunshine which lasted for the rest of the week. By noon the ground had dried out and His Excellency felt he could drop by and survey the progress without too much damage to his footwear. The Italian stall boasted a magnificent centrepiece with an enormous Sicilian donkey cart laden with packets of spaghetti and bottles of olive oil, wedges of cheese, giant salamis, dried tomatoes, anchovies, grissini, preserved truffles - every imaginable gastronomic delight.

Pyramids of bottles of wine, Campari, and Grappa provided a backdrop, and in the foreground were a number of non-edible but equally delectable temptations. Leather purses, wallets, card holders and key rings, silk scarves in every colour of the rainbow, designer ashtrays and sundry little gifts with the all-important Gucci emblem guaranteed to entice even the most hardened bazaar-goer to part with his or her ready cash. Returning from a tour of the other stalls around four o'clock when the pace was finally beginning to slacken, I was surprised to see all my co-workers in a renewed buzz of activity, apparently occupied in persuading some poor innocent to purchase anything that was left to sell. Edging closer to the table to see what the excitement was all about, I was amazed to see it was Michael.

"My God, back from the dead. We thought you'd been incarcerated at the very least." I thought he looked a little shamefaced but it was difficult to tell with Michael. Within five minutes he had charmed them all into selling him the remaining bottles of Grappa at a fat discount, told a couple of jokes, absent-mindedly opened a packet of grissini and proceeded to eat the contents, and disappeared after having put in a bid for the donkey cart. The wives thought he was delightful. I was less enthusiastic: I would have been happier had he removed his purchases from the scene instead of merely tossing down the money and clearing off to his office, and I had a couple of questions I would have liked answering.

They were destined to stay unanswered.

Giorgio was in London for the Summit, so I was managing to do more than my fair share of horse riding and tennis playing, dog walking and refusing luncheons. In between which activities, I would pop into the kitchen and help the Concitas bake and freeze little delicacies in preparation for our summer cocktail party which, with irrepressible British optimism, I was hoping to hold outdoors. With this in mind, I summoned the gardener who turned up at dawn and, instead of watering in new border plants, started creating a vegetable plot. When I mentioned that I had something rather more decorative in mind, he shrugged disdainfully and said, roughly translated from the Flemish, "them's only flarze, maa'm - make a splash for a couple of weeks and then wither away" and went back to planting his wilting lettuces, basil, tomatoes and radishes. He did manage to throw a load of fertiliser over the rose bushes (them's not flarze, them's roses), though omitting to weed them first, with the result that we ended up with the healthiest crop of dandelions in the area.

Left on my own in Brussels I noted that the phone was, needless to say, refusing to ring although he must have been aware that Giorgio was away. Ring, damn you, RING!

It worked. I always suspected I had supernatural powers.

"Hello?"

"Hello!"

"Oh *hello*. How very original of us. Where have you been? Insensible beneath a cloud of cut price Grappa, I suppose. How was it?"

"Um, I haven't got round to a professional tasting yet – well, apart from the one bottle I opened just to test on the night of the bazaar. Seemed to be fine. Bit small. Why are Italian litres always less than everybody else's? You'd think the E.U. would standardise things like that, wouldn't you? Did you know we have to have the same number of sheets on our bog rolls now?"

"Bathroom level humour usually signifies you've been hanging out with your beer-drinking compatriots for longer than is good for you. Time for spag type bog instead and Chianti and a little refined conversation, I think. What are you doing this evening? - Giorgio is in London, so we could even take in the latest Woody Allen film which I must see in the English language with a native speaker. But you would do at a stretch. The idea of Woody dubbed into French with Flemish sub-titles taking up half the screen does not appeal. Hello?"

"Yes, I'm still here."

"So why don't I hear you panting down the line in anticipation? Planned a night of debauchery with the ex-pats, I'll bet. Woody will be much healthier: he'll make you think, if that's still possible."

"Wrong again, not a debauch in sight, and I would have loved to but there is a very small logistical problem."

"I imagined. Driver is off duty and like all you guys, you've forgotten how to park. I'll pick you up - eightish?"

"Love, could you just shut up for a minute and listen? You go ranting on when a chap's trying to say something and a chap can't get one single notion into that head of yours once you're in full throttle. I just rang up to say hello, basically."

"Oh my dear God, not that all over again. We've *done* that bit, Michael - remember? Right at the beginning. You went "hello" and then I went "hello," and then we told each other how original we were, but we were only joking, weren't we? Tell me, please, I have to know, because maybe you're not my ideal companion for a Woody evening after all. Perhaps I should call up Derek Jamieson instead."

"Amore?"

"Yes, or ' hello', as you would have it."

"Listen hard for a second."

"I'm all ears. Or would be except for that infernal din behind you - don't tell me you just inherited a grandfather clock? How on earth do you get any sleep? Sounds like big bludi Ben in the background."

"Hooray! Now I *am* impressed. Underneath that deceptive façade there is an intelligent woman trying to emerge. I'm standing outside the Houses of P., Westminster, London, England, and as you so brilliantly observed, Benjamin is indeed booming. You may now look at your watches for a free time check."

"Why didn't you say so in the first place, you moron, instead of making me lose face inviting you out and having you refuse me. Health warning: rejection can cause serious damage to the ego at a certain age. Or at any age, I suppose, I can't seem to remember that far back. Are you there for the Summit too? Have you been recalled? Is it pouring? Could you bring me back a Harrods apron for Erlinda? She's convinced she won't get her uniform so spattered if she has teddy bears all over her tummy."

"No, no, yes, no, rubbish. In that order. Which by now you've forgotten, serves you right. Enough. This call is becoming far too expensive, and it's started raining with total dedication, so to my utter despair I shall have to leave you."

"Hang about, friend. I'm not that stupid. If it's wet, that was the "yes" in the series. Which means you're not there for the Summit nor have you been recalled. Taking a lot of leave these days, aren't we? Come on, now, you can tell Auntie. What are you up to?"

"Top Terribly Secret. As ever. And don't believe a word of the rumours. Bye now, give my love to the pissing mannequin. Cheers!"

He rang off, and I went to the cinema with Renata whose husband was also in London, and spent an interminable evening translating the dialogue in a hoarse whisper and wishing I could throttle her.

And, as I explained to the Security Officer who visited me later that month, that was the last time I had heard from Michael, and as it transpired I had been privileged, for he had disappeared without trace just as Big Ben finished striking the hour, though this time, apparently, it was for good.

CHAPTER NINE

The notoriously close relationship between the wife of the Italian Ambassador and a minor British double agent kept the diplomatic community throbbing for the best part of a month and a half. Tongues wagged, incidents were remembered, exchanged looks and intimacies recalled. The Corps had a field day. It transpired that during a prior posting to Moscow, Michael had become and remained over-friendly with the Russians, and had now been accused of passing them a classified Nato document.

I was just beginning to wonder whether I had, after all, succeeded in wrecking my husband's precious career when he was summoned to Rome upon Matters Unspecified. For two days I mooched around the stables in an old riding mac and head scarf, ferociously grooming the horse, cleaning saddles and bridles and polishing stirrups in an attempt to forget about Michael and the trouble he had caused us all. Finally Giorgio made contact.

"Got called in for a meeting with the Foreign Minister at 8.30 this morning."

"Omigod, You got shot down in flames? Shit. Shit. Shit. What did he say?"

"Called for a further meeting with the Under Secretary at 9.15."

"What are you talking about? Two days back in Rome and you're gibbering. Make sentences, for heaven's sake. Use verbs. What did your dreaded Minister and undersecsed boss SAY?"

"He congratulated me upon having dealt with the recent somewhat embarrassing crisis with discretion and forbearing throughout and promised to line me up for full Ambassador status. See you tomorrow evening, I'll be catching the late flight."

Lying in bed that night, I suddenly thought of Manuela who, like me, had always maintained that diplomatic wives really didn't count for much one way or the other, and for the first time in my life, felt thoroughly grateful that they didn't.

*   *   *   *

After an unprecedented week of clear blue skies and warm sunshine, I began to relax and think of the future. I finally persuaded the reluctant gardener to fetch vast quantities of border plants from the local nursery and transform the flowerbeds into a mass of colour. He continued to mutter darkly about late frosts, but this time I was adamant. Garden tables and chairs were scrubbed up and the awnings wound down for additional shelter. The cocktail party was now a celebration both of our National Day, and of Giorgio's promotion. Despite the fact that Beagle had succeeded in purloining a full tray of canapés just before the first guests arrived, that two of the waiters called in sick at the last moment, that the Greek and Turkish Ambassadors decided to use our bottle-neck of a hall to settle their latest dispute, that Giorgio spent a large part of the evening discussing a crisis on the hot line in his study, and that we ran out of Pimms within the first half-hour, I had to admit it was a considerable success. The shortage of Pimms was Giorgio's fault. He had maintained very firmly that as the wife of an Italian Ambassador, I could NOT serve Pimms at his parties, and that in any case no one would want to touch the stuff even if I did. Certainly the Italians preferred their Campari cough mix, and sniffed suspiciously at the aroma of mint as it wafted past on the evening breeze. Mint, as they all knew from their cradle, belonged inside artichokes and had no business floating around in glasses with slices of cucumber. The Belges thought it was charmant, and drank it down like lemonade. As usual a hard core of guests, convinced they had a special relationship with Italy, outstayed their welcome and had to be provided with steaming plates of pasta before they would go home. By this time everyone had moved back indoors and in desperation I let the dog into the house where she wreaked havoc with the ladies' stockings, knocked over a couple of glasses, snuffled around in the ashtrays, ran off with an ill-placed mobile phone, and succeeded in clearing the room by midnight. For which achievement she was awarded half a plate of spaghetti alla carbonara and permission to chase the neighbour's cat out of the newly planted flowerbeds.

CHAPTER TEN

August 1998

We were lying on a beach in Corsica when Giorgio's phone rang. It was that section of the beach which had always been frequented by tourists who preferred to do their sun worshipping in the state which nature had intended. A stark bollocks naked Ambassador (fully promoted by this stage,) shot to his feet to show some kind of respect and began an overly loud monologue.

Si, Ministro. No, Ministro, Certo, Ministro. Of course, Ministro. As you say, Ministro.

Up and down the beach, heads began to be raised in curiosity. Some Italian tourists even made half-hearted attempts to cover their most vulnerable bits, just in case. Sort of covering their bets.

With a silent but eloquent gesture, I motioned him to retreat behind the tamarind trees where, hopefully, the entire beach would no longer be obliged to participate in the ensuing conversation.

Inured to Foreign Office crises in mid-August, I resumed my interrupted dozing.

"That was the Minister!"

"So we all gathered. On holiday, one would have wished, but nevertheless blooming, one trusts?"

"Umm. Would you like to get some lunch?"

Slowly, very slowly, I opened one eye. Then another. And rolled over to observe, warily, the expression on his face. Lunch had not been an option this holiday. Latterly in Brussels some Belgian dry cleaner had quite obviously been shrinking his suits. All of them. Even the odd glass of rosé had been eliminated in the interest of saving his wardrobe from imminent demise. Despite, if one could dare to be so irreverent as to mention it on a nudist beach, appearances, Something was Up. I rummaged for some bits of bikini and we headed towards the restaurant at the far end of the beach.

"There's only one table left and it's only half in the shade."

"That's fine by me. I'll sit in the sun: I can never have too much of it. Even in Lagos I used to lie under it for hours with all the mad dogs and other Englishmen."

For some reason, this comment unnerved him to the extent that, almost without thinking, he ordered a couple of glasses of wine while we were waiting for our salads.

"It's no good for the skin, you know. You'll end up wanting a facelift like all your girlfriends. A cold climate is much better for keeping the wrinkles away."

One glass was obviously not going to be enough. What, in the name of all that had been considered sacrosanct, was going on here? Was he about to announce plans to elope with an Eskimo?

I sat back and waited.

"That was the Minister on the phone." Silence. Yes, we *had* registered that bit, thank you.

"He's in Rome." Silence.

"Doing a bit of shuffling ready for the Autumn." Large slurp of wine. Too large.

"He wondered if I'd be interested in a posting to Moscow." Choke. Bad one. The sort that goes up the nose and comes back through the eyeballs pausing to block every respiratory passage it encounters on the way. The sort that has helpful waiters running up with paper serviettes and anxious neighbours swivelling from surrounding tables with proffered water glasses and alarmed husband, bugger him, performing the Heimlich manoeuvre in front of everyone.

Russia.

I don't even *want* a fur coat.

PART THREE

MOSCOW

CHAPTER ONE

Autumn 1999

Aeroflot took off on time with all passengers obediently strapped fast into their seats beneath the stern gaze of First Steward Alexander. At your service. But without the smile. Not even when the Business Class passengers, the wife of the newly-appointed Italian Ambassador, her beagle and a couple of Mafiosi dripping with matching Louis Vuitton luggage were suddenly bombarded with a volley of plastic bottles (full) which came hurtling down the aisle as the aircraft tested its brakes. The bottles were followed in quick succession by stack after stack of paper cups and before long the compartment was a swirling mass of rolling cylinders. Collapse of Mme l'Ambassadrice giggling uncontrollably. Impassive First Steward was not amused. The beagle, which had no right to be there in the first place but had successfully claimed diplomatic immunity from travelling Russian dog class, leaped for the kill and hooked a passing bottle, pinning it down and ripping it to shreds in seconds. Business Class was immediately transformed into a paddling pool. Beagle shook herself vigorously over the Mafiosi before settling back into snarling at Alexander whilst endeavouring to snaffle the smoked salmon and caviar. Hardly an auspicious beginning to a new posting.

His Excellency looked disapprovingly at the bedraggled wife and hound as we emerged from the Ilyushin, skidded across the icy tarmac and fell into his sleek Alfa Romeo. The odour of wet dog mingled slowly with an even stronger stench of petrol emanating from the boot. In 1999, there was no unleaded fuel in Russia outside of a few pumps in central Moscow, so the Embassy car carried a leaky jeroboam in the boot. A little slopped out at every pothole, and given the state of the roads, we would have gone up like a torch had anyone dared to light a cigarette. In the middle of a five-lane boulevard, the owner of an ancient Skoda was trying to borrow a spare wheel from passing motorists. This was not an uncommon occurrence and tradition required that the wheel, once traded, be changed without the aid of a jack right there on the highway, the vehicle preferably parked sideways across as many lanes as possible.

I witnessed my first hand signal. The car in question, an ancient Lada, obviously had no electrics, so the driver merely opened his door and signaled with left arm and leg that he was intending to cross four lanes of traffic. Flag flying, our Russian bear of a driver, Nicolai, steered around him as if this too was a perfectly normal procedure. Nicolai had been a Colonel in the KGB until they had to let him go for lack of funds with which to pay his already meagre salary, but he maintained his connections out of loyalty. This was tremendously useful in traffic jams when he would either snarl through the closed window or, if the situation warranted, bark coded threats at the cops until they let him use the empty lanes still reserved for the highly privileged. It was later discovered that he was adept at pretending not to understand a word of Italian until a burning pride in his homeland got the better of him, at which juncture he would launch into a series of fascinating insights, first in Russian and then in fluent Italian.

Moscow grande città, molto molto grande. 10 stazioni. 6 aeroporti. 3000 turisti.

It took us two hours to reach our new home.

The Embassy was adjacent to the famous pedestrian street, the Old Arbat, where replicas of the Bocca della Verita invited the passer-by to have his palm read at 100 metre intervals and shady characters in beaten up cars would beckon him inside to reveal further secrets of his murky future. Matryoshka dolls in the season's colours - deep blue and shocking pink that year - sat side by side with peony-painted tin trays and army surplus gas masks. Lacquered boxes and military insignia from the Communist era encouraged the tourist to part with his roubles. Throughout the freezing temperatures in winter, there were ice-cream vendors on every corner, but why not? If the Indians were partial to hot tea and curry, there was most probably a very good reason why the Russians indulged in ice cream twelve months a year.

The Residence boasted a cook, a butler, a gardener, two drivers and a series of maids with all of whom Their Excellencies conversed in sign language. Valentina was a former ballet dancer and practiced her glissade up and down the corridors, hotly pursued by Beagle who thought it was all a great romp being put on for her entertainment. Coffee was served in a demi-plié position at great risk of a couple of kilos of solid monogrammed silver pot being launched into the recipient's lap. Cake and biscuits were presented in the second position. The show was accompanied by a dazzling gold-toothed smile. One morning she explained in graphic mime with the help of a lateral leg kick that Beagle had already been out into the garden and had duly peed. To which I could not resist responding in kind (with a controlled, slow motion deep plié) that dog in question was female, and as such, peed in a different manner altogether. It was in fact a revelation, and a great hindrance to my learning any Russian at all, how much vital information could be conveyed in this manner. Bearing in mind, however, my exalted status, of which I was constantly having to be reminded by H. E., I realized I would have to control this intercourse before it got out of hand. The day we ran out of toilet paper, I decided it was time to study the language. Miming a lack of loo paper exceeded even my idea of acceptable behaviour for an Ambassadress. I signed up for Russian lessons forthwith. They were not, I had to admit, an unqualified success.

Lessons One and Two:

Much smiling and pretending to take notes (not, one might add, in Cyrillic).

Lesson Three:

Open new text book printed, to all appearances, on recycled grey cardboard. A group of seriously boring students of the Russian language (Russki Yesik) meet to discover each other's names, how they are feeling, how many brothers and sisters they have, and what they all (even more boringly) do for a living. Mentally, I switch to more absorbing topics. Such as how to persuade Yelena the cook to refrain from serving blinis for breakfast, lunch and supper. We had reached saturation point ever since I had foolishly mentioned how delicious they were. Compared to her dumplings was what I had meant at the time.

Lesson Four:

Terminally boring Boris and his class of ill-assorted foreigners head off to visit formerly fascinating St. Petersburg and have immense fun getting lost on the Metro and ordering drinks in a bar. I take a personal mental trip to my none too varied wardrobe and try to imagine a way to diversify the tediously boring black skirt and friendly Department Store top which has been gracing all my dinner parties since arrival.

Lesson Five:

Aha! Sex is rearing its ugly head! Spanish student of the Russki Yesik, a certain Ramón has asked his German counterpart Ulla to accompany him to a Konziert this evening, whilst Klaus has been heard trying to persuade Ulla to join him at a Russian restaurant tomorrow night. Could be the end of a beautiful relationship if she goes for the dumplings. I wished I could warn her. 'Scajeetsie, pajalousta, NIET dumplingsov!" Hmm. Was obviously not paying attention throughout lessons 1 - 4.

Lesson Six:

It couldn't last. Corruption is setting in. With the excuse that teacher Boris celebrates his birthday next week, they have all decided to club together to buy him a tennis racquet. It so happens that their end of term exams are also, by pure coincidence, due at the end of next week, as those of us who have taken the trouble to flick through the ensuing chapter are all too aware.

Lesson Seven:

Surrender.

How can anyone learn a language which has twenty different verbs meaning "To Go", according to whether you've been but not yet returned, are going on foot, are using some means of transport, are just dropping by, or usually (abichna) go that way by foot (pishkom) but sometimes troll over on your velosipiede? It seems to me that life in general and postings to Russia in particular are just too short to merit the effort.

CHAPTER TWO

Apart from anything else, there were Credentials to be presented.

At the turn of this century, the Italian Ambassador to the Russian Federation had the privilege of being simultaneously appointed to Armenia, to Turkmenistan and to Georgia. The preparations for these four ceremonies to present the Letters of Credentials were considerable. His Excellency was under no little stress. The choice of tie, for example, was of paramount importance. It remains for posterity, after all, in the framed photograph which will adorn the sitting room (unless the rest of the family's pleas are heeded) wherever he will choose to hang his tricorne thereafter. In Moscow they did it in groups. Men only. Well, unless there was a female Head of Mission, obviously. The Italian Ambassador was set up for the occasion with his other newly arrived counterparts. This may be seen in the photographs. The vodka flowed. Evidence of this may also be perceived in the photographs. When he returned in full fig to the Residence, we uncorked some more bottles and celebrated the occasion with all the members of his staff and a select group of dignitaries and friends. Looking back, we had some difficulty remembering the precise details of that day. He accepted the framed photographs with diplomatic grace and began reading up about Armenia.

The frantic departure for the trip to Yerevan was made even more frantic by His Excellency's inability to locate his Letters five minutes before his scheduled departure to the airport. Leonid the butler and his harem of still tattily uniformed domestics were on all fours opening drawers, safes and cupboards, turning over the 1.200 sq. meters of Embassy in an attempt to locate the precious buff envelope. This was eventually run to earth by a Second Secretary soon, one feared, to be reposted to Siberia for the oversight because it had been sitting on his desk the whole time.

We were urged by the stewardess to have our duckuments ready - not such a bad idea given the amount of rain that was coming down. The Second Secretary lost yet another life for having got the weather forecast disastrously wrong and therefore obliging their excellencies to wade through the puddles for two days in highly unsuitable footwear.

Burdened with enough flowers to set up a market, we installed ourselves in our not over-large bedrooms where the combination of vast mountains of fruit and yet more bouquets soon exhausted what little there had been in the way of breathable oxygen. The discovery by H.E. that the heated towel rail in the somewhat inadequate bathroom was pounding away at maximum temperature sent him scuttling back to the foyer, where it was explained with considerable tact and forbearance that the choice was between a hot towel rail or cold shower water. His opting unilaterally for the cold shower was not considered to be in the best of democratic traditions, since he would thus have condemned the entire hotel to freeze its collective butt off whilst attending to their individual personal hygiene.

We went our separate ways. I was driven down the hill past a replica of the Sydney Opera House and the cruel black spike which was the monument to the Genocide and came to a halt in front of the offices of the All-Armenian Union of Women - every one of whom was lined up on the pavement awaiting my arrival. Between offerings of fruit, Italian chocolates, Turkish coffee and the local salty fizzy mineral water, (the effect of which upon the unsuspecting stomach is not something one would wish to describe), I was regaled with the fears and aspirations of this most worthy band of ladies. They were delighted that I had taken time to visit them, and said so, one by one with much ceremony. And at great length. Each speech was laboriously translated into Italian for my benefit by a heavily perspiring interpreter. Occasionally I would press the latter into accepting an apricot, and taking advantage of her momentary inability to communicate, would ask them all questions and receive their replies in English, which they spoke fluently. I eventually left promising rashly all manner of future contacts and visits and was yelled at upon my return for having kept His Excellency and delegation waiting for their dolmas and cucumber, to which I responded by wondering loudly whether the Queen received that kind of treatment when she returned from being gracious somewhere.

Back in Moscow, we had to leave again almost immediately for presentation of more arms or credentials or whatever to Turkmenistan and thence to Georgia. The prospect did not exactly shine like a burning star on the horizon.

Moscow, October 28th 1999

Dear Frankie and Alex,

Just back from visits to Armenia, Georgia and Turkmenistan, where we represented our country with charm and breeding as is our wont.

I hope the two of you are surviving without your mother's home cooking and your father's good advice, that you are both making ends meet on your respective allowances and studying very hard so that we won't need to cut off funds and send you out to learn a trade instead. I await news (and results) with trepidation.

I hope to be e-mailable by the end of next week, though I doubt I will be much good at it - it seems one has to be telegraphic at best or monosyllabic at worst in order to qualify as a Mailer, whereas I tend to suffer from logorrhoea as a result, no doubt, of being encouraged at school to cover multitudinous foolscap (whatever happened to foolscap?) pages on the meaning of literary concision. Discuss.

On Saturday we visited the market and your father, amidst much keeping of straight faces amongst the retinue, eventually invested in a fur hat for the oncoming winter. No amount of encouragement would persuade him to go for the Davy Crocket Siberian Wolf model, and although the one chosen was insistently guaranteed as mink, it has to be said that Beagle's rabbit/cat hunting instincts were clearly on full alert when we returned home and given half a chance she would have had it for lunch there and then.

My mastery of the Russian language after which you so charitably enquire, doth not proceed apace. Following this realisation I have decided that the quantity of roubles I had been sinking into the charade of not learning the Russki Yesik could be far better employed increasing my collection of hand-painted Palekh boxes whilst chatting ungrammatically with the vodka junkies. It occurs to me that I am not sufficiently motivated to speak the language correctly at this late stage in my life. I will happily settle for simply making myself understood and for this I merely need some infinitives, a minimum of nouns and the odd adjective which I shall then just string together. My Filipinos never had to learn the Imperfect Subjunctive, for heaven's sake, and we understood each other perfectly adequately. Anyway, I have resolved the problem of communicating with the staff by encouraging the butler to exercise his English, which he does with ever increasing proficiency. A whole week has gone by without a single blini. Once he had opened up a line of communication with the cook, my next endeavour was to drastically reduce the quantity of cakes which appeared with disastrous regularity at table, though the British Ambassadress was sceptical about my ability to achieve anything radical in this respect, asserting that she had thrown out all the rusting ovenware immediately upon arrival and had still gained a total of eight kilos to date. I have also decided that I will learn far more by chatting to the natives so, to the utter dismay of Nicolai, I have acquired an ancient car and a street map and started driving myself around. I am not prepared to have grown men sitting for hours with their car heaters set on "tropical" whilst I am in deep discussion with fellow doggy walkers in the woods. Rather than waiting for me to end an in-depth analysis of the political situation in Turkmenistan, they could be just as well employed back at the Embassy playing cards and drinking vodka. The only drawback to this plan is the problem of the "rasvarot", or U-turn. This is the first Russian word that any visitor to Moscow who ill-advisedly decides to drive himself will learn. It translates into the various languages of the European Community when speaking to one's chers collègues thus:

(Eng.): to rasvarot - Past Tense: I rasvarotted

(Ital.):   rasvarottare - ho rasvarottato

(Fr.):   rasvarotter - j'ai rasvarotté

And so on.

For some reason best known to themselves but surely not political, it is impossible to turn left anywhere in Moscow. Should one wish to do so, the alternatives would seem to be as follows:

a) Proceed to the nearest point where a U-turn is permitted by the authorities. This will involve going under so many rivers and over so many railway lines and around so many identical Stalinist-Gothic edifices that any sense of direction you may have had at the outset stands little chance of survival. On a good day, you may be lucky enough to catch a glimpse of your destination as it once again reappears on the wrong side of a ten-lane highway.

b) Drive on down to Georgia and bribe a policeman (probably quicker).

So I potter off daily to the woods with the dog in search of edifying conversation with the natives. Beagle has by this stage developed an attitude towards Moscow ducks, pigeons, rooks and salami-carrying babushkas, and is at dire risk of being deported. She has perfected the art of snatching lumps of black bread from the winos who are usually too pickled to notice. My first words in Russian were, of necessity "Excuse me" - which was as near as I could get to "Excuse her." She invariably does her best to taunt the local dogs into indulging in that frivolous Western habit of chasing fallen leaves. Russians are not amused by wayward dogs - they prefer them to stay close and OBEY. Diplomatic relations are not improved. The local pooch is brought up to work for its living. Thus it is expected either to reproduce to a high genetic standard (mongrels are not an option,) or chase the wild boar. Nicolai's dog is fed on prime beef and fresh vegetables in season. When I explained (in infinitives and nouns) that mine gets canned dog food, which it peps up with the contents of the Moscow dustbins, he mentioned that his dog caught forty-three mink last season. I did not ask from where, nor am I about to change Beagle's diet on the off chance she might turn her nose to more lucrative pursuits.

I hope this snail mail reaches you eventually. If it is true that the KGB can reroute the wires out of the chandeliers and down to my computer by the end of the week, I shall be able to stop these interminable letters and become terse. Shall you look forward to that?

Love, and keep me posted,   Maman

A series of technicians did, in fact, appear soon after bearing toolboxes and lengths of wire They received "help" from the resident handyman, Serafim, and were followed every inch of the way by a resident Italian carabiniere watching hawk-eyed for any sign of suspicious miniature objects being surreptitiously inserted behind the walls.

As if there were room for any more.

CHAPTER THREE

The days were long. The weeks longer. The worst part was getting out of bed in the morning, running the gauntlet from the near freezing bedroom, (there was nothing for it but to turn the heating off completely if one wanted to breathe at all,) to the bathroom, and to dress like an onion with discardable layers in order to survive the differing temperatures which the ensuing day would inflict. I immersed myself in a diet of (translated) Russian literature in an attempt to integrate, while Himself opted instead for a diet of cabbage and cauliflower which he had recently decided was necessary for the maintenance of his silhouette. Occasionally we remembered Michael and wondered what had become of him.

"I thought we didn't have an enemy anymore? What on earth did he find to leak that they didn't know already?"

"Nothing much. It was a question of principle, more than anything."

"So poor old Michael is condemned to a life in hiding and penury just because he spilt a few beans and spoilt all their little crypto-faxing japers?"

"I wouldn't worry too much about the life of penury. If you ask me, he'll be making himself a fortune in the world of industrial espionage, which is where he should have been all along. Never even used to turn up to half the Nato meetings, I seem to remember. Spent most of his time on the tennis court."

Time to change the subject, Sarah.

"Minestrone or caviar tonight? Or are we out somewhere? Yelena needs to know."

"We are supposed to be at the Bolshoi by 7.15. Dressed," he said, looking pointedly at the bare feet I had hoped were unnoticeable beneath the table. Little black number it was, then, and no doubt much singing for my supper afterwards with the director of the theatre and various other important personages who had kindly invited us.

The ballet was inspiring though, as usual, and the warmth with which we were entertained after the performance was, upon reflection, infinitely preferable to my customary aimless chatter about uncontroversial topics in the perfection of which, looking back, I felt I had spent the greater part of my life

Dear Mother,

As I write, I am hiding, not behind the green baize door, but the blue damask curtain, which is all that separates me and nailed-to-the-floor-Beagle from a men-only (brilliant invention) lunch. On the other side of said curtain I can hear H.E. demonstrating graphically in three languages (none of which, need I even mention, is Russian) precisely how and where a former German Ambassador, Graf von Mirbach, was assassinated by the Bolsheviks whilst taking coffee in our red (krasnay) salon. The colour scheme was subsequently thought up by an Ambassadress in an attempt to pay tribute to the good Count's guts which had been splattered across the wall hangings. Lenin paid a visit soon after to apologise, but it was too late by then, of course.

This will be brief because I am in training for the Internet. I am told that all mail is read by the secret service, which was par for the course at boarding school too, so I can probably live with that. I would love to watch them wading through my letters, though, searching for key phrases and wondering what dastardly concept the code word "Beagle" could possibly stand for. Speaking of whom, she had a very successful trip over here – you do get a fleshier class of ankle in Aeroflot, and it was well garnished with marinated sturgeon dropped from a discreet height so as not to offend those terrifying stewards. On Day Two, she ran the cook to earth in the bowels of the cellars (where the powers that be have thoughtfully placed the kitchen) and has been howling "Gone Awaaay!" at the top of the narrow spiral staircase which links it to the rest of civilisation ever since. Thus, in the manner of Squirrel Nutkin, I fear I shall not get to see this well-endowed lady until next Spring, or whenever my imported supplies run out.

In the meantime, Beagle's girth is increasing daily, but luckily for her the crows round here are as big as Ilyushins and so heavy getting off the ground that she is definitely in there for a chance.

Must go – some nice Russian ladies are on their way to take me to the monthly semi-precious gem market, having warned me not to set foot outside the house in these freezing temperatures until they get here in their warmed limo, obviously not wanting to carry yet another stiffie off our front steps, given the historical precedents.

So much for being brief. A great talker on little matters. Quote: Jane Austen. Love, Sarah

The strangest thing happened at the market. I was poring over a rather beautiful aquamarine, hemmed in on all sides by portly Russian matrons intent upon inserting their elbows into any available crevice, when I heard the voice. Nobody else had a voice like that, and although I could not be too sure whether it was talking in English or in Russian, I was quite sure that I recognised it as belonging to Michael. By the time I had managed to unhook myself from the elbows and look around it had stopped, however, and a mass of Russian babushkas had closed in upon me. I lost interest in bargain hunting and went home.

CHAPTER FOUR

H.E. having decided that three meals a day served by an obsequious white-gloved butler (and thus irresistible) were having an over-positive effect on his waistline, decided to frequent a gym. Not any gym of course, but the most exclusive available. Anyone else would have realised that the most exclusive would also be the most expensive and therefore frequented solely by the Mafia bully boys, but this strangely escaped the notice of our Sicilian. His accompanying spouse was scared too rigid to even approach any free machine in case she was picked off by an ear tip by some impatient hunk of tightly-packed, heavily tattooed muscle. Giorgio, by contrast, seemed to be oblivious to his surroundings, and pedalled away furiously for twenty minutes, resplendent in a dinky little pale grey short and top outfit I had picked up cheap in the local market. Fortunately he also seemed oblivious to the fact that said outfit was emblazoned across the pectorals with cartoon characters from The Simpsons, though most probably he had never heard of them in the first place, except possibly in the Wally context. The alternative activity for women, if that's what they were, seemed to be a step class: beginners, intermediate or advanced.. A printed warning adorned the door into the gym: "Please inform your instructor if this is your first time!" Otherwise, one assumed, it could well be your last. I sat in on the beginners session but they seemed to be in training to step the Lenin mausoleum and to my unprofessional eye I calculated they were breaking the urban speed limit by a good 30 kph and that at a conservative estimate.

Exhausted and demoralised, I took Beagle off to the local park where within minutes she was inciting a brace of Rottweilers to chase her and challenging them to her customary wrestling matches. These were obviously the doggy equivalent of the gym frequenters, minus the tattoos. Perhaps a little more intelligent. It was beginning to snow. I called it a day and went home to write some letters. Apart from anything else, I had lost all contact with Manuela again and was curious to know how she was surviving.

Dear Manu,
I am sending this to Rome, but have lost all track of where you are. Please inform and preferably come and stay for a few days. I would give anything for some fun girlfriend company in this cold, dark winter. Instead, I have the unwanted guest from hell right now, as we are harbouring a frightened Italian in the throes of a nervous breakdown. As far as I can make out, since we are only allowed to talk about it out in the woods or with the bathwater running, he spends his days chain-smoking in the spare bedroom handcuffed to a non-smoking carabiniere. Giorgio deludes himself that no-one knows of his shhhh! existence. Though somebody must be asking why in Hades plates of spaghetti should be ordered twice daily from the kitchens and carted upstairs with instructions not to use the House of Savoy crested

cutlery, please...

Meanwhile we are Awaiting Instructions and therefore can do nothing. Our pet Russian policeman who guards us 24 hours a day, minus 30° to plus 40°, has taken to walking constantly up and down in front of the main gates presumably in case someone makes a dash for it. He too has taken to chain smoking, though perhaps he always did and we just didn't notice in the days when he stayed tucked inside his little sentry box doing crossword puzzles or reading Dostoyevsky, windows hermetically papered over with copies of *Pravda* so that we could neither see him nor he us. After he had been with us for a week, our unbalanced lodger's local unlawfully-wedded made contact with the Embassy to say she'd lost him, so they rather shamefacedly had to admit he was cosily holed up in our 3000sq m of inviolable territory whilst she had been out roaming the streets in sub-freezing temperatures looking for him. They have now been granted conjugal visiting rights, but as H.E. was heard to mutter, not in *my* guest room, thank you very much, and especially not with handcuffs. Meanwhile our resident defrocked doctor turned aid worker who, strangely, claims to have known the guy in some dubious past life, pops in twice daily to fill him up with Valium to calm his jitters.

Do let me know what you are up to. Censored version, please. We don't want Big Brother spreading it all over town.

Love, Sarah

Dear Mother,

Apparently we can expect alternate snow and slush from now through until about next May, so I'll have to get used to it fast. Beagle was most amused at all this white stuff today and romped around the park creating havoc amongst the pit bulls and huskies. On more than one occasion only her lightning speed saved her from being mauled to sausage meat, and a few more weeks of scrounging titbits from the Embassy staff will surely curtail her speed and shorten her odds of survival. A couple of hundred kilos of Russian-speaking Rottweiler is used to a degree of respect, after all, not to having a hyperactive mini hound charging to and fro beneath its undercarriage at three second intervals. If she survives the posting we will both be amazed. A Rottweiler on a long lead, pees twice and thinks about it. Beagle, who never could fathom this male dog habit of pee before play, picks up the long trailing lead and tries to run off with it. Back home she has already terrorized the staff into unconditional surrender - poor old Serafim, our resident handyman and alcoholic who is recuperating from the intravenous vodka habit and still a bit groggy on his pins, was recently stuck up a 15ft ladder (where he'd been picking flies off the ceiling, or some such task related to his former affliction) for twenty minutes whilst Beagle howled "Quarry Sighted" beneath him. When tired of tormenting the staff, she frolics around the garden where Tonia the gardener, (released, I am beginning to suspect, without struggle from the Botanical Gardens because of her blue fingers), is busily scattering seed in the forlorn hope of creating a lawn before it all gets crushed under three feet of snow for the next eight months.

More news from Moscow With Love, soon......

Sarah

Serafim, did indeed have a considerable problem with his alcohol consumption, and was later found drunk in charge of a paintbrush, attempting to touch up the garden furniture, as a result of which the Embassy ended up with a white, weed-ridden lawn. Beagle, on the other hand, had discovered she could slip between the bars of the iron fence surrounding the garden, and was constantly being sent back at gun point by the Russian guard. Serafim was immediately relieved of his paintbrush and provided instead with a roll of wire netting and a pair of clippers. At the last check, the netting was definitely winning, to the delight of the assembled drivers, odd job men and general hangers-on standing around laying bets on the final outcome. The netting, he explained, if I was interpreting him correctly, was imported, and being thus of foreign origin did not have the Russian love of discipline. It was for this reason only that it persisted in wrapping itself around the Ambassador's car, neighbouring trees, the lawn mower and even Mikhael, our pet KGB cop, instead of laying itself obediently flat against the offending bars and rendering them instantly beagle-proof.

Time was, I could have found all this amusing, but what with the weather, my inability to communicate satisfactorily and the girls being so far away, I seemed to be losing my sense of perspective. That voice from the past hadn't helped, either, and as if I needed further provocation, I had just received the latest useless missive from the Association of Foreign Ministry Consorts. Whilst providing the customary priceless instructions concerning the number of saucepans and lemon squeezers I could legally claim on expenses, it included a curious new directive which essentially left the wives in no doubt as to the insignificance of their roles. Following a request to play musical teapots, in the sense that if the Embassy in Seoul happened to have a couple of spare ones they were encouraged to ship them off to a pot-needy colleague in, say, Tbilisi, we were in addition requested to note that Ladies Teas, Luncheons or Fund Raising Activities would no longer be reimbursed by the entertainment allowance unless H.E. the Head of Mission was also present. The Female Appendage of the Italian Ambassador to Moscow was consequently threatening to announce that any further activities rashly undertaken on her own initiative and excluding her worthy spouse would henceforth be curtailed and that all future engagements of such a nature should take place à la présence. Giorgio must come to all my coffee mornings. Despite The Presence, ladies would still receive encouragement, (should they need it), to cover their customary favourite topics: birth and breast feeding experiences, nannies from hell, the inadequacies of local schooling, recent operations or menopausal symptoms. They should equally feel free to swap addresses for reliable hairdressers, beauty parlours and health clubs, or to exchange recipes for How to Achieve the Perfect Soufflé. Especially when the kitchen was down a narrow spiral staircase, along 3kms of corridor and through approximately two time zones. Only a Russian cook could get a soufflé on to the table without it collapsing under these conditions, and I always suspected mine of borrowing from the same techniques used to preserve the body of Lenin who, seventy-five years after his death, continued to lie in impeccable repose within his mausoleum on Red Square.

I left for a (government subsidised) tea party at the German Embassy. Turned out of their Residence because of redecoration work in progress, the Germans had taken refuge for ten months in a luxury apartment designed for the son of a Novy Ruski. They had succeeded in persuading the owner to install partition walls so that their guests were not obliged to watch their dinner being cooked in the open plan kitchen, and to remove an excessive number of bathtubs to make room for a chest freezer, but in the spectacular glass roofed and walled penthouse where one might give lavish cocktail parties for up to 100 people, they had met with immovable opposition. The iron piping which coyly protruded from the middle of the sitting room floor was designed for a Jacuzzi, and no manner of protests on their part -"but ve don't *trow* that kind off party!" - could persuade the owner to remove it. An occasional table was instead placed over the offending item and it was turned into a conversation piece, whilst the rest of the modernisation of the Residence proceeded in fits and starts in the manner customary to workmen the world over. The installations in the ultra-modern bathrooms were causing them their worst sleepless nights: Frau Wife of Ambo was terrified that if something went wrong with the machinery or a guest's aim was inaccurate, the new laser flush toilets might be capable of rendering impotent all who ventured within firing distance. We reassured her to the best of our collective female ability.

CHAPTER FIVE

The barometer outside my bedroom window was declaring minus nine by the time I had prised my eyes open sufficiently to read it and it was with some reluctance that I forced myself into a pair of jodhpurs and a couple of sweaters, extra socks, two pairs of gloves and the dreaded boots. Dreaded because it took two people to remove them and because, not having been designed for walking on ice, the chances of my falling and breaking something were greatest during the interval between getting out of the car and on to the back of the horse. Skidding back to the car afterwards, I remembered I was scheduled to go to what would doubtless prove a deadly ladies' tea party at 4pm, and to visit a children's hospital on the outskirts of Moscow at 5.30.

His Excellency, it appeared, as I crept through the back door dripping snow and sawdust, was hosting a lunch for a group of influential Italian businessmen. Whoever had designed the Embassy had just not considered the possibility of unpresentable wives having to creep past the open door of the dining room in order to reach their private quarters for a much needed shower. I counted on a combination of butler and beagle to create a diversion, and with averted head, scuttled on down the corridor.

He joined me later as I was being served a late lunch

on a tray in my favourite refuge - my own personal mini-paradise of books, CDs, letters, radio and dog basket with papers scattered all over the floor.

"Couldn't you clear this up a bit?"

"Nope. There is a certain logic in this apparent mess to which only I hold the key. That pile on the floor is only masquerading as chaos. It is, in fact, a highly advanced and sophisticated form of file indexing."

"What's in it?"

"Begging letters. I am about to dispense largesse. Which reminds me: we are giving a concert plus dinner next month to raise funds for the soup kitchen which your Italian nuns are running in sub-freezing temperatures, and after that a ball to finance Leukemia treatments for thirty children who risk snuffing it without them. And your luncheon companions don't know it yet, but they are about to be hassled for blank cheques, because I have some handicapped children we need to send to Italy for hip operations. So next time you give them a free lunch, let them know the bill will be arriving later."

"What's wrong?"

"Nothing. Everything. Too much Anglo-Saxon cynicism, probably. The Jesuits didn't get to me in time before I blew the seventh candle off the cake. It's not easy: the last batch of medicine I had flown in for my Leukemia babies got sold off to the highest bidder, apparently. Everybody else knew you have to give it personally into the hands of the mothers. Not me. One learns by one's experience, but you look very stupid in the meantime. And then it's all just a drop in the ocean. How do you decide to save two children out of an orphanage and ignore the other seventy? Don't let it keep you awake at nights. I'll get over it. I'm off to a charity tea and then to visit a paediatric hospital - I'll see you tonight."

The tea party in question was to take place in the newly opened Pushkin Café, and as the heavily accented Russian lady had made clear over the phone, was designed to organise fund raising efforts for a worthy cause. Exactly which worthy cause, I had by now forgotten, I realised, as I made my way down to the cloakroom in the basement to leave my snow-covered coat and boots as required by the management. Nor did I have any recollection as to the name of the good lady in question, since the latter had been so confident that she was a household word within the walls of the Italian Embassy that I had not liked to ask for it to be repeated. I wandered back to the ground floor searching for a large party of noisy international females which would surely indicate I was on the right track. Downstairs there was nothing to fit that description, so I made my way to the floor above.

One single customer well ensconced behind a newspaper. Damn. I must have got the wrong day or time. Or café. The obsequious waiter was already hovering, terrified he might lose a potential tip. I was hesitating whether to sit down and order tea now that I was there, or whether to just run home and await the 5.30 appointment in the comfort of my own sitting room, when the newspaper was lowered, very, very slowly. A pair of dark brown eyes sparkling with amusement appeared over the top, and a heavily pseudo-Russian accent invited me to join it for "Earl Grey and cucumber sandwiches?"

For a moment I thought I was hallucinating, but he was already on his feet, supporting hand under my arm, persuading me to sit before I fell.

"Well, say something! Say you never suspected a thing! Say you're much happier to see me than the frightful old bag soliciting money you thought you were going to meet! Say you've missed me horribly and never believed one word of all the rumours flying around. Say HELLO, at least!"

But I couldn't, and it took two cups of alcohol-laced tea such as Mother never used to make, with or without the cucumber sandwiches, before I could even whisper his name.

Once over the initial shock, I asked him what had brought him to Moscow and he explained that he was now working as a freelance reporter and therefore came to the city on a regular basis. After three quarters of an hour, I rose to go to the children's hospital, and there was a distinct note of urgency in his voice as he begged me to stay longer.

"I can't. I have to be there by 5.30 and it's way out of town."

"Can I come too?"

"Don't be ridiculous, Michael. How would I explain your presence to the members of the Charity Committee who are accompanying me there? Pass you off as my bodyguard?"

"Financial Advisor. I'll trot out some figures. Or wait in the car."

Unprecedented. What *was* he after? I told him not to be stupid and ran out to the waiting car.

The visit to the paediatric hospital took place in the company of a delegation from the Embassy, members of the Charity Committee and an interpreter. We drove out of Moscow on snow covered roads which soon turned to ice as we left the city centre. I was to hand over an Electrocardiograph machine and a supply of medicines for the treatment of Russian chickniks. I found myself in the car with two officials whose names eluded me and who spent the journey endeavouring to explain at some length the technicalities of the latest equipment stashed away in the boot ready for presentation to the medical staff. I tried unsuccessfully to concentrate less on the driver's inability to keep the car in a straight line, and more on the briefing I was being given, presumably for inclusion in the speech which I suddenly realised with horror I was expected to deliver during the course of the ceremony. By the time we reached the hospital I was suffering from distinct cardiac irregularities myself. After half an hour of desultory conversation with the Deputy Director, it became evident, however, that the Director himself was holed up with a group of politicians from the Duma and that the chances of him being able to escape from the clutches of such worthies before dinner time were pretty slim. Watches were flashed, domino style, all down the line of the standing participants and a hasty battle plan was drawn up:

1) Present donation to Deputy.
2) Claim further pressing engagements of humanitarian nature.

3) Utter brief speech concerning nature of donation.

4) Withdraw with dignity still wearing snow boots (hardly worthwhile changing into the Ferragamos for a mere deputy), make swift dash to the waiting cars and be back in time for drinks.

*   *   *   *

A couple of days later, I was sitting in front of the computer, which was finally up and more or less running, about to compose an email when "Glasnet.ru" intimated its desire to forward an incoming message. Expecting the familiar "please could you tell that horrid bank to advance me something on next month's allowance? - I can't even afford to put petrol in the car this week," I froze as I read instead :

"Spies Anon. Meet at the Metro Voykovskaya 4 p.m. Destroy upon reception. Be there. Please."

Amused, I immediately typed back a reply.

"Mata Hari not available at such short notice due to prior engagement at Swedish Embassy to say farewell to her Belgian counterpart followed by necessity of receiving Courtesy Visit from Japanese Ambassadress." With which, I scrunched out of the front door and into the waiting car, determined that this time round he would be kept at a very safe distance.

CHAPTER SIX

Ladies Lunch at the Swedish Embassy - minus fifteen within and without. Everybody huddled around the modern Scandinavian designer fireplace in an attempt to keep their lips moving although in some cases it might have been preferable had some of those present frozen before they sat themselves down to lunch. We had no sooner begun to attack our first course than the token Russian lady present proceeded to intimate her wish to propose a toast to her dear departing friend. As she explained at some length and with a certain degree of emotion, she had given this homage some thought and wished to deliver it early on in the proceedings before she got too drunk. Despite being a nuclear physicist by profession and not a psychologist, she then presented us with a fairly in-depth analysis of our Belgian friend's character, attributes, achievements etc., which ended up with the speaker herself in tears and the rest of the table reaching for the Kleenex. Fine, but this kind of performance is a hard one to follow, and once it had drawn to its emotional close, there was a deathly silence until some mutt (me, of course, boarding school education wins again,) managed to defuse the situation with an inane remark. We despatched the cold entrée with something like relief, and had just started on the quenelles and leek juliennes when our nuclear physicist, flushed with the success of her first effort, rapped for further silence to propose another toast to her hostess. Cold entrées I can take, even if the external and consequently internal temperatures are, apparently, fixed in a downward spiral. Cold quenelles I cannot. I will not even mention that we had ice cream for dessert. I took my cup of mint tea as close to the dying embers of the fire as possible without physically sitting inside the chimney, and ran home to greet the Japanese Ambassadress who had elected to pay me her courtesy visit on this of all days. The driver kept the heating on "Pizza Oven" during the drive home, enquired as to how much vodka I had been offered, and was horrified that neither onions nor garlic had been on the menu. Every sane Russian knows that the only way to survive the cold is with a diet of garlic, onions and vodka. I noticed he followed his own advice, but there was no question of my opening the window, so I had to grin and bear it all the way back to the Embassy

Wrapped in a shawl, I received my Japanese counterpart as graciously as possible, though the ice was soon broken, in a manner of speaking, when she inadvertently flipped a contact lens into her cup of not very oriental tea. She later most kindly revealed her own secret for keeping warm ("May I show you?") in the form of a radio-active plaster which, when applied to any desired part of the body, generated heat in a manner unequalled by any common or garden onion, head of garlic or bottle of vodka. Desirous of furthering international understanding and cooperation, she promised to send her driver round with a free sample for me to test. I, in recognition of this kindness, revealed somewhat undiplomatically the names of certain Embassies where she would be well advised to adorn her body with the contents of half a dozen packets.

To: Sarah

From: Manu

You will never know what I had to promise some self-important vixen in your Embassy for her to release your email address. How's it going? Have you got rid of your house guest? Was he cute? I'm in Rome at the moment, just following up a couple of things. Nothing too important. Keep in touch.

Love, Manu

Plus ça change.

*   *   *   *

Returning from walking the dog up in the Sparrow Hills and manoeuvring with great difficulty through the Moscow rush-hour traffic, I mentally rehearsed the titles and ranks of the evening's guests. It was the annual Italian Armed Forces party which was always hosted in the Residence. I could never remember which World War they claimed to have won single-handedly, but that was the one they celebrated each year. Under H.E.'s watchful eye, I was under oath to refrain from jokes about tanks with four reverse gears, it being their Special Day and all.

Finally reaching home, I found we had been invaded. There were grouplets of Very Importants scattered all over the Residence - Ministers in the Library signing things, Minions in the Corridor taking notes and shouting into cell-phones, and Gentlemen of the Press (chain-smokers to a man) in the Krasnay Salon. I took refuge in a corner of our bedroom hoping that no one would intrude whilst I communed with Haydn and a face mask. Sub-freezing temperatures, I had been given to understand that day on the beach in Corsica, were supposed to conserve. I was still living in hope. The last of the military and their esteemed guests left reluctantly around midnight when a group of hardened drinkers with watery vision were winkled out of the Ambassador's private apartments and helped through the side entrance. Full of bonhomie and vodka, they were determined to do their bit for Italo-Russian relations and offered up a stirring serenade in rich baritones for a further half-hour following their eviction.

To: Manu

From: Sarah

What, pray, does "just following up a couple of things" signify?

I can't leave you alone for one minute, can I? You'll never guess, by the way, who I ran into by pure chance in a Moscow café? And again, perhaps you might. All news whenever we next meet – not that there's anything to tell, before you start phoning Hello magazine....

Dear Mother,

This morning I had a date with my personal trainer whose fee of $10 is worth every cent, in that she saves me from battling with the Moscow traffic and inhaling the pickles and BO which the average Russian gymnasium pumps through its ventilation system. I was thus lying beneath the sculpted bas-reliefs of over-nourished and under-dressed cherubs who, together with an ill-assorted selection of peacocks, goddesses and peonies adorn the ceiling of our salon, when I glimpsed a set of ankles. Recognizing these quite definitely not to be my own, since the whole point of this exercising was to bring such parts of the anatomy back into my sights after recent excesses, I followed them at length up an interminably long braided trouser leg and even longer braided jacket until I reached the apex - a saluting carabiniere standing rigidly to attention not a sword's length from my still supine body. Having taken so long to get my legs into the required candle position, it seemed a shame to wind them down again at such short notice, so I heard him out upside down, so to speak. In any case our resident carabinieri had long ago registered the image I was trying not to project when the new Italian Ambassadress was caught heading out of the back entrance to drive her own (filthy) car up to the woods in jeans and Walkman. The heels were never clicked with the same conviction after that sighting. On this occasion, it appeared that our impressive array of video cameras had spotted an intruder and our man was requesting permission to investigate.

Difficult to wave regally in that position, but it was achieved, and I returned to working the bum muscles with renewed vigour, pausing to wonder, as one so often does whilst working the pelvic area, who else could see me at it with all those video cameras. How, for example, do they *always* know which room to put my calls through to when I am alone in the house? Since I invariably wander around in a state of déshabille due to the excessive enthusiasm of the stoker in the basement, this question nags at me.

This afternoon, I had a Russian conversation lesson and have since being going around having the staff in fits asking them such basic questions as What is your name? and What is My name? which they think is pretty dumb since I've been here over a year now. Then I dedicated myself to our latest house guest. Took him around town and let him buy some appalling souvenirs which upped my credit with the Matrioschka sellers. Encouraged a bunch of Japanese tourists to invest in great dollops of amber whilst I was about it, telling them I lived here and these were the cheapest prices going. Bullshit. Much nodding and smiling and taking of pictures. Evlybody happy. Especially Matlioshka serrers.

I must, I fear, leave you with that image in order to prepare myself mentally and gastronomically for the imminent visit of a possibly influential and therefore useful, career-wise, Italian politician and wife. In cases like this I have to make very careful decisions concerning the menus. Do we drown them in caviar and earn their undying gratitude and admiration but risk them going home to tell everyone that the Italian Ambassador to Moscow is overpaid? Or do we give them tortellini and chicken and have them think we are making huge savings out of our entertainment allowance and investing instead in Russian art with which to finance our old age? Always a tough one, this. Somebody is hammering more microphones into my wall. Must go and investigate...............

Putting in new phone lines. A likely story.
Love, S
P.S. I hear the girls have opted to spend Christmas with you this year. Make sure they do all the cooking – if you can stand the thought.

YOU HAVE MAIL.
"Subject : Bond-ing

"Shaken and deeply stirred by our recent meeting, propose harmless walk in Sparrow Fields upon returning next Monday from top secret destination. Please specify time and date. Now."

Reply to sender:

Wrong time of year. Busy with kiddies Christmas party. Wrapping up 50 Russian Barbie dolls are the trickiest part. Lumps everywhere. Bet you wish you were here. You might enjoy that bit.
xx Sarah

To: Sarah
From: Manu
Just off back to Argentina for Christmas. Too cold in
Rome.
Wouldn't dream of contacting Hello unless I was
promised something in at least four figures. So either
forget it (as formerly advised,) or bludi make it
worthwhile. Can't stand all these wussy half
measures.
Ran into your friend Michael the other day, by the
way. He took me out to dinner except I was on a new
diet and could only eat oysters. Not very low
maintenance. He didn't seem to mind.
Luv, Manu

No, I thought. I'll bet he didn't.

To: Frankie

Cc: Alex

Isn't it reassuring to know that the expert in logistics
who has been here for three days preparing all the
minute details for the Presidential visit, measuring
the distance between banqueting halls and bogs, has
gone off forgetting not only all his caviar but even
his suitcase? And that we are now having to send
native runners (without cleft sticks) to remote
airports to reunite him with his goods and chattels?
Got up too early this morning having promised to go
and pick up new Belgian Ambo to take him riding.
Very proud, having booked horses all by myself in
Russian. Bit worried that I might have translated

"Wednesday" incorrectly, (oh yes, we are still at that level after one year and a bit...) but off we went. Managed not to take the wrong road, slid gently into the stream of traffic having collected him to the horror of his guards and domestics in my tatty dog-hairy muddy private limo 'cos I hate having clean chauffeur-driven cars waiting around for me when I emerge covered in dung and sweat from urging nags over sticks, and went slam into the mother of all traffic jams. Sat in it telling not very funny diplomatic anecdotes for a solid hour, rang the stables (another source of pride: " I no come. Many cars. Maybe next-day-tomorrow"), did a U turn round a couple of bits of Soviet statuary, and headed off in entirely the wrong direction towards the airport. Crawled another couple of miles to find a place for 2nd U-turn, finally made it home in time for lunch. Just. Highly frazzled.

Pause to consume plate of fruit sculpture which has just been brought to me. I offend the cook by only eating fruit when I'm alone, so they bring it to me beside my computer and go overboard turning it into a 3 dimensional work of art. The THINGS they can do with a banana......

Hosted an amazing concert the other night in front of a couple of hundred guests plus so many photographers, reporters and T.V. crews that they were sitting in my lap through most of the performance, (which meant I was sitting in the lap of the Foreign Minister and his wife who were also present). Yuri Bashmet played a piece by Shostakovitch which would normally have had me reaching for one of those little bags they thoughtfully provide on airplanes, except that he was so amazing I was Thrilled. No, as you would say, Really.

Afterwards your father decorated him most solemnly with the Italian Order of Something for Services Rendered, except that his hair was so long, as befitting a great artist, that M. l'Ambassadeur had great difficulty doing up the laces at the back of the neck without getting everything knotted and thus rendering him incapable of playing another note. Around 11 p.m. when we had planned on tucking into the newspapers or trying to discover how many house guests we still had lurking around the place, etc, they started on the vodka and eventually everybody had to be more or less forcibly removed.

I now have 200 guests tasting wine in my back parlour, closely to be followed, as I understand from the dog who has been down in the kitchens since yesterday, by an orgy of prosciutto, polenta, cheeses and trappings. Will thus have to stop hiding and get out there to sing for my supper.

Love to both, Maman

The Visit took up most of my time during the following week. I lost my voice completely on Day Four, which probably saved Giorgio's career for him, since by then I had a fair number of pertinent thoughts I was dying to relay to the bunch of parasites who formed the accompanying delegation at the taxpayer's expense. They went back with twenty kilos of red and black caviar between them, though Giorgio's future was hanging on the line on account of the sables they hadn't had time to purchase. The highlight occurred when a minion went to pay all their hotel bills and after a couple of glasses of vodka amused himself and us by relaying the extra expenditures incurred by each delegation member on mini-bar consumption and hours spent watching the porno channels in their rooms. When they finally departed, having borrowed extra suitcases in which to transport their quantities of amber and hand painted tea services, I took up the threads of my life with a sigh of relief.

CHAPTER SEVEN

Somewhat neglected of late, the dog was in need of some t.l.c., having been holding her tail very dejectedly pointing due south for the past four days, whilst any attempts on my side to find a scientific medical cure were having no effect whatsoever. These comprised, in order of application :

1) Endeavour to raise tail to upright position in case she'd forgotten how (frantic yelp),

2) Take no notice and hope it will go away (nope),

3) Apply Vaseline (yummy, lick, lick.)

Finally I sought names and addresses of vets, picked the nearest, armed myself with an interpreter and headed for the none too salubrious "Klinik." Larissa the interpreter was watching my reactions closely as we skirted the potholes, hopped over the missing stairs, tried not to trip over the exposed pipes and wiring, and braved it through some extraordinarily potent stenches I could not recall having ever encountered before. Finally we were confronted by a sour-faced babushka who demanded 120 roubles before she'd let us through the next door. Beagle's tail was by this stage even more firmly entrenched between her back legs, and the look on her face said very clearly that she was prepared to call the whole thing off and head for home. One X-ray, a couple of injections and a lecture about not going near the woods until next October because of the ticks, later, and we were informed that she had probably received a well-aimed kick in the backside which had left her with a traumatised tail. And as everyone this side of the Urals knows, apparently, the only real cure for such an ailment is to wrap the offending member in vodka-soaked cotton wool, and replenish twice daily. Oh, and some anti-inflammatory tablets as an afterthought probably wouldn't do any harm either. And if she still goes "yummy, lick lick," I thought on my way back home, I'll have two raging alcoholics in the Embassy instead of just Serafim.

I flopped in front of the computer in our not-so-private lounge once we were safely home and listened to Giorgio in the next room drinking coffee with a couple of Russians, a younger colleague from the Embassy, and an interpreter. The conversation consisted, I noted, of H.E. making controversial comments about which the Russians, knowing more than he did about the internal wiring of the Embassy, were being very cagey and non-committal. The young colleague was mute with terror. The interpreter had lost the plot halfway through dessert and soon abandoned all efforts to keep up and Giorgio was having a ball because, in the final analysis, he was the only one that got to say anything and could therefore legitimately hold the floor without competition. A lifetime's dream. He made a series of heavily politically incorrect ironic comments at which he laughed himself silly, seconded only by the young colleague who had a certain vested interest in this. Unfortunately, by the time the witticism had been translated into Russian, he had already sailed away to another topic, making it difficult for his listeners to participate in this spontaneous humour even had they wished to do so in the first place. Coffee over, liqueurs refused, he started the inevitable "well, that was such a useful exchange of...." and ejected them, leaving the stage free for Leonid to wheel in half a dozen round tables complete with pre-disposed flower arrangements and silver settings in preparation for the evening's concert and buffet supper. Logging on, I wondered fleetingly what the Chechen refugees were getting for dinner.

To: Manuela

From: Sarah

Subject: Happy Christmas and New Year

....and especially happy all the bits in between which are usually the most disastrous as you well know, like when you discover you've put on 2kgs from the turkey and trimmings and are heading straight for another debauch of caviar and blini, or in your case Argentine steaks the size of whales, without so much as time for a decent game of tennis/aerobic work-out/liposuction on the stomach before the next gargantuan onslaught.. I suppose you will be dancing on the beaches at midnight whilst we are tarted up in our penguin suits and frills to revel at the French Ambassador's. Hope it will be highly jolly, otherwise I'll just have to hit the fizz and be dragged insensible into the new Millenium.

Love, and let's wish ourselves all manner of Great Things for next year. Will drink silently to you without throwing glass over shoulder in traditional local manner - my Scottish blood forbids - at midnight.

P.S. Fancy your running into the dreaded Michael. What a coincidence.

Hmmmmm.

Dear Mother,

We must get you on line. Cannot do with all this paper and envelope business.

I have finally finished wrapping presents for the kiddies Christmas party which is scheduled to rock the Italian community during the festive season and have put our ex KGB driver on a strict diet so that he'll hopefully still fit into last year's costume, a poem in scarlet and ermine, and do his very passable impression of a bilingual Santa Claus.

Was toying (sorry) with the idea of pleading atheism and asthma to avoid all the Christmas Tree palaver - purchasing, erecting, hoovering up the pine needles hourly as soon as the Russian central heating hits them etc., but I am told it is Expected of Me. Story of my life.

Hope the girls make a decent job of the turkey and generally behave themselves. Feel free to impose curfews and T.V. restrictions no matter how grown up they think themselves. And try to have a minimally restful Christmas despite them.

Love from Sarah

The pre-Christmas season of concerts and dinners was well under way, and I hardly had time to notice that my snub had apparently taken effect all too successfully, for there had been no reply to my email. I fell to wondering as to Michael's whereabouts as I prepared to leave for yet another dinner invitation to a certain Scandinavian Embassy renowned for its bonhomie and vast unwelcoming structure. In Northern European countries the speeches invariably take place before any food is set on the table. This was, I presumed, so that participants with delicate stomachs could, if they had the nerve, rise and leave the proceedings immediately after the last toast, thereby avoiding all manner of complications and unpleasant scenarios when the dead fish swimming in mustard was placed before them. On this occasion, they would have been well-advised to do just that, as the pièce de resistance turned out to be a pudding basin bearing a giant turd possibly emitted from some prehistoric yak found in perfect state of conservation beneath a passing ice floe. Intrigued by the look of shock horror flashed by my neighbour upon catching sight of this offering, I reached for the menu.

"I don't have my reading glasses, but I think it says Moose."

My neighbour, a fairly newly rehabilitated writer and philosopher, with a background of persecution and hard winters survived on chopped roots and shredded birch bark, threw me a glance and opted for the generously large boiled potato and slab of steamed red pepper instead.

"Kak pa russki, 'Moose?' " he enquired politely.

About to explain that, beyond asking him how many children he had or the colour of his bathroom, our conversation was doomed unless he could come up with even a smattering of some other European language, preferably not Scandinavian, I took another squint at the menu.

"Sorry, Mousse of Reindeer. Not the same thing at all. Perhaps. Mojetbit. Ja ne snaio kak pa russki Mousse of Reindeer. I don't know. Nobody does." Flashing an apologetic smile, I left him looking bewildered as he toyed with his potato and swivelled hopefully to my left, praying for something innocuous like a G8 Ambassador or, even better, a pet journalist. Of all the satellites which habitually orbited around Embassies, the journalistic corps was one I had come to appreciate through many a long and deadly dinner if only because they were notorious for breaking all the rules, drank like sponges, smoked like damp chimneys and were splendidly non-deferential to Heads of Mission. They also hated having to dress up and pretend to behave at staid functions as much as I did, and as a rule would never waste time categorising people according to where they had purchased their ties.

I poked at the turd on my plate whilst trying to read the guy's name card for a clue to which language I should use but without my glasses could only manage to decipher a bit of his surname which ended in '-stein'. I hunted mentally for an opening banality in German, and was about to resort to the dreaded weather when he spoke to me in perfect English, give or take a New York drawl.

"Father Christmas gonna be using cabs this winter if our host keeps this up much longer."

I knocked the offending turd off my fork and played with the potato.

"Oh come, one reindeer doesn't deplete the whole pool, surely?"

"My second invitation this week. Same food each time. Must have just taken delivery from the North Pole. You been here long? Speak any Russian? Got any kids? What other countries you bin to? Ain't this weather foul? "

Jackpot, Sarah. Jackpot. Your entire gamut of conversational gambits gone, bang, wallop between two chews of reindeer and a slug of red moose blood. A diplomatic nightmare and the alternative on the other side necessitated philosophising in pigeon Russian. I was caught between two stools contemplating a stool. Abandoning the latter, I drew a deep breath and faced him.

"I must warn you," I said hopelessly, "that asking me my opinion of the weather could be a grave mistake. It is a subject I have developed so intensely over the years that my treatment of it is now considered an art form. Add to this, that in Russia they really have weather, even more of it than we British do, so the next ten minutes could be seriously damaging to your mental health. Are you prepared for the risk?"

His jaw dropped, revealing a section of partially masticated reindeer. This was beyond anything he had had to cope with since leaving the Big Apple. And he'd had to cope with some. Oh boy, he'd coped with some. Who was this dame, anyway? Looked like some eyetalian name there, but she talked like she just put that filthy great potato in her mouth. He shovelled down the red pepper - Doc. had told him it was great for the cholesterol - and looked nervously at his watch. It was gonna be a long evening.

To: Alex

Cc: Frankie

From: Maman

Having spent over an hour and a half driving back from the dog-walking park 10 mins. away, I have sworn a deadly oath that wild horses will not drag me out again tonight under any circumstances. Most especially not to go to Heidi and Hans at the Swiss Embassy for fondue and Fendant and candlelight carols. They can yodel themselves silly for all I care. Instead I am testing the fairy lights for the Christmas party and adorning the pillars with tinsel and kitsch angels and directing operations whilst two grown men swing from ladders to dress the tree. We are going to miss you desperately this year, but I am so relieved to think you will be taking care of your grandmother whose increasingly rare letters are showing signs, I fear, of confusion and loss of memory. Let me know what you think as I don't see how she can manage alone for much longer.

Hope that your New Year will be none too sober and that you will think of me as I dance to the strains of the Marseillaise at the French Embassy with a section of the Dip Corp who, on average, reach the wrinkles just above my knee caps.

Ceci n'est pas un email which, as we all know, have to be cryptic and abbrvtd. Trying to remember that Curt is Cool with great difficulty.

Love from Maman - if I can get this expletive thing to respond to my desire to SEND which I can't: "Server didn't understand the request." Thought *I* was dim...will try later.

Like (probably) in 2000. On a new computer. And most definitely with a new server. Kisses galore. Maman

And .....oh hell, why not? It was the season of goodwill, after all, and Himself was so busy entertaining Papal Nuncios and things he hardly had time to notice my existence.....

To: Michael

Subject: Merry Christmas

Big Brother who watches over my e-mails has just sent me a Dramatic Warning on line that if anything goes wrong with my computer over the New Year, it has absolutely NOTHING to do with Russki Y2K, and he bears No Responsibility. Unless, of course, I have omitted to pay up my dues well in advance (i.e. roughly back in May 1998), because it is highly likely that the banks will all be inoperable through till about March next year. So I'm reassured on that score and will take advantage of still being connected to send you best wishes for Christmas and New Year and advise you to stay well clear of brolly spikes.

But either the Millenium glitch or fate intervened, and no sooner had the message left my screen than everything blacked out, and I was left incommunicado until well into January.

*   *   *   *

We called up Alex and Frankie on Christmas Day – just long enough for Frankie to tell us that Alex was being non-committal about a Serb admirer she had met somewhere or other. And that she couldn't see why, because he was a) good looking b) extremely bright and c) making big bucks. Then Alex came on the line to inform us that Frankie had a steady boyfriend but that we were to keep our fingers crossed and not ask anything in case it brought bad luck. And while we were about it could we go and ransack the CD market for some pirated videos and compact discs because the Serb had told her they only cost sixty rubles in Russia? My mother sounded increasingly muddled, but with those two creating havoc around her and attempting to stuff and cook a turkey for the first time in their lives, it was entirely understandable.

CHAPTER EIGHT

Dear Mother,

I hope the house is still standing after the onslaught. Frankie and Alex seemed to have had great fun shopping and cooking for you over Christmas and assure me that nobody got poisoned and hardly anything got burned.

Giorgio and I survived and Beagle was her usual impossible self. In fact a diplomatic Euroincident occurred one morning as the wife of the Belgian Ambassador and I were walking our dogs along the river, chatting intensely about this and that. Beagle suddenly saw fit to chase the Belgian dog (three times her size) backwards over the edge of the parapet and into the ice-cold Moskva. Its brain cells frozen insensible, the hound in question promptly tried to swim up the side of the 3ft concrete wall over which two human and one canine face were anxiously peering. The only available solution necessitated the Italian Ambassadress lying flat out in 12" of snow in her maxi-mink holding on frantically to the feet of the Belgian ditto, likewise in full fur regalia to protect against the sub-zero temperatures, as she, likewise prostrate, edged her torso out over the freezing water in an attempt to grab the collar of furiously dog-paddling beast. All of this complicated by the necessity of kicking Beagle out of the way every three seconds because her single overriding desire was to join her pal for a swim. Upon being hauled out, the bedraggled animal proceeded to shake itself all over us and set off hell for leather in pursuit of Beagle in a) an attempt to get warmed up, and b) the forlorn hope of repaying the compliment, to an accompanying volley of Euroblasphemies echoing up and down the river bank.

And you thought granddaughters were uncontrollable? I just hope they didn't exhaust you. I am coming over in the Spring to Italy and England, so it won't be so very long now.

All my love, S

To: Manu

From: Sarah

How were the festivities? Personally I could do with a holiday. I miss the girls, I miss the sun and I miss people with a sense of humour. I managed to burst a tyre yesterday, right on the Boulevard where all the New Russians live and which is bristling with police every five yards and armed bodyguards every ten. They were not one bit amused by my limping up onto the pavement outside their heavily guarded palaces and I didn't feel I should crawl underneath the Alfa given my highly conspicuous diplomatic number plates, so I called the Embassy to send out a driver. Drivers all at lunch. They should have been so lucky: I eventually got mine at 4pm, which shows how long it took me to fix it. Not helped by the portable phone vibrating in my pocket whilst stretched supine under the chassis searching for the G spot to insert the jack. In any other circumstance......However. It was some Italian telling me he was stuck at Moscow airport because his visa had the wrong date on it. I mean, how DUMB can you get? And what, pray, did he expect ME to do about it? I gave him short shrift, told him to bribe the officials at the going rate of $100 and have a nice weekend.

Just spent another hour trying to remove black grease from hands, arms, shoes, trousers. Never mind, Haydn is working miracles, I'm free of house guests for 24 hours and am about to not go to the cinema as planned but snuggle up with a good book.

Nothing much else I can do, given that the car is doing a passable imitation of a Robin Reliant

Stay in touch. I need to know what has replaced the oysters.

Not to mention Stefano.

xxx S

*   *   *   *

In pursuit of congenial contact with the locals, we took ourselves off to the races. According to the Moscow Times, this already enthralling event was to be enhanced by the inclusion of a camel race. They had originally wanted elephants, but as it was, your betting man had to be content with four camels purloined from the local circus who surely never thought they would be galloping over snow and ice when they sprang from their respective mothers' wombs in Saudi Arabia. According to this highly informed newspaper, the animals in question were exceptionally worthy specimens, a fact that your average punter was invited to verify through a closer inspection of the humps. It seems that a healthy, well-fed camel has an erect hump. Anything displaying hump wilt is not worth betting on. It transpired, however, that these particular beasts had been trained to dance whilst in the circus ring, and that there was a very real danger of them executing a Viennese waltz all the way to the finishing line, rather than hot footing it in loping strides as warranted by a life and death race to the nearest oasis.

H.E. picked his way gingerly over the combination of slush and dung, an elegant state of the art pair of binoculars swinging casually from his slender, impeccably gloved wrist. He had been persuaded, with great difficulty, to leave his shooting stick at home. The combined aroma of pickled beetroot and onion soon had him searching for a secluded corner which, with an undignified whoop of unrestrained joy, he found in the form of a discreet door beneath a flight of concrete steps.

"VIP," it announced, proudly, and a couple of armed bodyguards were lounging across it to prove it.

"I am," he said, in his absolutely fluent Russian which by this stage permitted him to introduce himself with full title and to order a cup of decaffeinated coffee in one smooth sentence, "the Italian Ambassador." Pause for effect and to recall Lesson Two of the manual.

"May I?" Bit hesitant on that one. Bodyguards couldn't have cared less and carried on smoking themselves to death, leaning back just sufficiently to allow us through the door sideways. Once inside, we found ourselves in a well-heated room with a large bay window overlooking the racecourse, which was nice, in the company of twenty or so Russians who had obviously been raised together from birth, which was a little disconcerting, and facing a sumptuous buffet lunch laid on exclusively for the benefit of this very private party. Which was plain embarrassing.

We dobraydinn-ed (good-day) away like crazy and spassiba-d (thank you) furiously as these kind folk did their best to include us into the fold, pressing racing cards upon us as if their lives depended on it. H.E. was spotted trying to read his upside down which was unforgivable since he reckoned to be far more au fait with the Cyrillic alphabet than I was, and so he should have been for all the time he spent sitting in the back of a chauffeur driven car with the heating on full blast and nothing to do but read the road signs. Not like some of us, trying to keep a clear head with a beagle panting down one ear demanding Walkies NOW when I was stuck in the traffic wondering how to razvarot on the edge of a canal. So we watched a couple of troika races, thanking our lucky stars for whoever had thought to bring along those binoculars since, apart from the cashmere-lined gloves, the rest of the outfit could only be described as being designed to keep the wearer warm and the slush covered boots had begun to leak huge lakes all over the floor. The time between one race and the next might perhaps have seemed a little shorter had we not exhausted our limited conversational skills on the bodyguards at the door, with the result that a certain degree of heat beneath collars was soon being generated between us, and had I not saved the situation with an ostentatious look at the watch followed swiftly by a cry of concern, we might well have succumbed to the menopausal hot flushes. His Excellency, for once, managed to be a little less obtuse than usual and caught the hint reasonably fast, so that with much ohmygoshing in what we hoped was the correct tense, we departed with dignity, bowing and scraping.

Dear Alex, Dear Frankie,

Back to pen, paper and the diplomatic bag. Server has caught the millennium bug somewhat later than foreseen, apparently.

Just returned from the park where I had a brilliantly fluent conversation with a couple of other Beagle owners during which I managed to convey that Yes, it was indeed a Beagle, (in Russian: "Da, BEAGLE!!!") that she was three years old (3 fingers), and Niet Problem (standard reply to apologetic Russian owner who, as I interpret it, is saying "excuse me, my dog is trying to screw your Beagle"). This particular Niet Problem involves the removal of mittens in order to perform scissor movement with index and 2nd finger, ("don't worry, she's been sterilised.") After that I discovered they spoke Dickensian English and we had a lively exchange concerning our respective hounds' gastronomic habits (mostly pretty disgusting) whilst the animals in question cavorted licentiously and rolled in the snow in an exhibition of Italo-Russian cordiality and fraternity far more significant than anything we could have achieved within embassy walls.

Yesterday I took myself off to the riding stables. The Moscow Mayor who is so famous for spreading a lethal cocktail of industrial salt and gravel over the roads to ensure they are always passable, obviously has little interest in clearing the roads inside the Hippodrome complex. The ice beneath a deceptive layer of slush reaches a depth on bad days of around six centimeters, and since, or so I have always maintained, Alfa Romeos are like their compatriots and tend to skid out of control at a certain age under uncertain conditions, I usually enter stage left sideways on two wheels and exit stage right backwards in a cloud of spraying grey slush. This plus the famous Moscow rooks, ("I voodn't park under that tree if I vere you, Missis Djakomini"), is not doing much for the Alfa image. Once up on the horse, I spent most of my time avoiding a bunch of Russian suicide aspirants jumping everything in sight in any direction so that I would find myself half way up a five jump lane with 16 hands of Russki thoroughbred hurtling uncontrollably straight at me. My Instructor, (for "Instructor" read "girl who takes $30 off me for the privilege of slicking the bits of wood back up when we hit them,") was highly amused: "Wort you are seeing here iss Reassian *ann archy*, Missis Djako*mini*." Great – I can now study Russian politics from the back of a horse. Fine with me.

Got to go and get scrubbed up for a concert. Lots of love to both,

Maman

True I could not receive any emails, but you would have thought some people could have made the effort to use the telephone instead. Bastards.

*   *   *   *

A thousand odd people had been invited to the Tchaikovsky Hall for a charity concert and they couldn't start until His Excellency arrived to make the opening speech. Russians are rather punctual people, though how they ever get anywhere on time given the state of their roads is a mystery. I ended up having to walk through a hall full of slow handclapping to take up my seat in the front, (where else?) row, whilst His Excellency was sprinting round the back trying to find his way up on to the podium. Finally the concert got underway only to have a 3ft high formal flower arrangement crash down on to the orchestra's heads during the most rousing part of the Aida chorus. I rather enjoy the unscheduled bits – rather like when the bull finally gets to gore the matador.

With tears flowing freely as the flash bulbs flashed and the TV cameras whirred, the enormous soprano was given a standing ovation whilst Giorgio presented her with yet more flowers which I thought to be a somewhat superfluous gesture given the circumstances. I sidled round to the back stage to congratulate the Italian tenor who was venting his wrath about the cold which had done unspeakable things to his voice box, rendering him incapable of hitting the low notes at all and having to make a grab at the higher ones as best he could.

Interval drinks seemed like the best idea so far. Avoiding what I surmised to be the 50% proof pure alcohol in the thimble-sized glasses, I grabbed a more generous tumbler of red wine which, in the event, turned out to be Coca Cola. I went back and asked for WINE in three languages. I was directed firmly to the thimbles. Drank eight in swift succession, downed a couple of prawns, made some desultory conversation with the odd ethnic Ambo and resigned myself to the second half which consisted of an appalling Chinese soprano gargling shrill demitones fit to shatter glass. In Russian. Now if there's one thing more drear than Russian folk songs sung earnestly by Russian sopranos, it has to be Russian folk songs sung even more earnestly by Chinese sopranos. This was followed shortly but not shortly enough, by a series of be-spangled dancers doing that lateral thing with their necks whilst balancing a stack of plastic cereal bowls on their heads. For some reason this brought the house down.

Checking the programme notes, I perceived the act

was entitled, I swear, "Dance with Bowels on Heads." No wonder it brought the house down. A "Girl Wearing Feathers" sounded promising, but girl in question was covered in customary floor length robe with matching floor length pantaloons beneath her swirling skirts. The feathers in question were attached to bracelets around her wrists, and no amount of blowing on her part seemed to stir them into action. Which says it all. There followed a pièce de resistance in which a bunch of singularly unvirile men hopped around on their knees and performed buttock dances whilst shaking tambourines and rattles. One wondered how the race ever managed to procreate, for a series of unsexier positions has yet to be invented. After an hour of this, preceded and followed, needless to say, by speeches in three languages, we were led to the buffet table as sheep to the slaughter.

CHAPTER NINE

To: Frankie

Cc: Alex

Busy day today, what with a lunch for ten Archbishops, or something like that, (absolutely everyone was calling everyone else Eccellenza until no-one knew who the hell anyone else was talking to). My gelato ai frutti di bosco much appreciated by all since, as it was pointed out, even if they spilt it all over themselves, it would have matched the chasubles perfectly.

It is now 11 p.m. and I am on my way to the railway station where we have reserved an entire carriage in order to avoid the peasant bearing live hen scene. We are leaving for Nizninovgorod on a train which has only a Second Class, can you imagine? H.E. has furthermore been advised not to go anywhere near the communal loos, so he is taking his own empty mineral bottle, if anyone wants to know. He has also been under strict orders not to drink ANYTHING after 7 p.m....)

Will finish when I get back.

Later................

Reached NN, after not-sleeping on the overnight train on the equivalent of a draining board. Our designated carriage (for four anorexic dwarves) was equipped with a light which lit up brightly for 30 seconds to show willing, then immediately switched itself off, leaving the pair of us in highly claustrophobic blackness. Accompanying younger member of Embassy most chivalrously offered to switch compartments with us, maintaining that he never managed to sleep on trains anyway and not-sleeping in the light or not-sleeping in the dark made no difference to him. This will surely earn him a few extra points for services rendered outside the customary call of duty on his end of year assessment. His other duties during the course of the visit seemed to entail producing a scruffy piece of cardboard the size of a fag packet and jotting down the odd date or name whenever H.E. was trying to convince whoever he was talking to that he actually intended to make some kind of useful contribution to the worthy cause for which he was being solicited.

Am now safely back and just rushing to the opening of a new Italian designer's boutique.

Keep well, more soon. Luv, Maman

I skidded over the ice and on to the red carpet. There were arc lights and movie cameras everywhere and they were reluctant to let me in to start with since I hadn't rolled up in the official car as expected. It says something, I fear, for the degree of importance that I attached to my status, that I was still incapable of saying in Russian that I was the wife of the Italian Ambassador. This quite obviously stemmed from excessive modesty as opposed to total linguistic incompetence. However, I eventually gained admittance, though not without difficulty, since another of the things H.E. didn't believe in (together with such status-underlining details like not arriving on time) was the Carrying of Invitations. People were supposed to recognise one. I was dragged off to the centre of the floodlit podium where the designer herself had been awaiting my arrival in order to proceed with the opening ceremony. Someone actually pushed a mike at me and I nearly died, but managing to look deprecating and self-effacing, passed it on to Ms Italian Designer instead. After which we both smiled radiantly for the cameras and she breathed something highly suitable into the microphone before refusing the champagne. We skidded back over the snow and ice in an attempt to reach home before the 300 odd guests then transferred their affections to our own gastronomic offerings.

To: Sarah
From: Michael
Subject : Happy Birthday
Thumbs up. Happy memories. What are you doing tonight?

To: Alex
Cc: Frankie
From: Maman
Subject: Another e**ing year

Had half the Dip Corps for dinner on my birthday (I had the privilege of choosing the guest list, so it was the better half, i.e. the ones who know how to recognise a slice of Foie Gras when presented with it. Your father got all uppity about there being no risotto or Chianti, which is what he's here to promote, apparently. But in my most Wife of Ambassador tones I told him to sod off. He nevertheless laid on the dimmed lights and cake with candles (don't anyone DARE to count them) routine, which always gets me in the solar plexus. Happy B. to You and a dragon-sized blow (takes a lot of puff, these days) and that's that all over for another year, except that when I saw the photos afterwards I was demoralised to note that the best shot was without doubt the one taken from the back.

Sun is shining temporarily which means I'm singing and about to head for the woods with my high tech Jap. camera which, in the manner of tortoises, refuses to come out of its shell whenever the temperature descends below zero. Which it never does anything else than from Oct. thru' May. (Syntax?)

Sorry, still not got the email technique of being monosllbc - wkng on it. Cld do btter. also no caps. as in ee cummings, I seem to recall. Bet the Portughese are in amongst the front runners, given their propensity for removing all the vowels in a word and sitting on what's left. Cmpressd spch if ever I heard it.

Love and xxxxxxxxx maman

To: Michael
From: Sarah
Subject: The Unmentionable
Well fancy you remembering. If you weren't so morally disgraced, I would have invited you to attend the festivities, but I fear your presence might still cause a stir in former Nato circles. Just going to skip lunch and walk off the calories consumed. Cheers, S

I edged the car gingerly out onto the slippery highway and headed off with Beagle. Having ripped most of the front off the Alfa in an encounter with a large Russian lorry soon after I had acquired it, I now drove around with the number plate stuck inside the windscreen and all the Alfa innards exposed to the elements. The local coppers, always out to make themselves extra pocket money, tended to get very excited about there being no number plate in the front, though it always seemed pretty logical to me that you can't display a number plate if you haven't got a bumper to display it on, but neither my limited vocabulary nor their pea brains were up to conveying and comprehending that finesse. In any case, it fitted into the garage much more easily without all the extra bits, so I intended to leave it like that for as long as possible, since the alternative of forking out $4.000 to fix it rankled when considering this would be slightly more than we had paid for the car in the first place. And that was inclusive of hidden microphones being as it had formerly belonged to one of our military attachés. I had by this stage perfected my nark dodging technique and would drive away from the Embassy wearing maxi sunglasses, even in the rain, eye contact for the avoiding of, keeping the bonnet tucked as closely as safely possible beneath the rear bumper of the car in front. When eventually copped, as I invariably was by dint of some over-zealous policeman throwing himself bodily under the front wheels, I did the disarming slow smile, removal of glasses and stupid foreigner been here two years and still doesn't speak a word of the language, bit.

Sooo sorry. Would loooove to be of assistance, but....Ya ni panimayu.... The precious pink diplomatic I.D. card would be tendered judiciously at this stage, having been clenched firmly between teeth from outset of journey, thus eliminating earlier scenarios along the lines of "Just one moment, officer, while I jump out in the middle of this on-coming traffic and open the boot to get my handbag and rummage unsuccessfully to find my card, oh dear, it doesn't seem to be amongst the handkerchiefs, pens, makeup, purse, diary, hairbrush, dog lead, cell phone, nail file, Walkman, couple of spare cassettes, shrivelled conker, keys, unanswered correspondence, let's try the jeans pockets. No, not too much room in there for anything at all......

Meanwhile Beagle was usually ruining the whole idyllic scene by straining through the back window trying to rip his balls off, which was unhelpful to the extreme.

I parked up by the University and entered the woods.

I had been walking no more than five minutes when I became aware of footsteps behind me.

"I don't wonder you've wrecked that car – you drive like a scorched bat out of hell."

"Are you following me? How dare you! I could well have an Embassy carabiniere guarding my back, for all you know, and then how would we both look?"

"You haven't. I checked. That's how you managed to get here so far ahead of me. I'm a pro, don't forget. Or so everyone always liked to think."

"And are you?"

"I'm a journalist. I believe I mentioned that before."

"Why?"

"Why what?"

"What made you take up journalism?

"I get paid to travel and the hours are flexible. It leaves me free to play tennis, concentrate on the crossword puzzle and chat up wives when their husbands think they're having coffee mornings. And obliges me to nurture my drinking habit. Whoever heard of a journalist partaking moderately of alcohol? Bad for the image. Plus I get a hefty expense account and an excuse to ask impertinent questions like can I take you out to lunch, please? Now?"

But at that very moment a car backfired and complete mayhem ensued. Michael grabbed my arm and dived for cover behind a tree, pushing me to the ground in a pile of dirty snow before throwing himself on top of me in best rugby tackle mode. Beagle, never one of the breed's bravest hunters, uttered a yelp and headed for the hills. We spent the next two hours searching for her in a snowstorm before conceding defeat. Lunch was no longer on the menu. I returned home in complete despair.

*   *   *   *

Beagle was returned two days later by the Matrioshka sellers up near the University who had captured her after she materialised under their stalls sniffing for bits of sausage whilst her owner was searching the woods a mere half a mile away and shouting herself hoarse in the illusion that a little maternal love might prove stronger than the aroma of grilled shashlik. Luckily the stall holders in question all had mobile phones and Beagle was wearing a collar with her number inscribed on it, but it cost me a fistful of dollars and a promise NEVER to buy Matrioshka dolls anywhere else for the rest of my stay in the Motherland.

To: Michael
From: Sarah
Dog is back. 3kgs heavier. Now we are *all* on a diet.

To: Sarah
From: Michael
Am I forgiven? Has H.E. discovered I'm here yet?

To: Michael
From: Sarah

H.E., as you persist in calling him, despite my having spent many decades trying to reduce his ego to normal proportions, has most definitely not discovered you are here and with what the "gun shot" fiasco just cost me in bribes and dry cleaning bills, I would advise you to keep it that way. What could an investigative reporter possibly be investigating that might warrant such a demonstration of abject terror at the sound of a car backfiring? I'm not sure I want to know.

CHAPTER TEN

Even in Russia, Spring will materialize eventually, but Tonia the gardener was still concentrating her efforts upon growing cardboard boxes. She maintained, as far as anyone could interpret her eloquent explanations, that they were to protect the rose bushes. *What* rose bushes? one would have loved to enquire, but lack of vocabulary forbade. Surely she couldn't mean those sickly miniature buds which had dropped off as soon as they'd poked their heads through the yellowing foliage? As I surveyed the scene, I wished that she would at least use Moet and Chandon empties instead of Pal dog meat cartons for my guests to gaze down upon. And where were all those bulbs, I wondered, that I had seen her planting last Autumn? Could it be possible that she dug them up each Spring and sold them to someone else? Tonia maintained the snow and ice had been particularly unforgiving this year, but I was told by everyone it had been one of the mildest winters they had ever experienced. Beagle pee was also being blamed heavily and dark hints were muttered concerning the advisability of feeding dogs on a diet of stockfish and cabbage: this combination, once transformed into an end product, apparently having disastrous consequences on the average peony. *What* peony? I asked myself. I see only weeds, Tonia. Admittedly very healthy and flourishing weeds, but weeds nevertheless.

We took a trip to the Botanical Gardens where Tonia wanted to show me all the varieties of shrub and plants capable of surviving in this climate. I had been trying to impress her with my scant knowledge - thoughtfully studying protective walls, northern and southern aspects, and poring over the various catastrophes which seemed to be attacking every plant in the garden. I knew nothing about gardening, but was beginning to suspect that Tonia, with all her diplomas in horticulture and background in botanical research, knew even less. There were four of us headed out for the Botanical Gardens: Sergei our second driver, Tonia, myself and Sacha the interpreter. Still endeavouring to impress, I mentioned that, in my opinion, snails were eating everything she planted and her eyes lit up at my offer to import a gel from Italy which would deal with these pests. Flushed with success at my inspired diagnosis, I went on to describe how my mother used to dig snail pits and fill them with beer so that the little blighters would fall in and drown themselves. A muttered comment from Sergei as he swerved violently around the potholes was eventually translated back as a fervent wish to be reborn as a snail if this could be his demise.

The first signs of Spring were more evident in the Novodevichy park. Dandelions and professional drunks appeared all over the grass on the same day, the latter sleeping off their hard winter in the rays of warm sunshine. Two ducklings tottered into the water for a trial paddle. The carnivorous rooks were, I suspected, the reason for there being so few of these on the artificial lake which lay outside the ramparts of the Novodevichy convent: I later came upon one being unceremoniously plucked at the water's edge, yellow feather by yellow feather. Surveying the soft disjointed little puppet, I reflected that Beagle was in danger of meeting with the same fate if she persisted in chasing rooks in order to steal their lunch of bones and general rubbish scavenged from local dustbins. I now realised why the dog was putting on weight; it was not so much the diet of titbits from the kitchen where the staff had been threatened with instant dismissal if they so much as offered her a single strand of spaghetti, but her consumption of the trash dropped by the birds during their fly past over the Italian Embassy.

I found myself yearning for the oleander and jasmine which would most probably be already in bud throughout the streets of Rome

To: Manuela
From: Sarah
Subject: Ambassador's conference

I wonder whether you will be following instructions and presenting *both* your good selves (as I understand from certain highly-excited-at-the-prospect spouses (spice?) to be required behaviour,) at the upcoming Ambassadors' bash due, as I feel sure you are aware, to bring the entire Italian Diplomatic Corps to Rome next week albeit at their own personal expense. Because, or patte à mouche ta, as the Russians say, *were* you to be around that week, we might even skip the proceedings, which in any case none of us had the least intention of attending, and LUNCH. At the risk of incurring the ridicule of both my daughters who put LadiesThatLunch into an unmentionable category all of their own, and how right they are, but of course ours are purely intellectual encounters which makes it all right.

So this is merely to let you know that I'll be in Rome for the above, the sole purpose of which, as we all know is to massage the ego of our revered Leader at the F.O. Finally a captive audience for him to terrorize. I have it on authority that a gaggle of the usual eager-to-please wives are organizing their own enthralling meetings over that period. I therefore suggest that, since we are all supposed to be attending these knees ups for the consorts, we lunch as far from the Club as possible. Giorgio has very sweetly said I can leave a week earlier and that in any case I do not need to attend since nobody could possibly teach me anything about the Role and Function of the wife of a Head of Mission (isn't he just a sweetie?) Well, I may have paraphrased a bit: possibly the emphasis was a little more on the impossibility of the task, but that was the general gist. I also come out in spots at the mere idea of that gaggle of girls sitting around discussing how many tablecloths they are missing, and do not trust myself to remain silent through item number 6 on the agenda ("Other Business.")

To: Maman
From: Frankie
Forgot to say that Alex and I are planning a visit to Granny and won't be back until the day after you arrive in Rome. Feel free to clean the flat.

Think the Grandmother is losing it. Very garbled. Has wrapped up all the knives and hidden them down the back of the radiators, convinced someone is trying to murder her.

Haven't had any news for ages Are you forgetting to click on "send"?

To: Mummy
From: Alex
Subject: Remember me?
What's with the breakdown in communications?

To: Alex
Cc: Frankie
sod itm got both yoursm so you better get this one<
ЭГгарэ zc didn3t give Big Brother ti;e enough to read it

Right, this is what happens when you forget not to use the U.S. keyboard. Not writing it again. Consider it the epistolary equivalent of interpreting your maternal grandmother's speech patterns.

Breakdown in comm..s due to some analorifice who just blocked my entire computer sending me an attachment from Rome with not-very-funny jokes copied from a notveryfunny site. Mouse paralysed with terror, screen in advanced state of Parkinsons. My rheumaticky Mac can't handle that stuff at all, and freezes solid at the very thought. All the other important messages, such as yours, were stuck in line behind and nothing was getting through.

However, having finally chucked the last remaining

guest out of the front door reasonably early (11.30) by dint of not offering any cognac/liqueurs, I have just spent a profitable half hour swapping around half a dozen cables with something approaching expertise, and succeeded in downloading it onto a little lap-top. Which just goes to show that size doesn't matter after all. This, fortunately, liberated the constipated Big Mac, and we are now back in business, though all this computer activity is seriously interfering with my learning Russian. Now *that's* a good joke.

Cu both soon

P.S. Actually, I did learn 3 words of Russki last night and promptly fell asleep on the sofa. Never fails.

To: Sarah
From: Manu
See you in Rome.

To: Michael
From: Sarah
Thought you might like this one, since you spend so much time on Russian trains.

Quote from today's Moscow Times: "Diarrhoea sufferers will be forced to get off trains," the Moscow Railways said in a press release distributed last week. Further down; the announcement explained that by diarrhoea sufferers, or ponosniki, it was referring only to carriers of infectious gastrointestinal diseases such as dysentery, cholera and typhoid, and that passengers suspected of carrying these diseases would be inspected by doctors and sent to clinics.

The word amongst the usual bunch of expats hanging out in the Djon Booll Peb (John Bull Pub) at the top of the Arbat is that said trains are such a load of shit anyway it's a wonder anybody would notice or care.

To: Sarah
From: Michael
Just off to Reggio Calabria, following a story line.
By plane. Thought I wouldn't risk the train.
Be in touch when I get back.

Only by then, I thought with grim satisfaction, I would be sunning myself in Rome. And, know what? I wasn't even going to bother to tell him.

Grass was finally showing through the snow - brown, muddy grass, but grass it was. According to the Moscow Times, the temperatures were due to soar to a stifling 18° so, optimistically, I exchanged my fur-lined boots and jacket for ordinary shoes and a raincoat for the first time that year. Not my best move. Driving back to the Embassy in a sudden snow flurry, my mobile phone rang. Answering with one hand as I tried to clear the windscreen, I could hear a group of well-tanked Calabrians singing Neapolitan love songs for my delight whilst they enjoyed a boozy lunch on the beach in shirt sleeves. As the lead singer eventually took great delight in informing me in his distinctly British Public School accents.

Spring or no Spring, I was hit by a blinding snowstorm on the way to the airport. Visibility was down to two yards and I skidded out of the car and into the VIP lounge on my Italian leather soled moccasins, ill-advisedly the only ones I was taking with me. The temperature within the aircraft was no more than two degrees above that outside on the tarmac, which at least reduced the risk of swelling feet. The jack-booted stewardess ordered me to partake of "breakfast" and was mightily offended that anyone at all, most especially a paltry foreigner, should refuse the smoked salmon, shrimps, caviar, mixed salad, cold meats various, hot roast chicken with vast assortment of vegetables, cheese platter with crudités, fresh fruit, cream cake and vodka a-gogo at 9.30 in the morning.

I lay back and dreamed of the forthcoming days in Rome which I had every intention of spending eating clams on bruschetta on the beach whilst everyone back in Moscow was still clomping around in boots and furs.

CHAPTER ELEVEN

I fell into the Rome flat, tripped over a pile of the girls' dirty washing and tried to grab the phone before it stopped ringing.

"Amore"

"What? How on earth did you get hold of this number?"

"Phone book. All spies worth their salt know how to use a telephone directory."

"And how the hell did you know I was in Italy? "

"Research. The email was just to throw the minders off track. What are you doing this evening?"

"No idea. I've only just arrived. Why? Where are you? I thought you were in Calabria."

"I'm – dare I say it? On the train. Can I take you out to dinner?

"Well – why not? I was going to get an early night, but I suppose I need to eat first. Only don't stand me up at the last minute because I get very uptight about sitting around waiting for no-shows."

"I never stand people up - what are you talking about? I'll come by and pick you up around nine."

I set to work on the flat. I made the beds. I tidied away the old magazines. I emptied the dishwasher. I attacked the pile of ironing. Then I lay down on the bed and fell straight off to sleep.

The phone rang again.

"There's this dinner thing in the country not too far from Rome, but we need to leave now. No-one you know - guaranteed. I'll pick you up in ten minutes. Can you wait outside on the pavement for me? We're running a bit late."

Huh? I just finished cleaning and tidying and ironing. Been awake and travelling since dawn. Nothing to wear. Go away. I'm too tired and I wanna go home. Wherever that is.

I threw on a kaftan I found in Frankie's wardrobe and shot out of the door with wet hair. The "dinner thing" turned out to be a lavish party in Frascati in the garden of an English journalist. I was introduced all round as an old friend from Dorset, and spent the evening in terror of being questioned about my origins since I'd never set foot in the place. A couple of my slightly drunken compatriots took me off to dance. Michael, I noticed, was busy inviting all the beautiful young Roman girls and flirting preposterously with at least three at any one time. Did somebody mention gay? How wrong could they be.

At two in the morning the party started to break up. He drove me back home, kissed my hand and watched while I let myself into the empty flat. Ten minutes later he was on the phone.

"Buona notte!"

"I thought we'd done that bit."

"To whose satisfaction?"

"Nobody's, probably, but that seems to be the story of our lives. Buona notte. Thanks for a fun evening."

"What are you doing tomorrow?"

"Being maternal. The girls are due back from checking out their grandmother and will need to de-stress." He hung up, promising to ring in the afternoon.

The girls flew back in from England in the early afternoon. Two wheelie suitcases were left just inside the front door for ease of tripping over. The handbags were dumped a couple of paces further along the corridor. The jackets were abandoned outside the kitchen. Scarves were strewn across the dining table. The passports and reading matter made it as far as the sofa.

"Where is everything? What's been going on here? I can't find a thing. Where are my magazines?"

"Not to mention my notes. And who's been fussing around in my bathroom. Since when did you go all minimalist?"

"Mummy, you have to do something about Granny. She's gone all funny and can't find anything and keeps accusing everyone of moving her stuff or stealing it. She had me looking for her watch for two days and then it turned out she'd hidden it in the teapot. When are you going?"

At this rate, after due deliberation, given the circumstances, and taking all manner of things into consideration, tomorrow morning would seem to be as good a time as any. So much for the tennis and girlfriends. So much for Manuela. So much for the non-attendance at the Ambassadors' conference. I reached for the phone.

* * * *

My mother was comfortably housed in a warden-controlled residence a mere half hour away from London. I arrived in full daylight and was immediately concerned to note that the curtains were drawn. I rang the doorbell twice but there was no answer so I went round to the warden's cottage and borrowed a key.

The key turned in the lock without any problem but the door wouldn't budge an inch. I went back to the warden for advice.

"Oh that's all right, dearie. Your mum does that sometimes. She likes to pile all the furniture up against the door to stop the burglars coming in. Don't you worry about it. You can get in through the French windows round the back. She always leaves those open so she can get some fresh air. She'll be watching T.V."

Not only did I find furniture wedged up against the door to discourage intruders, every knife in the house had been meticulously wrapped in layers of newspaper and hidden under the mattress to foil any potential murderer who made it through the window, all the jewellery was stashed into old socks and piled up inside the hollow pedestal of the bathroom washbasin and her purse had been safely hidden and lost, by all accounts, over a month ago. There was a policeman's truncheon by the side of her bed. It was not looking good.

I rang the G.P., managed to exact a promise he would send someone round to assess her condition the very next day, and began removing the furniture so we could use the door again.

The assessor cum social worker cum shrink cum, more probably, first year psychology student, had tattoos all up one arm, a stud in her nose and three piercings in her left ear. My mother took one look at her and locked herself in the bathroom. With her jewellery but no knives. It took half an hour and the promise of tea and biscuits to persuade her to emerge.

"Now then, dear," said Ms Multi Piercing soothingly, "let's see how our memory is doing, shall we?"

Back in her favourite armchair with a comforting cup of tea at her elbow, Dear perked up considerably and even gave me a wink.

"Yes, dear. Mine's fine. How *is* yours?"

Nose stud quivered imperceptibly.

"Can you remember your name and address for me now, dear?"

"Oh yes, dear. Thank you. Look, it's written on the top of your form there, in case *you've* forgotten it."

Perplexed scribbling of notes.

"And your telephone number?"

She reeled it off. Together with her granddaughters' number in Rome and her daughter's in Moscow. Complete with international prefixes. Then relaxed back into her armchair and reached for the teacup.

"Now then, dear," she said with a wicked grin. "Let's see just how many of those numbers *you* can remember, shall we?"

CHAPTER TWELVE

To Alex

Cc: Frankie

Managed to sort fulltime help, a lovely lady called Grace, for your Grandmother before leaving yesterday. I think she will be alright for a bit. She has good days and bad, but the warden pops in regularly and keeps an eye on things. I'm afraid it's only a temporary solution, but we'll have to cross that bridge later.

The impact upon returning to Moscow was not good, but will soften as soon as the sun comes out. Have changed my computer screen background to a field of scarlet tulips while I'm waiting!

To: Michael

From: Sarah

Back in Moscow in case your info. service hasn't caught up. Had to go to the U.K. for family emergency.

Lunch?

*　　*　　*　　*

I needed fresh air. Sunday May 7th, 2000 was the day of the inauguration of President Putin. A men only ceremony which I should perhaps have watched on T.V. except that I decided to go for a walk in the park instead. As usual the ring road was blocked off at every corner by baton swinging cops who kept telling me to go back and turn left. By the time I had obeyed this order five times and thereby crossed the river thrice, I was so hopelessly lost I had to call in to the Embassy and have someone talk me through how to get home from the unattractive and probably unfriendly suburb where I found myself. Meanwhile the men, in keeping with tradition from Tsarist days, were standing in a side room of the magnificently restored Kremlin hoping to catch a glimpse of Second President Putin as he swung down the half kilometer of red carpet towards his place of honour beside his predecessor Boris Borisovich.

In the park, Victory Day preparations were already underway three days in advance - stalls everywhere were selling patriotic books, bird tweet simulators, rabbit ear headbands, handicrafts and the inevitable ice cream. On a podium, a military band was playing a series of stirring medleys for the edification of the ducks. A lone toddler was practising her ballet steps in time to the music to the evident pride of a hovering babushka. They played their hearts out all morning, each number ceremoniously announced with much pomp from a tuxedo clad compère reading from a leather bound notebook, though at any given time the maximum audience figures never exceeded five persons. On the day of the Parade itself, there were no planes, no tanks and hardly any weapons. Rumour had it amongst the grumbling ranks that there were insufficient funds to provide the fuel for either of the former and that the weapons were all in use in Chechnya. We were treated instead to a clanky march past of veterans followed by one from the military. The former was by far the most amusing: hats blew off in the wind, an excess of medals made walking upright a feat in itself, three somewhat sclerotic dodderers had to be roughly pushed back into line by a commanding officer in spite of their obvious desire to halt proceedings there and then and wave instead to admiring friends and relatives in the crowd. The latter, a succession of fresh faced youngsters presumably about to be packed off to Chechnya as cannon fodder the minute festivities were over, was more sobering.

To: Alex

From: Maman

No, I was not whooping it up with the plebs on Kutusovsky with your Serb friend, whatever *he* was doing there. You forget that Excellencies are condemned to watch the military festivities from the VIP stand in Red Square as opposed to getting wasted in the streets with the natives and tourists. Trust he was not dressed for Roman temperatures as the barometer has descended (again) to Arctic levels.

Gotter go. Mobile ringing. Hope it's not in Russian.

Xxxxx m

"Strastvitzie!"

"*Now* where are you?

"Filing a story in Rome- fly over and join me. We'll pop down to Tuscany once I've given birth."

"You're crazy - I've only just got back. Also I have a delegation of politicians arriving by private 'plane tomorrow and three days of world-shattering consultations lined up after that. All interspersed with formal dinners and buffet lunches necessitating extravagant flower arrangements."

"And every one of them a Men Only. And the 'plane is going back to Rome empty once it has dropped them all off. What a waste. Stand on the tarmac with your thumb in the air. Your Maitre D can organise the rest and Cook will cook, as she always has done. The flowers are on their way. Call you later."

I collapsed into an unaccommodating Louis XIV chair as he rang abruptly off. Ten minutes later one of the maids materialised to ask where I wanted to put some flowers which had just arrived. The man was mad - there was no way I could possibly justify jumping into a plane at 24 hours' notice.

But the fates were conspiring. I thought nothing more about it until just before lunch when there was a hysterical phone call from Frankie in Rome saying that the bedroom was flooded due to a burst pipe in the flat upstairs, that the apartment was transformed into a highly convincing replica of Venice during a high water crisis and that she herself was leaving for a weekend in Ireland with her boyfriend and could not possibly be expected to put her love life in jeopardy waiting around for a plumber. Alex, it seemed was up a mountain somewhere. Studying rainfall patterns.

And my phone was ringing.

"Well?"

"Tell me, does Interflora run a remote control pipe bursting service too?"

"What *are* you talking about? Did my flowers turn your head? You don't have to say who sent them, of course."

"Well, I wasn't exactly about to blazon it around, now that you mention it. Thank you, they are rather beautiful but you definitely shouldn't have ......can I know why Monsieur Insouciant is coming on so strong all of a sudden? Do I have some kind of classified information you need for your next comic strip?"

I almost believed he was taken aback, as far as it was possible to sense other people's feelings down the echoing tube of a satellite phone. He knew nothing about the plumbing predicament, obviously. Was paranoia hereditary?

Tactfully he was not waiting for the plane as it touched down at the military airport in Ciampino, and I picked up a cab to get home. Water, I was relieved to note, was not seeping out from under the door, though the smell of damp was overwhelming as I let myself into the apartment. Pausing only to read a hastily scribbled letter from Frankie, I began to investigate the damage. The mattress had caught most of the flow and would have to be thrown out, together with a sodden upholstered armchair. A polished table could perhaps be restored at a price, but the ceiling and parquet flooring were disaster areas. The bathrooms dripped with condensation and smelled strongly of blocked drains. I headed upstairs to talk to the owners of the flat above and discuss insurance claims.

His phone was switched off, there were no flashing messages on the answering phone when I returned home and my own mobile was sulking in silence at having to exchange MIS. RUS for TELECOM. IT.

I hauled the scooter out of the garage, revved up its reluctant battery and took myself off to the Club for a late lunch. The usual crowd were there, and shouts of joy greeted my unscheduled appearance. The food was as bad as ever and the same old complaints were being made about the showers being under repair yet again. The customary sarcasm was being bandied around concerning the eyesores which kept appearing in the name of Art - somebody, they reckoned, was making a bit on the side buying particularly nasty bits of statuary and ruining the beauties of Nature by sticking them incongruously amongst the rather beautiful trees and lawns. Half a tree had recently fallen on top of an innocent new member reclining in the shade beneath it, breaking most of the bones in her body, and the general consensus of opinion was they should quit spending so much on artistic monstrosities and invest in a little pruning. They ridiculed the latest Club rules whereby one was only allowed to approach the swimming pool if securely enveloped in a burqa style towelling bathrobe. Only the gossip was half-hearted. Manu and Paolo had been posted to Peru and were due to leave, hand in hand, in the summer. Good material was sorely lacking. If only they knew. Or again, perhaps not, as the phone refused steadily to ring. I took my leave and went back to the flat to wait for the loss assessor from the insurance company.

By the time the phone eventually rang at 8.30 that evening I was fuming and ignored it. It rang again ten minutes later and I ignored it again. I was certainly not going to let him think I had been waiting for his call. I waited ten more minutes then rang him back.

"Sorry, I only just got in - did you call?"

"Yes, hours ago."

Liar.

"The train was late, so by the time I get over to you it will be well after 10 o'clock. I don't know, what do you think? Maybe we should postpone it until tomorrow. If I'd managed to get hold of you earlier...."

So I told him what I thought. Most fluently and in no uncertain terms. I even permitted myself the use of some of the more colourful Roman insults which, I felt, depicted his mental and physical attributes more succinctly than anything my native vocabulary could supply. I let fly. Then I slammed the phone down on him. It rang immediately.

"We got cut off. Don't get mad, I'm on my way over, wait for me."

I yelled that no, he was not on his way over, that I was going out for what was left of the evening and that no way had we been cut off. I had merely slammed the phone down on him. And proceeded to repeat the act.

It rang again.

I ignored it and ran out of the door.

"Manu?"

"*Hellooo*! I didn't think I'd hear from you again today. How are the soggy bogs?"

"Manu, what are you doing? Can we meet?"

"Sure. If you don't mind my receiving you in my bedroom slippers. Come over here and I'll show them to you. Three inch heels and pink pompoms. They wreak absolute havoc with the parquet. Why should I care? I'm only renting. Bloody woman downstairs doesn't like them one little bit. Accuses me of clomping around the flat in Dutch clogs. Listen! I've got terrific news - you'll never guess! What's wrong? You've gone all quiet?"

"Chance to get a word in would be welcome. I'm coming. Break open a bottle. It's pay back time for all that nurturing I gave you in the past."

I switched off the mobile and went off to confess everything to Manuela.

*   *   *   *

"Have you eaten? I'm just about to fix a snack. Paolo isn't back yet. Went to play bridge or something. Waste of time, if you ask me. No money in it. Now poker, that's a different story altogether."

"I'm not very hungry. Anything will do. What are you having?"

"Latest diet. Liquids only, but I have to have them all the time. Six meals a day. It's an awful bore - I hardly have time to sleep. Terribly healthy, though. I'll make double quantity and you can join me, it'll do you good. Pure vitamins. Don't you want to hear my news? Paolo has agreed to let me have a face lift. Reckons it'll probably save him money in the long run. You know what? I think I could fall in love with that man all over again. Especially since he's got us posted to somewhere nearer home."

We went out to the kitchen and Manu started preparing a huge bowl full of peaches and strawberries. By the time it had all been through the liquidizer, there was enough to fill a small bathtub.

"Right. That should do it." She tasted it gingerly and wrinkled up her nose.

"Pretty disgusting. Luckily I'm a pro. Like all the best cooks, I have my own secret ingredient."

And in went half a bottle of champagne.

Finally we settled down on the sofa for a good long talk.

*　　　*　　　*　　　*

There were fifteen missed calls when I turned the mobile back on.

Just one message.

"Sarah? I'm really sorry. I had to file an article. Had a deadline. I'll pick you up at nine tomorrow morning and we'll go off somewhere."

I did not set the alarm clock. I did not pack a bag. I went straight to bed and was awoken by the doorbell ringing.

" Oh hi! Finished the article?"

" Yes, thank goodness."

"What was it about?"

"Economic situation in Italy for Forbes magazine. They're running the issue with a big plate of spaghetti and clams on the cover."

"Michael, do you ever tell the truth?" He raised my imprisoned hand to his lips and his eyes twinkled.

"Are you ready?"

"What for?"

"To go to Tuscany, of course."

"Oh I'd forgotten about that. No, sorry, I can't make it. Got some friends coming over. We're off to spend the day on the beach to get away from this smell of rotting wallpaper. They'll be here any minute, in fact, you'd better scarper. Must think of my reputation."

He hardly flinched. A huge grin lit up his face as he took hold of my shoulders and stared deep into my eyes.

"No hurry, love, no hurry. Things are better taken real slow, you'll see."

CHAPTER THIRTEEN

To: Manu

Subject : Did it!

Sorry, no time to phone before leaving.

Mission accomplished as recommended.

Queen of Cool now safely back in Moscow in one piece.

I definitely owe you one, so have decided to come and hold your hand when you go under the knife and not to leave until you have emerged from the chrysalis.

July would suit fine.

P.S. Thanks for everything

Arriving back I had been greeted by hordes of rampaging Russians who were being kept out of the Embassy by machine-gun-toting militia. Having been escorted by the police into the residence, I spent the rest of that day and the next barricaded within whilst T.V. cameras and marauding demonstrators were marauding and demonstrating outside my front door. They stayed there all night. There had been some question of the Visa section having had to close its doors after issuing only 1.000 visas in one day, as per usual, to the immense dissatisfaction of a street full of further hopeful applicants who were left standing out in the open air feeling somewhat let down. Giorgio, I learnt to my surprise, was on the point of departing for Chechnya together with a delegation from the Foreign Ministry, leaving Beagle and me alone to be eaten alive. Around midnight both dog and I were in such need of a walk that I replaced the scruffy jeans with the Armani trouser suit for the benefit of the cameras and emerged through the front door to brave the throng. Beagle wanted a couple on toast immediately, but I thought that might not improve already soured relations. It being the season of white nights, the Arbat was still buzzing with people and I took my time getting back home calculating, only partly correctly, that with any luck they would all have gone to sleep in the backs of their Ladas by the time I returned. They were eventually persuaded to move on with their cameras the following morning, but not before they had taken extensive footage of a reluctant hound emerging into the cold morning air for her pre-prandial pee.

To: Sarah

Subject: Patriarch Ponds.

Given that sources usually classified as infallible reveal temporary absence of H.E., propose we meet at the Café Margherita next to the Ponds for supper. 8 p.m.

P.S. Remember to point that proletarian mob outside your door in the direction of the wine cellar if they breach the defences: it is believed to have saved almost everybody not dressed as a woman at the Winter Palace on a cold night in 1917.

Reply to sender:

Such a coincidence – or did your sources tell you that, too? I did the Bulgakov tour fairly recently, flying in and out the windows of the Writers Union and avoiding the tramlines and feeling intellectually v. superior through knowing twice as much about the Master and Margherita as the tour guide. Made up for the time I did the Fallen Monuments tour with Giorgio and the guide kept asking historical trivial pursuit quiz questions all the time. For prizes. Had to keep hiding behind pillars to avoid eye contact.

Sorry about tonight. Have to take care of one of our famous Italian sculptors who is in residence for the next few days overseeing the transfer of his delightful statue from the student campus, where it was being peed on and used to paste lewd telephone numbers, to a more suitable site in front of the Modern Art Museum where it need fear nothing more than the ubiquitous pigeon.

All the best, S

Wow. Queen of Cool strikes again.

I fell into bed with Count von Mirbach who had a tendency to crash in and out of the oak and mahogany panelling all night long when I was alone in the house, though usually only when the heating was turned on.

Leonid gestured eloquently the next day as I returned from my morning walk, giving me to understand that H.E. was back in residence and reading the newspapers in the library. The warning was superfluous: Beagle was already hot on the scent and with a full throated cry of "Hunt in Progress," charged straight down the corridor at the gallop and into the library with a howl of recognition. She threw herself at her master's feet, spraying him with a putrid mixture of dog hair and slush. Strangely enough, he hardly flinched. I noticed in passing that he was reading Pravda. The right way up, for once.

"Welcome back. How did it go?"

There was a non-committal grunt as he turned a page and absent-mindedly brushed a trail of white dog hairs from his trouser turn ups. My eyes widened as I noticed the socks.

"GIORGIO!"

He peered over the top of his paper.

"Where on *earth* did you get those socks?"

He glanced at his feet with an air of surprise. They were purple, the exact colour of a Cardinal's hat and whilst they did not actually have "Made in the Ukraine" stamped all over them, they were clearly not his preferred brand of transparent Italian Filo di Scozia, obtainable exclusively from a tiny specialised boutique in an indisputably respectable area of Florence.

"Ran out of socks in Chechnya. Had to buy these. By the way, I've already had lunch, so you go ahead and eat."

He had, too.

No wonder Beagle had shown such enthusiasm.

There was an unmistakable smell of pickled onion in the air.

Which reminded me that it was time to organise the logistics for our National Day bonanza. At a lengthy reunion to finalise details for this event, fourteen soberly dressed career diplomats and high ranking military attachés assembled around the dining table armed with notebooks and newly sharpened pencils. Their task was to decide the best way of dividing the multitudes so that the most illustrious guests might be shepherded through the fast channel into the Presence in order to greet and be greeted. They discussed in detail the providing and placing of musicians, ice cream, mortadella and parmesan and the necessity of stripping the place bare against the inevitable light fingered kleptomaniac. The festivities were scheduled to stretch over two days so as to accommodate not only the Military, foreign diplomats, top Russian brass and notables, but also the sizable Italian community. When it seemed they had covered everything, members of the assembled company were unwisely asked if they had any further suggestions and at this point a bearded military attaché not noted for his intelligence, rose ceremoniously and in all seriousness brought up the problem of the flying cotton from the poplar trees in the Embassy garden, great dollops of which had invaded the house, the garage and everybody's eyes and nostrils for the past ten days. In the opinion of this worthy gentleman, a very real threat would be posed to all wearers of beards who ventured out into the garden during the party. The image of uniformed and other dignitaries transformed into Santa Claus lookalikes cheered up the bored participants of the staff meeting visibly, and the snapped response from H.E. that such participants could choose to remain indoors or even refrain from participating for all he cared did nothing to dispel the evident delight of his pen-twiddling colleagues around the sombre mahogany table.

To: Frankie

Cc: Alex

Just about to instruct twenty assorted waiters in the distribution of food and drink to eight hundred assorted guests.

O.K. correction.

Just about to walk the dog in the rain whilst Leonid instructs etc. Hoping fixed smile can be retained throughout the greeting of afore-mentioned merry eight hundred (possibly somewhat less merry after having to wait outside and half way up the Pereulok in the pouring rain in the receiving line.) Your father and I do this, need I add, quite fluently in five languages. Not necessarily matching correct language to nationality being shaken, but you can't have everything. Three foot nothing secretary cum interpreter stands on tiptoe throughout the performance trying to breathe translations into H.E.s unreachable ear and inevitably gets taken for his lady wife, which pisses both of them off something dreadful. Stack of paper napkins kept at close range, sweaty hands for the wiping of. All for the honour and glory of the homeland.

Evviva. M

The socks had reverted to funereal black, I noted, though he would splash out at weekends in a snazzier shade of burnt charcoal. On the other hand, he was suddenly receiving an inordinate amount of wrong numbers on his mobile phone whenever I was around, and seemed to be going to an excessive number of working lunches all of a sudden. Whilst Beagle's nose might twitch at unforseen aromas floating upon the air, my antennae were equally on high alert. What appalling timing.

We had catered conservatively for eight hundred VIPs for the National Day Mark One ceremony, as rumours were abounding that the drivers had chucked most of the hand-delivered invitations straight into the River Moskva. Over a thousand guests turned up and the indoor temperature turned consequently from chilly to cosy to suffocating. The crush was considerable but no-one seemed to care. Ice-cream was served in one corner of the dining room, and went down a treat, a great proportion of it onto the carpet, judging by the state of the latter as observed during the aftermath when a multitude of maids strove to scrub it back to something like its former pristine condition in time for the next bash. A bilingual slicer, complete with shiny machine and accompanying giant basket of bread, was detailed to stand guard over the prosciutto and salami and ensure that all guests left with the same number of fingers they had possessed upon entering. In another corner, half a wheel of Parmesan cheese was hacked to death by a hard core of vodka drinkers whose aim became increasingly inaccurate as the evening wore on. An unknown lady rolled her eyes to the heavens, or more accurately, towards the painted ceiling of the ballroom which, in her defence, bore a strong resemblance to the heavens, and possibly confusing illusion with reality, proceeded to pass out cold in a heap. Willing hands transferred her to a delicate Louis XV sofa upon which, following much slapping of face, raising of legs and massaging of various body parts, she eventually came round and rendered back to the Embassy that which had belonged to the Embassy. An un-uniformed maid who had been happily washing glasses in the kitchen for the past three hours was quickly summoned with pail and extremely grubby floor-cloth. The carabinieri were most helpful in assisting the last drunk horizontally out of our historically renowned Red Salon, doubtless causing posthumous anguish to Count von Mirbach who, in his day, had left it in the same position but for the nobler reason of a Bolshevik bullet through his brain. Finally getting the assembled company down to a mere fifty or so lingerers, H.E. and Madame hoofed it discreetly down a beagle-guarded corridor, reprimanding said hound for chewing her basket to shreds in frustration at not being able to reach the canapés, exchanged the glad rags for something more accommodating and escaped through the kitchen, pausing to royally wave, congratulate and personally thank the twenty hired waiters lined up backs to wall with outstretched hands awaiting the pay off. Donning dark glasses, we kept our heads down until reaching an unmarked car waiting with engine running to take us off to the nearest Italian restaurant for supper.

Exhausted, we hardly exchanged a word until the food arrived and then, over the third glass of wine, both started talking at the same moment.

"Giorgio, I need to ask you someth..."

"Sarah..."

"Sorry, no, after you..."

"No, no, go ahead."

"No really, mine can wait."

"Me too. Really. What were you going to say?"

"Oh - I've forgotten now."

"Me too. Another glass?"

"Please."

There was another silence whilst we attacked our respective pizzas and fought to restrain the unruly mozzarella in case anyone in the restaurant had recognised us. Italian Ambassadors and their wives must be seen to be in complete control of melted mozzarella at all times. The head waiter was spotted oiling his way over to the table, with much wringing of hands and obsequious bowing from the waist.

"Bugger. That's blown our cover. Quick, you've got tomato sauce on your chin."

He stared hard at me for a moment and then, unaccountably, started to giggle. Giggling was not something he did, normally, but this time he was a lost cause. To the consternation of the waiter, he buried his face in the over starched napkin, flapped a regal hand and disappeared towards the cloakrooms, leaving me to reassure the anxious staff that everything was absolutely fine. Thank you. Perhaps we could just about force ourselves to manage another carafe if it was not too much trouble. Just a small one. Half a litre would be more than sufficient. Thank you. No, thank you, there was no need to worry. His Excellency would be finishing his pizza any minute now. Thank you.

"What the devil was all that about?"

He controlled himself with difficulty and shrugged.

"How do I know? Women are the ones who spend their time analysing situations. We men just react as nature dictates."

"So I should tell you why you're laughing? Well, I think it's relief that your stupid party is over and even more relief to be eating plain Italian food without having to make polite conversation to anyone. Then I would like to think it's relief that after all it's just you and me and a blob of tomato sauce we can still conspire about. Probably that's the best bit."

I thought about it some more.

"Though I'm not sure that should be funny. We still have one more to get through. Will it be any less exhausting, do you think?"

"I doubt it. That's why it's important to laugh about it. Rendez-vous right here tomorrow night. Same time, same place. Unless you get a better offer, of course?"

"ME? It's old purple socks that needs to ask himself *that* question."

He raised an eyebrow. Just the one. Come to think of it, he was actually very attractive with one raised eyebrow and a quizzical look and his handmade suit with the handmade shirt and the black socks tucked into the made to measure shoes. Despite the remains of the tomato sauce on his chin. Or perhaps because of it. Suddenly I realised that maybe life wasn't only about clandestine lunches or getting a buzz every time the phone rang or one heard that little ping that announced "You have mail." It was also about not feeling obliged to make conversation if you didn't want to, and being able to tell someone they had tomato sauce on their chin. Or spinach in their teeth. Or that their new deodorant wasn't working. Because you loved them enough to take care of their image too. Because you were in this together and needed all the help you could get. Both of you.

He looked up and studied me as I was studying him.

Gently he leaned over and drained the last of the carafe into my glass.

"You're drinking too much," he said. "Better control it before it's too late."

Yes. Let's both do that. Control it before it's too late.

CHAPTER FOURTEEN

To: Alex

Cc: Frankie

One down, one to go.

Increase in Beagle body weight throughout Nat. Day Mark One : approx 3 kilos.

Starvation diet imposed but no great hopes being held for adherence to same.

Can only pray that she will eventually be too top heavy to negotiate the famous spiral staircase down to the kitchen. If I'm to take her to Corsica this Summer, something radical has to be done (canine lipo?) as theoretically she is weighed and I get charged for excess baggage.

Xxxxx maman

It turned out that VIP day preceded VVIP day, which was not so clever since guests to the second effort ran a grave risk of being served with the leftovers and serially refrozen ice cream which by this stage had been shuffled between too many freezers of irregular temperatures for its own good - the passion fruit was looking decidedly depressed, I noted sadly. The visit of the Italian Foreign Minister was fortunately not due until the following week, for the bath tub in his elegant suite was filled to overflowing with ice cubes generously donated, as a result of a frantic last minute appeal, by a number of Italian restaurants.

The temperatures had now soared to 33°, something which would have mattered less had it been possible to shuffle a proportion of the guests out into the garden. Annoyingly, it had also decided to pelt with rain, the garden was reduced to a paddy field and the general level of sweat was profuse to the extreme. A more idiotic and useless exercise, I thought, as I shook the nine hundredth hand and murmured greetings, thanks and appreciation in English, French, Italian, Spanish, German and even, (for by this stage I was beyond caring about tenses,) Russian, has yet to be invented. Refusing to spend a couple of hundred dollars on adequate floral arrangements, I had persuaded the gardener to dig up all the newly planted hydrangeas and arrange them artistically in baskets. The result was spectacular, though our horticultural expert refused to speak to me for the rest of the week. As the last hard core of guests was about to leave, I headed for the shower, stripping off my finery as I went. There was a gentle tapping at the bedroom door which I took to be the dog, banished as usual to the private apartments for the duration of any festivity. Only when it became increasingly insistent did I don a towel and explore. A highly embarrassed Second Secretary begged to inform me that the staff of the Russian Foreign Ministry's Italian Desk had just turned up en masse and H.E., in the light of a lunch for fifty people we were supposed to be hosting the following day, had invited them all to the local Italian restaurant to avoid having to interrupt the staff from their bottle washing, furniture replacing and carpet scrubbing activities.

So much for our romantic diner à deux.

To: Manuela
Subject. Exhausted

Just got over shaking (I do not exaggerate, for once) 3,400 hands (1700 hellos, 1700 goodbyes), during the course of our (two) National Day ceremonies. More precisely, 3,401, since the Ambassador of Kenya, despite having had more than his ration (the strong two-handed clasp) when I was still on the receiving line, came up to me whilst I was Circulating Graciously amongst my guests, and asked who I was.

Am now about to give an interview to some unknown magazine who wants to know my impressions of the glamorous Diplomatic Life. Giorgio is looking very worried and treating me with kid gloves. And well he might.

To: Sarah
From: Manuela
Have scheduled the face lift for July 12. Cancel absolutely everything you might have in the diary and book your flight now. No way can I go through with it unless you are there holding my hand.

And then, two days later, the inevitable happened.

We were invited to the Hungarian Embassy for dinner. It was the usual dip gathering –a couple of token (English speaking) Russians, a token representative from the Commonwealth, a couple of up and coming musicians struggling in a kommunalka with one bathroom between five families and the occasional use of a gas ring. These would most certainly be playing and singing for their supper before the evening was out. All eyes turned as a most beautiful blonde Russian girl walked in and strode confidently across the room to greet the Ambassadress who wilted slightly. There were now thirteen people in the room, and she had visions of having to swap the name cards around at the last minute and coerce her teenage daughter out of her torn jeans and into something more respectable before they could all sit down at table without fear of some catastrophe befalling the party.

"Svetlana! Have you come alone?"

"No, he is on his way. He was held up. He was coming back from Chechnya but met with slight inconvenience. He will be here in a minute."

Perfect English. Stunning figure. Amazing cheekbones. Translucent skin. Legs right up to the delectably fragrant armpits. Five foot eleven and a half and fully in control of four inch heels. She charmed her way around the room providing a welcome diversion from a somewhat nauseating aroma of goulash which was emanating most persistently from the kitchen.

Giorgio was facing the door and I happened to be looking his way when Michael walked in. His jaw dropped and he ground to a complete halt in mid-sentence - an unheard of occurrence - so I guessed immediately what was happening behind my back. In any case, that voice was unmistakable. The hostess fluttered around introducing him. Whatever crime he was supposed to have been guilty of in Nato days, he had either been exonerated or news of it had yet to reach Hungary. He was once more the darling of the diplomatic circuit, brimming with the latest news from the battlefront, informed yet witty and *so* decorative with his charming young Russian companion. Such an asset. What an attractive couple they make. Don't you think?

I was in deep conversation with the Papal Nuncio by the time he reached our group. Never had the possibility of future dialogue between the Catholic and Russian Orthodox churches seemed so vitally important and totally absorbing. I was, as usual, acutely aware of his approaching presence heralded, more unusually, by a distinct aroma of garlic sausage. The Russian influence was already at work. The rest of the evening proved to be as nauseating as the goulash.

Giorgio refrained from comment until we were safely back in the car and on our way home.

"Did you know he was here?"

"Somebody did mention he had been seen around these parts. Did you find out what he's doing in Russia?"

"Recycled himself as a journalist, apparently. Investigating links with the Mafia. Commutes between Chechnya and Calabria. I hope his companion has friends in the right places, or his days are numbered. Stupid man. Always did have to stick his neck out. If he walks into a gun-toting Vespa in the market place of Corleone, I for one will not be held responsible."

CHAPTER FIFTEEN

To: Maman

From: Frankie

We seriously need a cleaner. Alex leaves glossies strewn all over the flat and I don't see why it should only be me to sort the mess.

xxx F

To: Maman

From: Alex

Bullshit. If she wasn't so busy with her boyfriend she might even notice that I do, *so*, pick up my stuff. Every Friday night when I'm looking for my tennis gear. And anyway, you should *see* the colour of the water in the vase of roses he gave her about three weeks ago. Syrup of figs. Don't know how he stands it. She doesn't deserve him.

xxx A

To: Alex
From: Maman
What's he like?
xxx M

To: Maman
From: Alex
Too good for Frankie.
Xxx A

To: Alex

From: Maman

But what's he *like*? Details. Adjectives. Pref. within comprehensible sentences and swaddled in recognisable syntax.

Xxx M

To: Maman

From: Alex

Commitment phobic.

Xxx A

Oh shit, not another one. Like Mother like daughter. We must attract them.

To: Alex

From: Maman

How's Frankie?

xxx M

To: Maman

From: Alex

Miserable. And grumpy. Loses it if I so much as leave ONE dirty plate in the sink. In love. Ugh.

xxx A

To: Frankie

Cc: Alex

From: Maman

Thinking of you both immersed in your glossy mags this Sunday as I study Soviet Constructivist architecture and the philosophy of Tolstoy. Hope you've resolved the cleaner crisis and will soon start on the flower arranging classes. Am on my way over to hold Manuela's hand throughout her little adventure.

See you both Tuesday.

xxx M

To: Maman

From: Frankie

Umm, Tuesday not good. I'm staying with a friend for a long weekend and Alex is off dog sitting someone's Great Dane.

How about lunch on Friday?

Xxx F

Well it was good to know the pair of them weren't nursing suicidal tendencies or counting the hours until I arrived.

To: Sarah

From: Manuela

I'll be at the airport tomorrow to meet you. If I'm a bit late, wait for me. You always were so nit-pickety about punctuality. And don't drink too much vodka on the plane – we've arranged a girls' night out as a send-off.

Love, Manu

Michael? I wondered briefly as I paced the departures lounge the next day waiting for my flight to be announced. Caught in cross-fire in Chechnya or swimming across the straits of Messina with a pocket full of pebbles for all I knew or cared.

*   *   *   *

I knocked myself fairly senseless on Aeroflot's Georgian wine, flew into Rome in a haze and, once she finally turned up at the airport, went straight to Manuela's, there being nobody at home waiting for me.

We had such a riotous night out that, as I accompanied Manuela to the clinic the next morning, I was almost envious of my friend's opportunity to sleep off the effects for twenty-four hours. There must have been more than enough alcohol still hanging around in her bloodstream to render further anaesthetic almost superfluous. I checked her in with a particularly nasty nun who quite rightly felt she should have been administering last rites to the sick and dying in war torn outposts or earthquake zones, rather than filling out forms for people with nothing more life-threatening than an odd wrinkle or three. To add insult to injury, this supremely healthy example of human vanity standing before her had the audacity to claim that she would not be requiring a pre-op. blessing: it hardly seemed worth sharpening the scalpel for one so manifestly predestined for a spell in the furnace. Manuela was asked to sign a couple of dozen declarations in which the clinic disclaimed every possible responsibility that could have been remotely held against it. After the first three or four, we lost interest in nun baiting and gave up bothering to read the small print, signing away every right and privilege with abandon, anxious only to get to the seclusion of that private room where we could nurse our respective hangovers. A smiley nun from Bangladesh ushered her into a lift and up to the top floor where apparently the operation would take place, while I made my way to the room, unpacked her overnight bag and laid out an impressive array of face creams in full view of the bed. That would cheer her up when she came round from the anaesthetic – she could lie there and calculate how much money she would be saving in future. In the manner of Goldilocks, I then proceeded to curl up on the patient's bed, solely in order to test it for comfort. I was brought back to consciousness four hours later by someone playing bumper cars with a large metal trolley and then trying to park it parallel to the bed, using about the same amount of finesse that your average Italian driver would use to slam his third hand wreck of a Fiat into a parking space too small for it by about half a meter. A drugged voice from beneath the sheet was heard instructing everyone in unrefined Spanish to get lost pronto and leave it to sleep for about another week and a half.

"My God, you look just like a baby with a motorcycle helmet."

"What mobikle pelmet? What you on about?"

"Oh sorry - haven't you had a feel yet? Your head's all wound up in a shroud. But the bits in between that I can see are as smooth as the proverbial. Wow! Me next. What did it cost you?"

"Arm and peg. Gemme drink."

"You're not allowed. That old bag of a nun threatened me with an eternity in the underworld if I brought up the bottle of fizz. Said it would make you throw up. I told her it never had yet, and you'd been practising pretty hard for nigh on half a century."

"Not fizz, water. Need water! Canttalk. No slyva."

"I told you, you're not allowed. You'd vomit. You haven't got any saliva because they stuff tubes and things down you with the anaesthetic. Dries you all up something rotten. Don't worry, it'll come back. Try not to talk - you look fantastic - want a mirror?"

No, she most definitely did not want a mirror. She wanted water and then to go back to sleep for another four hours. She was denied the first but achieved the second of these aspirations so I took the opportunity to leave her in the hands of the smiley nun and went off to get some lunch.

Manuela swam back up the black spiral just as ice-cold pads were being placed over her eyes and immediately began complaining loudly that someone had omitted to remove a squash ball from her throat before dismissing her from the operating theatre. People were talking over her head, making approving noises, but she left them to it and sank back down the tunnel again.

"Manu! Come on, wake up. Can I take your pads off and have a quick look?

"Uggg. Water."

"Right. Here, can you hold the glass yet? Oh, whoops! no you can't. Wait, I'll go and ask for a straw. What's this sponge thing for in the glass? Why are you nodding like that? Ah, got it. Thieves on the cross and all that. See how useful Bible studies are in moments of crisis? Wait, I'll dunk and drip on you. Better? Can I see your eyes now? Oh yuk. Doesn't that hurt? You must be crazy, you never looked a day over fifty-three in the first place."

"Ffoff."

Armed with a good book and a smuggled Thermos flask of prosecco, I curled up on the sofa and prepared to pass the night administering to the sick. I slept soundly through until 6 a.m., oblivious to everything and everyone.

Manuela, by contrast, apparently slept in fits and starts until 10 p.m. when, wide awake and bored, she thought she would by-pass the nun and nip to the bathroom, not realising that both ears were wired up to some kind of a drainage system and had been quietly bleeding into a couple of containers throughout the day. Succumbing to the dreaded nun, she requested the even more dreaded bedpan and meekly accepted to be filled up with sleeping pills to see her through the rest of the night. The following day the helmet was removed together with all the tubes and some of the stitches and she was sent home hiding behind a pair of dark glasses. Her be-wimpled friend at the reception desk looked even more disapproving as she groped her way out into the sunshine on my supporting arm. I dropped her off and headed for home.

The flat was deserted. A minimal attempt had been made to clean it up for my return: the rubbish bin was empty and though the dishwasher was full, the plates in it were clean. Even the beds were made and, exploring further, I noted that for once there was no rotting food in the refrigerator. One could almost imagine that no-one was actually living there, or at least not on any permanent basis. I refrained from conducting an in depth inspection of the girls' rooms and confined myself to a couple of lengthy phone calls to them, from which it transpired that Alex's Great Danes were fine and Frankie's friend was in the best of health, thank you. And could we make it dinner on Friday, not lunch?

I went round to have lunch with Manuela instead and searched for bruises, but there were none. Just a bit of swelling.

"Hey, do you want my creams? I don't need them anymore, and my surgeon says they never did any good in the first place."

"Don't tell me that - I still need to believe. Here, have some vino, your glass is empty."

"That's a water glass, treasure. I've given up the vino."

I stared open mouthed at the look of smug self-satisfaction on her face as she reached for the bottle.

"It was such a massive investment I thought I ought to contribute something. And I couldn't bear to think of going back prematurely to the bottled apricots in alcohol texture, so I decided to quit. Coffee too. In fact any minute now I'll be seeking some exciting new vices, so if you have any original ideas on the subject, just let me know."

Frankie turned up in time for dinner the next day looking radiant but giving nothing away. I couldn't help but notice that a considerable amount of time was dedicated to sending and receiving messages whilst we waited for our food, but with great restraint I refrained from comment.

"Frankie, come shopping with me tomorrow, I feel the urge to buy a jeans jacket."

" Sure, that'll wow them at your next ladies' charity committee tea party. What's all this about? Your best friend having a face lift? Forget it. You'll be wanting blubber lips next. I don't want my mother to be taken for my sister, thank you very much. And besides, I've got a date tomorrow and I honestly don't have time."

"Who *is* this guy? And will I be allowed to meet him if I promise not to inject any toxic substances into myself in the meantime? Come on, I won't bite. I can't sit around holding Manuela's hand for another three days – it depresses me."

"Shoot down to Sicily and pay a visit to Nonna. She could do with some cheering up – she's getting deafer by the minute and is refusing a hip replacement so she can't even get out of the flat without two strong men to help her down the steps. I'll be back in time to run you to the airport."

"What do you mean, 'back in time'?" You've only just *got* back. Where are you going this time? And where is that little sister you should be looking after? We spoke a couple of times on the phone, but I couldn't hear a thing for dogs barking."

"She's making herself a fortune at some farm in the country looking after the animals. She walks the dogs and rides the horses and feeds the pigs and comes home stinking of manure with her pockets full of undeclared cash. She'll be fine, don't you worry about her. Go and sort out your mother-in-law."

So I went down to Sicily to visit Nonna, though "shoot" turned out to be the joke of the week. A one hour flight, they said. Then Etna started its little capers, and I was stuck in Fiumicino airport for five hours trying to get out of Rome. Eventually we creaked into Reggio Calabria instead of Catania and, given the backlog of passengers, took a few more hours to find a place on a ferry to cross the Straits of Messina. Total travelling time: ten hours. Total number of signs of cross executed by mother-in-law upon eventual arrival: thirty-two. Or maybe more. It could be I'd missed a couple when I was in the bathroom. It had to be said that Nonna was not on top form but at something undisclosed over the age of ninety it was only to be expected. There was a big mystery surrounding her age: not even her only son was supposed to know how old she was or even the date of her birthday. In an era when those of her generation had to be married off by the age of fifteen, she had been thoroughly on the shelf until well into her thirties. She had then given birth with immense difficulty to Giorgio and sat back on her laurels considering that her happiness was complete. Only it wasn't. Firstly she had been tragically left a widow just as her husband's career was getting off the ground. Secondly her only son had upped and married a foreigner. Thirdly he had chosen a career which would keep him well away from her beloved Sicily. And fourthly, he was now posted to Russia, just as she needed to move back in with him so that he could repay all her sacrifices by looking after her in her dying days. Because, having threatened him with it for the past twenty years, she was now intending to die. Just as soon as the good Lord permitted. Sign of Cross. Number thirty-three. Or thereabouts. Now, regarding this imminent event, she had something very important she had been waiting to tell her daughter in law. When she was Called, (but she was ready for the Call, they were not to worry themselves on that score), she wanted Sarah to promise upon the heads of her children (number thirty-four) that she would be sure to reach her deathbed before Giorgio did. Giorgio was not to be allowed within sniffing distance for at least twenty-four hours. She had an absolute horror of being tipped into the grave prematurely and she knew how distracted he always was. Her best friend's cousin's sister's husband's mother had regained consciousness a day after the last rites had been administered by that cretinous priest from the church down by the market. And the last thing she was prepared to put up with was her son standing over her inert body with a mobile phone clamped to each ear going "Si Ministro," "No, Signor Presidente," whilst the doctor was signing her death certificate. Ti raccomando. Thirty-five.

The return journey was even worse than the outward one: this time they not only closed Catania airport, they waited until I had more or less swum across to Reggio Calabria to close that one, too. I was then coach-lifted with a bunch of ill-shaven Calabrians and their multitudinous possessions to some obscure strip of concrete in the middle of nowhere and eventually landed back in Fiumicino in the early hours of the morning half-starved and in an advanced state of mental and physical exhaustion. Not that anyone was staying awake on my account, for once again the flat was silent and empty, though decorated with a large fluorescent stick-it note from Frankie apologising in advance for not being back in time to take me to the airport. She was in France, and had got caught up in the pilot's strike.

CHAPTER SIXTEEN

Moscow.

To: Manuela

From: Sarah

Trust you are still bruise-free and that Paolo is fully satisfied with his new wife. Do not forget that you must now revise your conversational gambits: No, you hardly remember the Beatles, or not having a T.V. or central heating. The Biafran war? When was that, you say?

You will also have to become adept at freezing personal remarks with ambassadorial hauteur and apologetic smile – hopefully you can manage the apol. smile by now without fear of cracking. This is a tactic I myself use frequently. When asked, as a simple example, what I think of someone called Svetlana, or whether I have seen anything of someone else called Michael recently, I change the subject to an in-depth analysis of our newly appointed President's choice of close collaborators. A conversation stopper if ever there was one. Is Putin about to adopt Yeltsin's "family"? or will he aim to free himself from the past? (elaborate). This usually gives me sufficient time to compose a non-committal reply and infer that I have far more important matters on my mind right now than to waste my time thinking about anything so futile as couples in love.

Except for Frankie, of course, but that's another story.

xxxxx Sarah

To: Frankie

From: Maman

Subject : Quickie.

Not the expression to use when I've got a religious service beginning here in ten minutes. We have a religious fanatic staying who requires mass to be said every morning before breakfast. On occasions such as these, the painting of the rather rude nymph which hangs in pride of place on the wall of our sitting room, is carefully removed and stashed behind a curtain. Which is where I'd found her in the first place when I moved in here. She'd obviously been axed by some puritanical Ambassadress before me. I restored her to pride of place the first time Serafim was sober enough to be entrusted with a hammer and nails, and she's helped me through many a dreary evening since then.

So since I am being religious today, I shall pray to your own personal saint for your success and happiness. You are forgiven for not being the dutiful daughter during my brief visit to Rome ONLY if the guy is worth it. If he turns out to be a sonofabitch, you owe me a couple of lunches at the very least.

Can c y folk abbrvte emails - u wldnt get anything done all day, othrwse. *very* addictive. hve a nce dy. let me no u r ok.

xxx M

To: Maman

From: Alex

My sister is about to write and tell you something. You'd better be sitting down.

xxx A

To Maman:

From: Frankie:

HE JUST ASKED ME TO MARRY HIM!!!!!!!!!!!! YESYESYESYESYESYESYESYESYESYES!!!!!!!!! A Spring wedding. I think I'm going to burst.

xxx F

*   *   *   *

The administrative officer in charge of the purse strings finally dismissed Tonia. A couple of undernourished university students were engaged in her place and, by dint of standing over them with a horsewhip in the pouring rain, I finally achieved rows of border plants in geometric patterns struggling bravely against the elements. I even managed to get the dandelion lawn chewed – by a goat from the look of it, but better than nothing. As a final gesture, I called in a garden architect who presented me with a pile of magazines picturing cascading fountains, rampant rockeries, and nooks and glades surrounded by kitschily paved walkways. I tried to explain with eloquent gestures and simplified vocabulary that we could not even get financing to restore the main building before it fell apart, let alone to create Kew Gardens in our own back yard, but Foreign Diplomat is equated with dollar signs in Russia just as much as Russian Expat is equated with multimillions abroad. We compromised with a fish pond.

To: Sarah
From: Manu
My only problem is that I never saw myself as an aged crone in the first place, and when I looked at photographs or caught sight of myself in direct sunlight, I just used to think I was having a bad day. So that now, when I look in a mirror, I think "Yes, that's right. That's me. So what's new?" Nine thousand quid down the pipe is new, that's what. I still drink only water on all occasions, or tomato juice. No coffee either and I am currently working on the chocolate habit because my skin now thinks it is 15yrs old and keeps breaking out in acne.... Well, you know me, it has to be all or nothing (Stefano didn't know what he was missing, did he?) I have to say that the temptation to tank up during boring dinners is pretty strong, but so far so good. Am obviously seriously in need of some new distractions, just in case you've got any suggestions, though as mother-of-the-bride-to be, I don't suppose you'll be much good for anything for the next six months.
Thanks for the support.
All love, Manu

To: Manu

From : Sarah

Great to hear your latest news: we've both come a long way when you think back, dear, haven't we? I must say it is almost a relief to stop running....

You, though, are quite clearly in need of some new and legitimate distractions. I am worried by your tone of resignation. A lift is supposed to do just that, not force you backwards onto your laurels. Tee-total, indeed. How retrograde.

I cannot aspire to your dizzy heights of self-denial, the odd glass of grape juice is still an essential part of my daily diet, but certain other extra-curricular activities have been firmly eradicated with surprisingly few withdrawal symptoms. I have also become a dedicated gardener. We have created a fish pond in the garden beside which Giorgio and I meditate of a summer's evening. The fish, I am told upon authority, freeze solid during the winter months but remain delightfully warm and cosy under the layers of snow and ice. They then re-emerge, fresher than ever and wrinkle free, in the spring and take up where they left off. What a saving. Some folk have it made. Beagle and I spend many a contented hour watching their antics. Their movements mesmerise us as they swim in the pool flicking their tails and gyrating around the breadcrumbs. Beagle leans further and further over the water trying to reach them without falling in.

Fatal attraction. You can almost hear her thinking "Yum. Sushi."

One of them has a positively seductive wink.

I call him Mike. Mike the Pike. Filed. On a spike.

Much love, Sarah

To: Sarah

From: Manu

Since you are being so cool about it, I may as well confess that I saw your friend Michael a couple of times. Purely in a spirit of revenge.

So I shouldn't let the thought of Svetlana keep you awake at nights, if I were you.

And you can rename the Pike. Call it Mick.

Draw your own conclusions.

Best love, Manu

CHAPTER SEVENTEEN

Giorgio and I flew back together to meet our future son-in-law. As soon as Aeroflot heard that the Italian Ambassador had preferred to travel with his luggage on one of their shaky old Ilyushins rather than arrive without his luggage on an Alitalia Airbus, they upgraded us to Oligarch Class. As we slid into our allotted seats, the back rests obligingly collapsed to a semi-supine position at no extra charge. Vodka and caviar were served. The oligarchs were already on their second helping of the day. Or third. It was, after all, well past breakfast time. His Excellency accepted a tot of tomato juice just to calm his nerves. Given that he was on his way to encounter some kind of village idiot who would undoubtedly prove to be unworthy of cleaning his daughter's boots, let alone keeping her in the manner she deserved, he considered this excess justifiable. In between praying that this shaky old crate of an aircraft would succeed in reaching Fiumicino airport in one piece, he prayed that heaven would preserve him from having to meet this gibbering idiot's parents too: he shuddered at the very thought. Supposing they said "dinner" when they meant "lunch," or didn't know it was unacceptable to say "buon appetito" before eating? He glanced sideways at me, wondering if I was sharing his fears.

"It's all a bit scary, isn't it?" I said, reading his thoughts. "What do you think he'll be like?"

"Awful," he said firmly. "Nobody could be good enough for Frankie, and she always did have dreadful taste in boyfriends." Together we thought back over a series of undesirables who had appeared at intervals only to disappear again, fortunately, as our daughter moved on to the next country or phase in her development.

"But if Frankie is so happy, what can we do?"

"Nothing. Hope. Make sure she has a good job to fall back on and a roof over her head."

"Perhaps he'll be lovely. We never thought of that."

"Hmmm."

Eventually we fell asleep on each other's shoulders, and not even the vodka-induced snores from the oligarchs disturbed our already troubled dreams.

*   *   *   *

The door to the flat was ajar. Nobody in the sitting room, nobody in the kitchen. The sound of running water coming from somewhere.

"Frankie! We're here."

"Cooeee! I'll be right with you." A strangely falsetto voice issued from the bathroom. A faint smell of jasmine was in the air. The door opened and an apparition emerged. Five foot two in his (no, surely not?) Cuban heels, purple shirt embossed with daisies and three, yes three, earrings.

"*Darling* people. You must be the lucky *lucky* parents of our *darling* Frankie. She just popped out to buy some bikkies for tea. *Such* a joy to *finally* meet you."

A lily white hand with impeccably manicured nails and the merest hint of varnish advanced towards us.

We clutched at each other for support.

I was the first to recover the use of my vocal chords.

"Oh, what a surprise," I said faintly. "We weren't expecting....I mean we sort of thought you would be Italian...."

A bit lame but given the circumstances, masterly. A true professional. Even Giorgio looked impressed. Or would have done if the situation had been less terrifying.

The apparition fluttered his lashes and beamed at us delightedly.

"Dadsy was an all Roman boy, but Mumsy was *gen-yew-ine* Essex," he said proudly. "They met on a beach in Rimini and I've lived in this un-*holy* city all my life. So I know it like the back of my hand." The lily white member in question palpitated vaguely in the direction of the Coliseum, the Forum, St. Peters, wherever.

"So our darling Frankie needn't worry her pretty little head about *anything* at all. I shall *personally* take care of absolutely *every* little detail. Now do come right inside and treat the place as if it was your very own. She'll be back any minute."

But we seemed to be having some trouble getting any co-ordination in our leg movements. Those wretched Aeroflot seats. Behind us the door was pushed open and our beautiful, beautiful daughter greeted us, radiant behind an armful of groceries.

"Ben arrivati! Good old Russian airlines – bang on time as usual. *And* with accompanying baggage, I see. I hope you've been extra especially nice to

Robin because I couldn't live without him. He's taken all my worries away and completely changed my life. He's my wedding planner. Isn't he divine?"

He was, indeed, divine. Quite remarkable. Knew which churches could be bribed into agreeing to marry a couple who had absolutely no connection with their parish and hadn't walked down an aisle since their First Communion, except for the odd Christmas Midnight Mass. Knew where the most scenically impressive villas were available to rent for the reception, where to find the best caterers, dressmakers, printers, hairdressers, musical quartet, disc jockey - he had them all at the tip of his pampered fingers. He even came up with a series of suggested itineraries for the honeymoon. Nothing was too much to ask of him. With just the one teensy exception, of course. With all the best will in the world, he could not substitute the groom. He was prepared to take them to the very brink of their future life together, but once they were safely in their little love nest on whichever romantic island took their fancy he would, regretfully, have to leave them to it. Each to his own, sweetie.

Absolutely by far the best thing about him, though, as we confessed to each other later that day, was that he was not Marco. Whom we were to meet over dinner that night and who at this juncture only needed to be half-way normal to satisfy our re-dimensioned aspirations.

*   *   *   *

Having feared the worst, of course, Marco was wonderful. We couldn't believe our luck. We exchanged delighted little nudges under the table and caught each other's eye in conspiratorial euphoria throughout the evening. Furthermore he was obviously besotted with our daughter, which showed him to be a human being of superior intelligence. Giorgio was riding on such a wave of relief and admiration he even suggested they might stop somewhere for a nightcap, an unheard of occurrence, to discuss, man to man, a few technical details. It was pointed out that it would be considered somewhat eccentric to order a glass of mineral water at room temperature in the kind of sophisticated bar he had in mind, but it seemed he was prepared to even risk consuming a little alcohol to celebrate this special occasion. Wonders would never cease. Marco was definitely a positive acquisition.

Frankie and I left them to it and headed for home. We had been deep in conversation for a couple of hours before we heard them coming back. Marco put his face round the door first. He was looking utterly mortified.

"Had a bit of trouble getting him into the car," he said. "He seemed to think it was the Aeroflot luggage compartment. I'm really sorry. Perhaps he's allergic to cocktails? I didn't know, but we only had a couple."

A couple? A COUPLE? Giorgio?He was completely plastered. Giggling like a looney and waving the inevitable mobile phone around his head like a maniac.

"The Minister," he managed to splutter eventually, "I invited him to the wedding, and he said he would definitely think about it. And he would very much like to pay an official visit to Russia if I could organize that in the meantime. Next week." For some reason he seemed to think this was even more hilarious. Aware, finally, that the assembled company were not sharing his mirth, he made an attempt to sober up.

"Do not," he said, heavily, "mistake my apparent euphoria with intoxication. I am perfectly sober. Just very very happy."

So saying, he fell backwards onto the sofa, snuggled into my shoulder and passed out. It was at this point only that the hilarity of the situation hit the rest of us simultaneously, though our combined hysterics failed to wake him or even minimally disturb his snores.

Leaving all the arrangements for the Spring wedding in the be-ringed hands of the capable Robin, I flew back to Moscow with Giorgio and tried to concentrate on absorbing some vital statistics in time for the Minister's visit: Italian population of Moscow, date of construction of Italian Embassy, current state of Russian politics, economic progress since the collapse of the USSR, names of most important politicians, architects, ballerinas etc. Along the way, I toyed with the option of Sorry, I Haven't a Clue. And why don't you oblige us by most kindly posting my husband to the Court of St. James instead? But with age, I guess one just learns to stay calm and carry on.

CHAPTER EIGHTEEN

To: Manu
From: Sarah

Lucky spy - He, at least, came in from the cold, whereas I just exchanged Roman sunshine for unsexy woollen tights, boring grey trousers, three sweaters (grey), jacket made out of an eiderdown (grey), fur boots and 2prs of gloves, and still came back from Beagle walking looking blue. Or probably grey.

I guess you are in Peru by now and trust you are confining your affections to Paolo and Paddington Bear as opposed to searching for new vices as threatened. I personally have found an excellent outlet for my frustrations and am now regularly contributing to a monthly publication where I let rip about Diplomatic Dire Doings. Anonymously, of course. I don't want to wreck Giorgio's career quite yet.

My usual mega depression at the thought of returning to Moscow is slightly better now I'm here. I just hate moving around all the time and realise I can't relieve depressive symptoms by Tidying a Cupboard - every intelligent woman's answer to the doldrums, in case you ever need to know. Here I have a squadron of Russian helpers who whip my discarded clothes back into geometrically acceptable shapes before I'm half out of them.
And I'm *complaining*?

Not that I am exactly underemployed. I have just had 200 guests including two Foreign Ministers, theirs and ours, for a concert and supper, together with a couple of dozen TV crews, secret service personnel masquerading as waiters and the usual bedlam in every corner. The Italian bodyguards got offended and refused to eat cook's 3 star delicacies off the solid silver plates with matching cutlery, Murano glassware and linen tablecloth served by our white gloved butler in his none too copious free time between serving the rest of the hangers on and the Minister himself in the dining room. Apparently they turned their plates upside down, or whatever it is that bodyguards do when incorrectly placed at table, and stormed out of the Embassy. It transpired that although their table had been set up within regulation firing distance of the Minister they were supposed to be defending with their lives, it was, nevertheless, set up in a cloakroom. A polished mahogany panelled cloakroom which is roughly two and a half times the size of my dining room back home and very cosy too, what with all the coats acting as draught proofing, but nevertheless a cloakroom. So our poor Minister was left to survive unprotected.

I managed to mention the Court of Saint James to him once he was well mellowed with vodka and caviar, but Giorgio was checking out my body language from way down the other end of the table, so I didn't dare go down on one knee and actually *beg*. Anyway Our Man in London has only just unpacked his chattels, so we would have to wait a couple of years at least until he has exhausted his wine cellar. Or done something unforgivable – like not managing to prevent the free British press from publishing sarcastic articles about our great Italian leaders.

I shall live in hope.

Trust you are well and wrinkle free and won't invite you to come and visit in case it undermines your alcohol free resolve. Anyway, our days here are numbered, and for once it will be perfect timing, what with the wedding coming up.

By the way, what was all that about Mick the p***k?

Love, Sarah

To: Sarah

From: Manu

Just settling a few debts for you, since you will obviously be far too busy writing your memoirs in the future.

Forget it.

xxx Manu

*   *   *   *

Frankie's wedding disrupted most of Tuscany for about a week and a half.

Neither of the grandmothers managed to be present at the marathon, and perhaps it was just as well. The English one was sound in body but not in mind: the Italian one was sound in mind but not in body and the stress would not have improved either of their conditions. The pair of them then waited until we had left Russia and were back at the Foreign Ministry in Rome, almost as if they hadn't wanted to put us to too much trouble, to fall asleep and not wake up. Nonna had reached the age of ninety-six: my mother was ninety- four. They died within three weeks of each other, considerately giving us just enough time to organize one funeral and begin on the next. We had a three day lying in state for my mother-in-law to be quite sure, and mobile phones were strictly off limits.

The family was suddenly shrinking. Frankie had gone off to live with Marco in America for a couple of years and Alex was studying to be a Vet in Brussels. We ploughed through our home posting feeling depleted, with only Beagle and occasional sightings of our younger daughter to relieve the daily routine.

Then everything suddenly began moving at once. Frankie came back to Europe and started having babies in quick succession. Alex moved back to Rome and started working. And one famous Saturday, the phone rang when we least expected it and it was The Call. The body language, though restrained, must have worked after all, because there was the Minister himself on the line wondering if, were he to ask very nicely, we might just see our way to stretching a point and accepting the London posting? Would that amuse us? Would we mind too dreadfully? He knew we hadn't been back in Rome so very long, but a vacancy was now looming and the idea had just occurred to him, no pressure, of course, take your time to think it over and perhaps discuss it with your wife – had he remembered correctly that she was English? So perhaps she might just be persuaded....

I was booking the tickets on the computer whilst Giorgio was still rambling on about how expensive London was, how the food was so awful and the weather so depressing and the work in a European bilateral Embassy insufficiently challenging.

Tough. Let me at it. Gotter get out there and stake my claim before it occurs to any of your chers collègues that it might just amuse them, too. Hang my hat. Plant the flag.

London, here I come.

PART FOUR

LONDON

CHAPTER ONE

The Embassy was large. Six floors in the centre of London overlooking a park. Drivers and household staff all had self-contained accommodation up on the top floor, and the basement was occupied by four separate private apartments for our resident carabinieri and a series of not very charming cellars. The remaining four floors were for our private and public functions of all natures. Smiling Filipinos occasionally appeared from where they had been lurking, duster in hand just in case, in unused bedrooms or condemned bathrooms and it seemed I was supposed to spend my days playing hide and seek up and down the six floors checking on whether they were actually doing any work. At least where the cook was concerned this activity was unnecessary. It was all too clear from the outset that he wasn't. Not so much from lack of good will as from complete lack of any culinary ability.

He was given the benefit of the doubt for the regulation three months and then we started to search for a replacement. One morning, as I passed the door to his office, His Excellency was overheard dictating a telegram of extreme political sensitivity, the gist of which was a plea to the Authorities That Be to permit the Bearer to travel in the company of his private collection of kitchen knives. Our new chef never went anywhere without his equipment, you understand, and just as well, given the disastrous state of the Embassy kitchen. Whilst I could not claim that the gastronomic masterpieces which began to emerge were achieved over a Bunsen burner with the help of a billy-can and a couple of twigs, it was an indisputable fact that he performed miracles in the face of considerable opposition, for the Powers that Be were not at their most generous where refurbishing kitchens was concerned. Ask the Admin. Dept. boys for cash to replace an ageing cooker whose thermostat hadn't worked properly since 1993, and they would sigh and shake their heads regretfully whilst surreptitiously installing yet another coffee machine in the staff common room. Point out that the extractor fan hadn't worked since last summer, so that all the cooking smells permeated throughout the entire Residence every time we gave a dinner party, and they would commiserate and tell you to open more windows. I also paused occasionally to reflect upon what Health and Safety would have to say at the sight of our food processor which was attractively held together by fluorescent masking tape. You could almost see the microorganisms clinging to its blades despite the fact that it had not actually been put to use since the summer of 1997.

Replacing the Filipinos took longer – they were just too sweet. Useless, but sweet. Eventually I managed with great tact to retire them and they were replaced by a couple of new models who went around dusting the insides of all my cupboards and drawers and putting things back in rigid soldierly rows so that I was unable to find so much as a stapler for a whole week and was much too scared to ask. I was also obliged to Throw Things Out in order to keep up with their high standards. It goes without saying that they were called not Concita or Maria Jesù nor even Divina (who came for a trial run one morning and was still ironing the first of H.E.'s shirts four hours later,) but Gretel and Margot. No, they did not yodel or dance as they brought me my fresh orange juice with which I sought to combat the odd free radical still doggy-paddling valiantly through my veins having miraculously survived the previous night's onslaught of chocolate and pure alcohol, but they changed my life quite dramatically for the better nonetheless.

Beagle was thrilled to be in London. She was now 15 years old but not any wiser. If she were approached with one of those dinky little machines they used to check radiation levels in the Moscow markets, she beeped disconcertingly, proving to the world she was micro-chipped, rabies proof, tattooed and whatever else is required to keep my animal loving countrymen content. It had taken six months at twenty euros per day for a dog sitter whilst she waited for her permission to enter England, so she was roughly worth her weight in gold. Whereas I had taken three days to find my way down to the kitchen which, as in Moscow, the Foreign Ministry had once again situated in the basement thus rendering the serving of food at anywhere near the desired temperature well nigh an impossibility, Beagle had it sussed in four minutes flat. From there she made her way to the offices which were joined to the Residence via an impenetrable corridor protected by a system of security locks and keypads requiring code numbers or, at the very least, Written

Permission. The Embassy staff tended to bring packed lunches in to work. She sussed that out in record time, too. The rest may be left to the imagination. As usual, we made lots of friends during our daily excursions into the local park bearing the regulation doggie poo bags and as usual the ensuing conversations were extraordinarily edifying.

"Excuse me, your dog just dropped a packet,"
"Oh, shit."
"Yes."
Owner of large labradoodle starts walking backwards in search of offending pile.
"No, no. Left hand down a bit. Twenty past ten......MINEFIELD! Look – there. Mine's just peed on it."
"At least she didn't eat it."
"No, prefers horse dung."
"Really? It's goat droppings with ours."
"Goat droppings? That's just a snack! Like M and Ms."

I would sneak back into the house in my muddy jeans and re-emerge in all my splendour, driver standing to attention with car door open ready to tuck me into the shiny limo and whisk me off to some official function, whilst the doggy friends gaped from under the tree where I had left them a mere seven minutes earlier. They were a mixed bunch: the owner of the little black pug, I learnt after a year and a half, had an impressive title and belonged to one of the most illustrious families in England. He had just sold a house round the corner for more zeros than I could manage to digest in the course of conversation. The beautiful boxer bitch belonged to a Welsh lady with an accent which took me a good three months to comprehend, but once I had mastered it, I realised she had a sense of humour that would put me in a good mood for the rest of the day. I think she was a concierge in one of the nearby mansion houses on the square. Diego, Beagle's best friend, was exercised thrice daily by Rosy, a lovely Indian who had the most amazing collection of saris in jewel-like colours over which she would throw one or other of her employer's Barbour jackets whilst she hand fed the little devil his lunch. Diego would only touch food if he thought someone else might want it, so she fed him in the park under Beagle's nose. One handful for Diego, one for Beagle. It kept them both from starvation, not that Beagle was at risk on that particular count.

We never really went into personal details: it took us all our time to keep our respective hounds' noses out of each other's backsides and everybody else's picnics in between parcelling up their droppings and posting them into the doggie mail boxes.

To: Alex
From: Maman

Have just had very smart Carabiniere in full uniform straightening out my computer glitches in his copious free time between volleying anthrax envelopes back to sender, or whatever it is they do down in the basement all day and night. Anyway, I am now up and functioning. So keep me posted please.

To: Frankie
From: Maman

Did you celebrate St. Patrick's Day in Italy too?
Just been to the Irish Embassy to congratulate them, as one does, on their National Day and found they were generously distributing shamrock to adorn their guests' buttonholes. Rumour has it the Japanese Ambassador pronounced it delicious and asked for more.
Any idea what Alex is up to?

To : Manu
From: Sarah
Where the hell have you disappeared to this time? Haven't had a cheep out of you for ages. Make contact please, if only to cheer me up as I go about my glamorous duties as wife of ...etc.
So far I have overseen the repainting of an entire flat on the sixth floor for the new cook, gutted two bedrooms and three bathrooms on the third, resurfaced five baths and six basins (rust stains on all eleven the size of dinner plates: think fifth class Bognor boarding house) and found somebody to dismantle the chandeliers bit by bit, number all the pieces, clean each petal until it gleams and then reconstitute and re-hang. The hardest part in all this? Parking the car underneath Wandsworth Bridge at 8 a.m. in such a manner that it is impossible to read the number plates whilst I load two new bidets into the boot. You get a good class of bidet at a very reasonable price under Wandsworth Bridge, should

you ever need to know, but if you present yourself with diplomatic number plates, the price, logically, goes up by 15%. I have furthermore ordered new beds for future visits of the President of the Italian Republic and my grandchildren, been measured for new curtains and "voi-ills" (sic) throughout to replace the grey, torn, shrunken monstrosities currently gracing the newly-washed windows (quote on arrival "window cleaner has been discontinued due to lack of funds.") Which, being interpreted, means I have to pay him myself. Together with the installation and maintenance of the window boxes, but so what, I gotter live here, innit?

And now, as I write, exactly what I needed after a bad day.

Polish plumber just bored a hole right through the bathroom wall trying to hang a cupboard, knocking down half the bedroom on the other side. Giorgio, meanwhile, is trying to justify employing Italian workers in some god awful northern factory so neither of us are going to make it to the Dean of Westminster's cocktail party tonight because *he* is busy being interviewed on Channel 4 and *I* am trying to hold up a wall.

I exaggerate a *bit*, but you get the picture.

Plus, my literary career is currently suffering a setback because I am having a tiresomely bad relationship with this new supersonic computer. It suffers from premature wotsit. I only have to look at it and it Sends. So you may well get half a msg. That's just the effect I have on it, what can I do.....

Most phrustrating - the German Ambo wrote me a note recently thanking me for the phantastic party, so now I use it all the time – phantastic phood, philm, you name it.

And whilst we are on the subject of phantasy and phantoms, accustomed as I am to your disappearing into the ether, a sign of recognition once in a while would be appreciated? If only to show you were still alive, kicking and not sinking into depression? I might even be prepared to forgive you for Michael, concerning whom your uncustomary silence speaks volumes. Bitch.
Write. Please.
Love, Sarah

To: Maman
From: Frankie
Little sister says she is investigating her childhood influences for an advanced research project based on Freudian psychology.
Basically this means she is dating a Nigerian.

To: Frankie
From: Maman
You got me worried there. I thought you meant she'd reverted to walking round with a stuffed rabbit and a bit of blanket.

CHAPTER TWO

"The Lord Mayor and the Lady Mayoress present their compliments and hope that those ladies who care to do so will wear tiaras."

Not many cared to do so, I noted, studying the assembled company. Times were certainly changing in this classless society which was now Great Britain. I could only spot half a dozen at the most, and three of those were Butler and Wilson. I sneaked a passing sausage and applied myself to the task of recognising people of significance.

"I fail to comprehend," said the Impressively Highly Placed Representative of Her Majesty's Foreign and Commonwealth Office, "why it is that the Media treat us so appallingly. They seem to think we spend all our time quaffing champagne and dressing up like Christmas Trees."

I do love IHPRs of HMG who are unstuffy enough to talk through the tongues in their cheeks whilst sipping at alcoholic beverages.

The occasion was the Lord Mayor's Easter Banquet. Apart from those (in sadly increasing numbers) members of the crowd conspicuously waving glasses of fresh orange juice, the rest of us were, it is true, having no qualms at all about quaffing. I personally was well into my second quaff of the evening and just warming up. Units be damned, I was most certainly not about to include the Ladies Lunch earlier on that day in my calculations of glasses imbibed on a weekly basis. No way can I get through a LL quaff-free.

I wandered around the room, pressing the flesh.

Christmas Trees were the order of the day. The prize went to a well-travelled representative of a South American country who would have put Mussolini to shame except that he was listing very heavily to the left with the weight of all his gold and enamel. Down amongst the baubles though, he confessed that somewhere there was a FIFA medal secreted. I moved on to parlay with some of the more beautiful caparisons and headgear and ran straight into the person I had been wanting to meet since arriving in London: the Queens very own Riding Master.

In need of exercise other than the raising of the elbow, I had been looking for a horse to ride, but as far as I could see it would take the entire day to drive out into the country to find anything with hooves smaller than large dinner plates. Even the trek to Richmond would put me at risk of being late for lunch and thus not to be contemplated. I could not fail to notice, though, the rather splendid black specimens of Irish extraction pawing at the ground within Hyde Park Barracks, a mere ten minute cycle ride from the Embassy. There were, if you will pardon the expression, a couple of not unsurmountable difficulties to overcome, but nothing too worrying. First, one needed to be awarded classification as a "civilian rider." This involved getting to know the Queen's Riding Master, passing a test in the indoor ring and subsequently riding out in the park accompanied by two superior officers. There was one other minor drawback to the whole scheme: riders had to present themselves, correctly dressed in velvet collared hacking jacket, shirt, tie and pudding basin hard hat by 7 a.m. in order to identify the horse which they had been allotted, to find a saddle, bridle, stirrups and girth which might conceivably fit, unearth a body brush and a hoof pick, groom and polish it, get it saddled and bridled and be ready for the off by 8 a.m. latest in groups of twos or threes. This, presumably, in order to avoid 18 hands of Irish blood mowing down the joggers, commuters, Nannies with their babies and other insomniacs who began invading Hyde Park at that hour.

So I was thrilled to meet him in such convivial surroundings and immediately invited him to the Embassy the following day for a late tea, hoping very much that he would stay on for something a little stronger which might have pleaded my case for me more eloquently than the vision of my rather rusty abilities to canter around in circles without stirrups. But, quite rightly, rules is rules, especially where Her Majesty's horses are concerned so I puffed off to do the test and presumably was considered good enough to be allowed to proceed to Stage Two: the Exhibition of Skills in the Park Itself.

On a gloomy, grey, cold and drizzly morning I pedalled up on my bike, chained it to the nearest tree, and headed for the trial.

We adjusted our stirrups, climbed aboard and set off in stately fashion, chit-chatting of this and that, as one does with a couple of stunningly handsome and sexily uniformed officers accompanying one upon either side with ramrod precision along Rotten Row at what seemed like dawn. All went very smoothly, everything under control. give or take an Irish tendency to throw its head and weight around. At the walk, however, this was not too much of a problem. We proceeded to a trot. It may be of interest to note that when ridden out on parade, those beasts have everything but the kitchen sink in their mouths. Civilian riders are given the option of a plain jointed snaffle or a plain jointed snaffle as far as I could see when tacking up in the gloom. The trot needed a little more concentration. Wisely it was decided that I should go on ahead of the other two and begin the canter alone to avoid any misconception on dobbin's part that he was heading for the straight in Tipperary and should give it his best. We were supposed to be talking Perfect Control, after all. Remembering all the many hours of insults I had had hurled at me as a child in Kent by misogynistic instructors, I sat firmly in the seat in the approved "F*** the bl***y horse" position, heels down, elbows in and not so much as a glimmer of daylight betwixt knee and saddle. We were taught to canter with tiny slips of paper tucked under our backsides and inside each knee, and woe betide anybody who arrived back at the stable door with even one slip missing. Years of riding in Italy had left me somewhat lax about sitting to the canter, but I needed to impress the Brits, here. Or so I thought.

The first buck hit me as I was merely contemplating the application of heel to flank, and once into a canter proper, they grew in proportion. Gritting my teeth, I kept as close to the saddle as possible and was still on board, just, when my two companions rode gracefully up on either side of me. Using the forward, Caprilli position. The forward position for the uninitiated, is when the bum is not in the saddle at all because the rider is suspended over the neck of the horse thereby avoiding any turbulence which may be taking place beneath him.

"You may notice, Signora," they said respectfully, "that we have adopted the Caprilli seat in your honour as an Italian." I was, indeed most tremendously honoured. And no less relieved.

Upon returning to my tree, I discovered it remarkably free of bicycles of any description. A stern looking soldier in camouflage was keeping watch.

"Lost something?" he enquired suspiciously.

"Yes – I thought I'd left my bike here....."

"They've taken it away to be blown up," he said. "Controlled explosion. Third this week. Can't leave bikes chained to lampposts or trees no more," he said regretfully. "If you run you might just be in time to save it."

I ran. I found it surrounded by sandbags and managed to save its life, though not without getting a right earful from the security guard. I mean, how much Semtex can you fit into a ladies bike? And why would I want to blow up a tree anyway? Beats me. I pedalled off home in the rain to prepare to meet the Queen and other Members of the Royal Family.

Once a year the entire Diplomatic Corps to the Court of St. James is invited to a dinner and dance at Buckingham Palace. Decorations and National Dress, long gowns and gloves, jewels – it is a spectacular affair. Ambassadors are lined up throughout a series of State Rooms according to the order in which they had arrived in London. Drinks are provided but whisked away before the Royal Party makes its entrance. The old hands refuse them anyway. No point in applying all that unaccustomed lipstick in order to leave it on the rim of a glass just when you need it to smile at her Majesty. One year they served spinach at the buffet dinner. Not a good idea. Avoid at all costs.

The Ladies in Waiting and the Marshal of the Diplomatic Corps appeared in the doorway. We stopped vying for elbow room and stood to attention, intelligent expressions and fixed smiles at the ready. We rehearsed, or rather our Heads of Mission did – the rest of us reckoned we could wing it with a dazzling smile – a little repartee in case we were asked to be Conversationally Eloquent. The royal party made its way around the room, pausing to exchange apposite niceties with every representative of every country represented. Never will I understand how her Majesty does that. She never gets it wrong and has something suitable to say to each of them with virtually no prompting at all.

The Italian Ambassador straightened his tie for the sixth time that evening. I don't know what I do to bow ties. They are the embodiment of perfection when we leave the house, but once into the throng and they wilt into a foetal position and are in need of therapy at ten minute intervals if they are to survive the rest of the evening bearing any resemblance at all to an item of neckwear. He rehearsed his most serious political and cultural gambits. He practised mentally a couple of linguistic turns of phrase. He reminded himself that ma'am should rhyme with jam or spam and not palm. He took the extended hand and bowed with infinite respect.

She paused in front of him and thought for a moment before looking at me.

"I hear," she said, "that you are riding my horses in the Park?"

Ha! I am Addressed Therefore I Exist.

I *love* this country.

CHAPTER THREE

Most Ambassadors consider themselves lucky, or unlucky, depending upon their point of view, if they have one Presidential visit to contend with during the course of their careers. We had survived two by this stage and were heading for another semi private one. The difference between official and semi private is that during the latter variety everybody of importance sleeps under our roof instead of getting B&B in Buckingham Palace. Thus, three days before The Arrival, I was running round in circles checking for soaps, shower gels, room sprays, coat hangers, adaptors for Italian plugs, mineral water, spare blankets etc. in four bedrooms whilst Cook (why Cook?) was pouring litre upon litre of caustic soda down all the loos in a vain attempt to eradicate a sudden persistent smell of drains. Tables were set up in the downstairs dining room, (dinner Monday night), a table was set up in the first floor Venetian room, (dinner Tuesday night), a table was set up on the third floor, (breakfast for the "also rans"), a table was set up on the landing (bodyguards), a table was installed in the President's suite (private breakfast for the serving of...) and a dozen tables were set up across the entire Piano Nobile to accommodate a hundred or so Special Guests at our own intimate Banquet for the Queen.

Thank God, I thought, for the official luncheon at Buckingham Palace. At least it would give them time to wash the dishes.

Emerging one morning from my bedroom, I perceived six foot of hand made pinstriped suiting crawling up and down the staircase with a spirit level and a tape measure. On closer inspection I recognised it as containing a highly placed colleague of Giorgio's who I had been warned would be coming to prepare the ground for the visit. I hadn't realised they meant it literally. He had, to my sure knowledge, a degree in Politics, Philosophy and Economics and spoke seven languages, some of them even in a reasonably grammatically correct fashion and with an accent that could be understood by the natives of the country concerned. He had an impressive title, one which gave him the right to be addressed as Excellency, but there he was, on all fours, crawling up the stairs. When he had finished with the staircase, he turned his attention to my teaspoons and table cloths which, with a certain sense of foreboding, I could see he would feel obliged to trash. He had already condemned the bath towels and made copious notes concerning the flower vases. Prior to measuring the staircase, I should mention that he had been spotted skating around the guest suite on the bedside mats in order to test their degree of stability, and was heard to be ordering rubber underlay in a voice of shocked horror. Rubber underlay, it would seem, is essential to the life or death of a visiting Head of State and it is upon such things that the future careers of Heads of Protocol may well hang.

Having counted the stairs, he began pacing out the number of steps required from the dining room to the nearest loo, from the sitting room to the nearest loo, from the front door to the nearest loo and from the nearest loo to the next nearest loo.

After which, I was given to understand, he would personally engage an electrician, a full time plumber, and a lift technician, all of whom would be on twenty-four hour alert throughout the ensuing three days. Furthermore, an ambulance would be on constant standby within whistling distance. I was not brought up to whistle, and on the rare occasions that I have attempted this facial gymnastic, usually in a desperate attempt to separate a headstrong Beagle from a half-empty crisp packet or a four year old's ice-cream, I cannot say that I have had much success. But then Beagles, as is well known, are acoustically deprived and unless it is dinner time they suffer from selective deafness. Rather like husbands. I could only trust that either Giorgio or I would be up to the task should the need arise.

The best, however, was yet to come.

Since all our silver, glass and porcelain was firmly engraved with the royal coat of arms of the former King of the House of Savoy, it would have to be hidden in the back of a cupboard – or more precisely, several cupboards - for the duration of the visit. A President of a Republic entertaining her Majesty the Queen could hardly be seen eating off royal plates once the property of a former Italian monarchy. Republican plates were, therefore, flown in specially in sealed crates and left lying around my admittedly extensive hallway for everyone to trip over until such time as the Quirinale Palace could spare their only technical expert with the necessary security clearance for opening crates of tableware and send him over to the London Embassy to unpack it all.

A matter of hours before we sat down to dinner in the presence of two Heads of State and innumerable members of the Royal Family and of our respective governments, the usual parasites managed to wriggle themselves on to the guest list by dint of begging at the doors of people in high places. Never one to miss a chance to make a dramatic entrance, sidle up to VIPs and drop a couple of dozen curtseys, Ms. Peacock skidded around in her tent of many colours, intent upon getting her face photographed for publication in next week's glossies. Personally I loathe the whole paparazzi bit. Is there anything worse than having a bevy of professional photographers aiming their lenses at you for two solid hours throughout, for example, what would otherwise have been a charming concert if you could just have been permitted to concentrate on the music rather than upon presenting your least worse profile to the camera? The whole thing is frightfully unnerving since after the first half hour you realise that their patience is also wearing thin as they search for your least unattractive angle. Confirmation of this arrives with the photos themselves two days later when you realise they are four in number, despite the fact that you remember with crystal clarity at least 673 flash bulbs popping during just the first movement. Mr. Party Gatecrasher also managed to get himself invited at the last moment, though not without some huffing and puffing from our pet butler who had spent days aligning the numerous knives, forks, glasses, menus, bread plates, name cards, salt cellars, napkins and similar bric-à-brac on the tables in order to leave room for the flowers. Now he was asked to add an extra place. Just like that. And for a large gentleman, too. One who would require elbow room. He considered briefly seeking alternative employment with the

Canadians next door, but realised he would never fit into their uniforms. We ourselves had been most accommodating in this respect and, having given up trying to find him a jacket in his size over the Internet (and you cannot imagine what comes up on the Internet when you are searching for maids' and butlers' uniforms....) had been obliged to permit him to wear our predecessor's cast-off suit jackets with a pair of Moss Bros bespoke striped pants. Our predecessor, one should understand, had not shared Giorgio's predilection for a diet of mineral water and boiled broccoli.

Everything went smoothly: the butler buttled to perfection and the cook cooked with inspiration. Apart from his brilliance in the kitchen, I privately suspected the latter of having degrees in computer sciences, management and accounting, economics, building and construction works, and advanced psychology. He was the only one who could reset the central heating system when global warming gave us snowstorms in July and heat-waves in November. He was the only one who could chivvy the handyman to repaint a whole floor in the space of a week without dripping pots of deluxe eggshell over the carpets and furniture. Only he could cook a buffet dinner for a hundred and fifty people and then spend the rest of the evening hanging out of a third floor window in the pouring rain trying to repair the T.V. cable. And only he would have the nerve to scrape all the mud off the latest delivery of mushrooms and send it back to the suppliers, weighed and neatly packaged in cling film, with a request they should replace it with the equivalent weight in mushrooms. As ordered. And paid for.

All in all, we spent a lot of time eating and drinking for our country. This has, of course, always been one of the requisites of a successful diplomat and I could understand why Manu tried to escape her obligations so frequently. Ability to consume vast quantities of food and alcohol without incurring permanent damage to the arteries, to the liver or to one's ability to make a coherent speech or semi-intelligible conversation was part of the job description. There was a time when a new entrant to the Italian Corps would be invited to a formal meal during the course of which he would be encouraged to demonstrate his prowess at wielding a knife and fork whilst simultaneously sustaining a meaningful conversation in a minimum of three languages. A career could be truncated before it even began by a single strand of wayward spaghetti. A high ranking German colleague once confessed to me that ultimately he owed his success to having unflinchingly pursued an argument about macro economics in fluent Mandarin despite his Foreign Secretary having thoughtlessly spiked a chicken Kiev with excessive fervour, thereby releasing a stream of hot liquefied garlic butter all over our friend's new suit. According to the country to which it has been assigned, your diplomatic digestive tract is expected to deal with all manner of culinary horrors:, trotter of pig, tripe of cow, leg of frog, tail of ox, crackling of grasshopper. The hair of dog is manna from heaven after such abuse.

CHAPTER FOUR

June had been a hat, glove and take a blanket month, what with Ascot, garden parties, Trooping the Colour, open air operas and various charitable fetes. July was spent trying to cram at least three cocktail parties into an evening before heading off to dinner with muddy heels - the result of sinking into soggy lawns whilst huddling into a pashmina. All too soon autumn and winter were upon us. With the dark beginning to descend over London ever earlier in the afternoons, Beagle and I retreated to our den, she to her basket, me to my computer. I completed an article for an otherwise intellectual magazine for whom I wrote fairly innocuous bits of Diplomatic Gossip under an assumed name and then turned my attention to the emails.

To: Maman
From: Frankie
Forget Nigeria. The latest one is Sicilian.
xxx F

Sicilian. As if one in the family wasn't enough.

To: Manu
From: Sarah
????????????????????

I was halfway through the line of question marks when the phone rang.

"Sarah?"

"In person. Who is....?"

"Paolo. Come stai?"

I held forth for a few minutes. Usual stuff. Giorgio, the children, the grandchildren, London, the busy life, the weather. When I got to the weather, I thought I had probably overplayed my part, so I shut up for a second.

Silence. Can't have that. I started again.

"Paolo, where are you?"

"In Rome. Home posting. We missed each other by a matter of weeks."

"I had no idea you were in Italy. Is Manuela with you?"

"That's why I was ringing. I was rather hoping she might be with you."

Oh no. Not again. Now what?

"Paolo, I haven't heard from that unpredictable wife of yours for ages. I send emails into cyber space and get no answer. I don't get offended because I know by now that she occasionally disappears off my radar – usually when she is fighting a losing battle with her weight and that she will reappear when she has kicked the depression or lost half a kilo and feels like re-establishing contact. That's the way she is. But no, she isn't in London- or at least not with me. When did you last see her?"

It was not reassuring. He had moved back to Rome on the understanding that she would follow from Peru via Buenos Aires three weeks later just as soon as he had rented a new flat for them both. He had managed the move single-handedly. The flat was all ready for her arrival, but she had told him she was going to travel for a week or two before reaching

Italy, that she would call from time to time because her mobile phone had been stolen and because she did not want to be disturbed. He had not had any news for three weeks.

"How was her weight?"

"Never been so good."

"How was the face lift?"

"Fine."

Something was wrong. Even allowing for his preoccupation, he was not sounding particularly enthusiastic. He had taken delivery of an almost brand new wife, after all, following that face lift. Was he cross about the £9.000? What was £9.000 between husband and wife, these days, in exchange for a sleek wrinkle-free new model? He should be so lucky. Some of us were obliged to sit with our backs to the light, spend fortunes on useless face creams and still have to airbrush the photographs.

"Paolo?"

"What?"

"Are you telling me everything?"

There was another pause. I refrained from mentioning that the weather in London was grey and that clouds were gathering and that it looked like rain. I flatter myself that I know how to judge the moment.

Eventually he spoke.

"We had a row."

Good. Nothing new there, then.

"She was a bit upset."

I could imagine the scene. Manuela, with all her hot South American blood did "Being A Bit Upset" along the lines of Norma discovering that Pollione has betrayed her with Adalgisa.

Betrayed. I had a sudden suspicion.

"Paolo? Do you want to tell me what happened? I can't help you without knowing what her reasons might have been this time. If it was the weight problem, you'll probably find her hiding in some health farm with a quack feeding her illegal slimming pills. If, on the other hand, sex is rearing its inevitable head, I'm afraid I need to know a few details in order to point you in the right direction."

Another silence. Men are such rubbish at this game. He had, however, been playing the ostrich for long enough and was now getting seriously worried. A confession was near and I was the only one who might just be able to help.

"Sarah you must promise me to be discreet. It hasn't always been easy living with Manuela – you must realise that. She's pretty impossible at times."

He had a point. But what the hell had she gone and done this time?

I began to feel sorry for the poor man.

"I do know that, Paolo. I was the first to try and talk sense into her each time, but keeping Manu under control is not an easy task. Is there anyone else, do you think?"

I remembered all her past follies. With a facelift taking twenty years off her age, she was probably out there cavorting with a teenager somewhere. No wonder she hadn't dared reply to any of my emails. How could she?

I cursed her silently for the unprincipled, unfeeling selfish cow that she was.

Wasn't.

He cleared his throat nervously and took a deep breath.

"She discovered I was having a relationship with a younger woman. A girl I met at a conference during a trip back to Rome. One of the Foreign Office secretaries who were there taking notes and things."

For "things," read "husbands," I thought, resignedly. Poor old Manu. Gave up the men, gave up the wrinkles, gave up the booze and then got displaced in middle age by some damned singleton out to get herself a sexy little diplomatic passport. I could see both sides of the argument but obviously I was only prepared to commiserate with one of them.

"Paolo! Should I congratulate you on your new lease of life and happiness and wish you a exhilarating future with your new young lady friend? Are you madly in love, both of you? Are you feeling liberated and light headed and completely over the moon?"

I laid it on a bit thick, admittedly. Like I said, it was not too hard to foresee which side I would come down upon. I also reckoned that by now he would most probably be under some degree of pressure from the new plaything and would most probably be feeling he had already lost his illusory freedom. For someone who was in the throes of an exciting new affair, he didn't sound particularly besotted.

"Sarah. We have to find her. I need her back."

Aha! We recognise that symptom. Ms. Totally Dedicated piling on the pressure? Demanding a commitment? Ready to leap into the convenient vacuum? How very useful wives can be at times for getting one out of tricky, ultimately undesirable situations. Come back Manu. All, but ALL will be forgiven. Just get this Other Woman off my back before I have to go through a messy divorce, pay lots of alimony, alienate my children and lose the 20% allowance I get to feed and water a spouse.

I promised to do my utmost, though beyond praying that she had taken flight with her computer in her hand baggage, I wasn't sure where I was going to begin.

To: Manu
From: Sarah
Manu you shithead. Make contact, for goodness sake.
I promise I won't tell Paolo where you are, but we are all of us worried sick. He more than anyone. Come and hide in London for a bit. I swear not to tell him you are here and will feed you only undressed lettuce leaves until you are back to svelte and competitive proportions.
We love you.
Sarah

To: Frankie
From: Maman
So excited that you are coming over.
Can't wait to see you and the small things. Hope I have remembered all the fine details regarding nappies and dietary requirements. Memory not improving with age. Senior moments abound. Am even stuffing myself with some pill (must not be working - can't remember what it's called...) which is reputed to be a homeo-pathetic memory enhancer.
Will expect you all in time for lunch.
xxx M

I was awaiting the arrival of twenty females for morning coffee, tea, juices and babble in order to organise some Charity Do Dah. In the midst of this, a group of hefties were going to be winching a grand piano in through the windows of the salon where the ladies would all be gathered to discuss (mainly) the quality and variety of my biscuits. The piano was for a concert we were giving for another charity that evening. This, in turn, was to be followed by a seated Black Tie dinner for the hundred odd concert goers who were paying a fortune per plate to consume the remains of the biscuit crumbs transformed, doubtless, into a dessert of such delectability that I would have difficulty getting rid of them until well after midnight. During the course of my coffee morning, the grandchildren were expected to turn up on the doorstep with their wheelie suitcases bearing enough clothes to see them through till next Sunday whilst their parents hove off to a wedding in Scotland. Also Giorgio had a working lunch, so my main problem was going to be to get the ladies out in time for his guests to ascend the magnificent staircase with dignity, as opposed to being bowled over by the full force of the chattering magpies descending, late, to pick up their kiddies from school or wherever it is they go at that age. The timing was out on all sides by a critical ten minutes, so the scene half way up, or down, depending on your perspective, bore a strong resemblance to a busy Underground station in the middle of rush hour when all but one of the exits has been closed for emergency repairs.

To: Manu
From: Sarah
Ever heard of Internet cafés?
Great places for pickups. Nice dark, salacious atmosphere perfect for groping. Depending upon which country you are in, ideal for asking that handsome stranger sitting next to you where the hell the asterisk is situated on the French/ German/ Chinese keyboard confronting you.
Press Reply to Sender NOW.
Please.
Love you – Sarah

But I might have been talking to myself.

CHAPTER FIVE

Our predecessors did not share the same bedroom.

There will be those, I suppose, that would consider this to be too much information.

But wait…. You *do* need to know this.

Frankie and Marco went off to the wedding leaving us with the toddlers. We tucked them up side by side in the room next to the master bedroom and threatened them with all manner of punishments if they dared to wake us a minute before 9 a.m. and they snuggled down very cosily with teddies and bunnies.

And, bless them, refrained from waking us until 09.30, at which civilised hour they crashed through our door and started jumping on our heads.

Well, weren't you good boys and girls, then. Did you only just wake up?

No, we've been doing somersaults on our beds. And then the policemans came. And the big one let me try his hat on.

Yeah, ok, guys. Don't tell stories, now. What have you been up to?

No, it's TRUE! She pressed this button and then the policemans came into our bedroom.

No I didn't. HE pressed it first. And they had guns too. But they let us try their hats on.

DIDN'T SO! SHE pressed it first and then …..

And so on.

Right. No more adventure videos before bedtime, that's for sure. Overactive imaginations I do not need in the under sixes whilst in my care.

Since it is pouring with rain, we plan a game of hide and seek around the Embassy to take their minds off all these imaginary exploits.

Round about 11 o'clock the phones start ringing.

First a highly apologetic security officer who had taken it upon himself to personally escort the Diplomatic Protection Squad up to our private apartments and perform a commando style eruption into the bedroom of his former Excellency who, they were at this stage convinced, was being abducted at gunpoint by terrorists. Then afore-mentioned Dip. Prot. Sq. wanting to know why the current Excellency was sleeping so far away from his panic button, thereby potentially rendering all their best efforts useless in the face of an eventual attack. Finally daughter and son-in-law anxiously wanting to know how the little darlings had slept first time away from home and whether they hadn't been too overawed by all those big rooms and being so far from mummy and daddy?

We reassured them on that account.

To: Alex
From: Maman
Pity you couldn't manage to get over this week too. Grandchildren are definitely the best invention since daughters.
Xxx M

To: Manuela
From: Sarah
Ok, I am trying desperate measures. The *things* I do for you at the risk of totally losing all face. I just cannot think of anyone else to contact who might

possibly have any inkling as to your whereabouts. To show I'm not just looking for an excuse, I will copy you into the correspondence. So there.
Love, Sarah

To: Michael
Copy: Manuela
From: Sarah

Dear Michael,
We have lost Manuela - do you by any chance have any idea where she might be hiding? Please use your inexplicably efficient networks to do something useful and hunt her down. We are all desperately worried.
Anonymity guaranteed, promise!
Regards to Svetlana,
Sarah
P.S. Please note new email address. We are in London now.

CHAPTER SIX

Still nothing from Manuela.

Paolo was becoming increasingly hysterical and wondering whether he should risk starting a scandal by contacting the police. He rang every morning and I tried to listen sympathetically and offer useful advice, but we were both of us becoming very worried. I persuaded him to leave it one more week, put the phone down and slid silently out of the house dragging a reluctant Beagle who had caught a whiff of hot croissant and homemade scones. Some important personage was having a working breakfast with H.E. in the Small Dining Room which was, as usual, un-strategically placed between me and the front door. I was dressed, (if you could call it that), picturesquely but with great practicality to deal with mud and dog crap. I had two whole hours of freedom before cutting the tape at a Charity Bazaar, checking the monthly accounts and overseeing the arrangements for the evening's jollities.

It should have been a perfectly normal dinner party. Chaps and chapesses from various walks of life, a sprinkling of lords of the land, a few respected titles, the odd Ambassador, the usual bevy of non meat/ fish/ wheat eaters. A couple of pregnancies but nothing so advanced it might require urgent bowls of hot water between courses. The odd late arrival but not enough to ruin a soufflé. A handful of smokers but once they had registered the news that ashtrays were not an option and that the Embassy was a fag free zone, they dutifully went out into the rain or up a nearby chimney to inhale. Nothing to startle one out of one's self-contented diplomatic rut. Except that the husband of the Guest of Honour, tearing himself free from the delectable young buttock he had been guarding with his life, suddenly bounded over like an over enthusiastic puppy.

"You still writing that crappy column?" he twinkled.

Of course – *that's* what it is that I do. I'd quite forgotten. What with trying to convince the Foreign Ministry to inject enough cash into our coffers to prevent the top floor bedroom from crashing down into the kitchen. And dissuading the ensuing bevy of builders from stuffing their empty beer cans down the waste pipes thereby causing a blockage which ensures that the first floor loos explode every time anyone takes a shower. And begging the Immigration Authorities not to deport the only one of my Filipinos who can recognise her left hand from her right. Or at least not until after our next dinner party. And encouraging one of the afore-mentioned Polish plumbers to check into rehab before he chips any more paint off the decorative flowerpots adorning the entrance to the garage with his white van.

"Because you've got some seriously salacious material here tonight," he winked. "Keep your eyes peeled."

We sashayed on down to the dining room, my literary antennae waving furiously. In the manner of Beagle running to ground a discarded bagel, my nose twitched its way around the table in search of salaciousness and the scent of scandal.

The Chinese Ambassador was holding forth about hawkish attitudes vis-à-vis Ilaq and Ilan. A peer of the realm was discussing other people's taxes. I zoomed in on an earnest couple on the far side of the table, watching closely for any signs of extra marital activity beneath the damask table cloth. Not so much as an elevated napkin. Not a hint of dastardly doings in the entire room. One person texting furiously under cover of her handbag. Probably just checking the au pair hadn't gone out clubbing. Nobody even got up from table to visit the Embassy cloakrooms, which was a relief because at the rate the Poles were going, they'd have had to climb over raw sewage to "powder their noses." If you see what I mean. Whatever it was that was happening beneath all those respectable outward appearances, I was clearly not getting it.

Perhaps that was the trouble.

Perhaps I should get out more. That's the problem with us famous authors starving away in our garrets. We miss out on life. We don't get in on the act. We spend too much time being screwed by our computers. Wonder what happened to Michael. Not a thought for a grandmother to entertain.

To: Sarah

From: Michael

Actually I spotted you in Kensington Gardens this morning being taken for a walk by that Beagle, but being the soul of discretion, as always, I popped into the infamous men's toilets. The things you make me do, really.

I am working on your Missing Person dilemma and in exchange for a lunch date I could possibly help to throw some light on your friend's whereabouts if you were particularly nice to me.
Tomorrow, 1.15p m., outside Westminster underground station.
Best regards,
Michael

Telepathy or what? Now I know what it must feel like to have a stalker, though I suppose he has every right to return to the UK too every now and then. Wonder if he came back alone.

Ping!

To: Sarah
From: Michael
P.S. Which Svetlana?

Not telepathy. Thought police. Must have this room swept for hidden mikes just in case.
At least he had avoided fixing a rendez-vous in Chelsea where most of the Italian community were to be found lunching these days. Westminster. House of Commons? More likely he's got a friend with a houseboat.

CHAPTER SEVEN

And there he was, on time for once, recognisable by the customary copy of The Times, open at the crossword page, under one arm. Looking a bit older but twinkling as usual with amusement at my embarrassment.

"Sarah! You haven't changed a bit! London obviously suits you to perfection."

"You too – though is that a hint of grey I spy around the temples? And you haven't finished the crossword – bad sign that. How are the Russians and Calabrians getting along?"

"Better than ever. Kindred spirits. Follow me, there's a pretty sleazy pub somewhere round here where we can get something to eat without fear of being spotted by anyone we know."

It was 4.30 before we finally emerged from the pub, arm in arm and the best of friends. Just as it should have been right from the beginning. We had laughed together, looked back over old times, remembered all our old friends in Rome, in Brussels and in Moscow and generally had a wonderful time. We had, after all, known each other for a good many years, and there was an awful lot of catching up and explaining to do. Best of all, he knew exactly how I could contact Manuela and I was so grateful for that piece of information I didn't even bother to ask how he knew.

To: Manu
From: Sarah
No wonder I wasn't getting through to you – how dare you change your email address without telling me? PLEASE (shouting) get in touch AT ONCE and stop being so bludi selfish. Paolo is desperate and so are we all. Please get on a plane and let us discuss it at least. I promise not to give your new address to anyone just as long as you keep the lines of communication open.
Miss you, love you, need you back. All of us.
Sarah

To: Sarah
From: Manu
Go away.
I am wallowing in deep depression and do not wish to be disturbed, especially not by Paolo. How dare he. After all I went through making myself 20 years younger just for him and renouncing the sins of the flesh. I hate all men and I especially hate all Italians. If you continue bombarding me with messages I'll end up hating you too.
Anyway I have this mega problem with answering your emails.
Whereas to the majority of the stuff that used to hit my In Box I could apply one of the foll. formulae:

Ha Ha
Gosh

No, Really?
Noted. Will Be There
Can't Do It
Sorry
Effoff

...yours' require an in-depth, intellectual, humorous (um, how do you spell that?) well, witty, response which could one day be published in serial form when I might need to eke out my twilight years as a divorcée earning peanuts instead of silver surfing.
So just go away and leave me alone.
P.S . So that toad gave away my new address? I always warned you he was a bastard. What did it cost you? Not that I care.
M

O.K. I had made it through the fog and prowling black dogs to reach her and apparently the sense of humour was still alive and well even if she couldn't spell it. The next step would require all the diplomacy and insouciance I could muster.

To: Manu
From: Sarah
Silver surf yourself. Just because you gave up dentists and I developed an allergy to military attachés doesn't mean we are over the hill. Any boringly common complaints associated with age can, I have discovered, be cured instantly by increasing the supply of white wine and chocolate. Pref. intravenously. Same remedy applicable to boring dinner parties.

Recommended reply to above :

Gosh, really?
There. Have even saved you the trouble.
xxx Sarah
P.S. Keep in touch, love, do. We all need you.

To: Maman
From: Alex
Can you DHL me your blue hat? I have to go to a
wedding next week in Palermo, and refuse to spend
money on headgear as well as an outfit.
Alex

To: Alex
From: Maman
To my immense distress, hat in question bears, at
time of going to press, close resemblance to our
Russian cook's blinis. Cleaning up the flat I found it
wrecked beyond belief under a particularly heavy set
of earthenware pots inside a cupboard stinking of
mould emanating from a culture of advanced life
forms growing out of the walls. Result of the leaking
 pipe which I had to fly over especially to fix when
your sister was too busy introducing her latest beau
to the leprechauns somewhere on the Emerald Isle.
And you were paddling round the Dolomites in
boots. You may remember. Nor did I have time to
send it for re-blocking. Can supply numerous
funereal substitutes in varying shades of black, or a
serious mistake I once made in bright green. Nobody
wears hats to weddings in Italy anyway. Just wear
your own hair.

To: Frankie
From: Maman
What's going *on* here? Since when does Alex go to weddings in *hats*? Dare I hope for a civilising Sicilian influence at work? Or was that last week?
xxx maman

To: Manu
From: Sarah
My wedding anniversary, would you believe? How many of our colleagues do you know that can notch up 35 years?
Your time is running out, and anyway, where the hell ARE you??
Sarah

To: Sarah
From: Manu
Congratulations! Not many. The odds were/are pretty much stacked against us.
They all end up re- marrying their secretaries, as far as I can see. No imagination at all.
M

To: Manu
From: Sarah
You just stick in there, love. You are still very much in the running. If it is any consolation, it looks very much to me as though the fascination of Miss Typing Pool has already worn thin and anyway, who are you to act the offended party? I have it on authority

though, that like all men he might need a little face saving scenario which I am prepared to write for you when you decide you can face the world again.

So please hurry up and come to your senses.

Waiting, Sarah

*   *   *   *

"Paolo?"

"Sarah!" The intensity of hope in his voice vibrated in my ear all the way down the line. "Any news?"

"A bit. She won't say where she is hiding, but once in a while I get an answer to my emails. She's really taken it badly. You men do choose your moment. Why do you always manage to dump the dutiful wedded right bang in mid menopause?" Even I had my doubts about the dutiful wedded bit, but it had slipped out of its own accord and in any case he was so anxious and miserable he didn't even seem to notice.

"Do you think I should notify the police after all?"

Oooooo. Men? Ask me about 'em. Bring her back in handcuffs, perhaps? Bad psychology, Paolo. "Not if you want her ever to speak to you again, no. Tell me though – how's it going with the girlfriend?"

In fact, I was fairly sure that it wasn't going at all. Not anywhere. By all accounts, she had given up waiting and was currently launching a two pronged attack on an ageing colonel and a younger First Secretary. Not that Paolo would give me any satisfaction by releasing this information: I'd had it from the Foreign Office information service, alias one of the drivers who, faithful to tradition, were still sitting around playing cards and following Ministry gossip whilst awaiting assignments.

Paolo, of course, could not admit all this over the phone with, probably, one of her cronies listening in on the extension. He pleaded calls coming in on other lines and promised to ring back later in the day. He needn't have bothered. I knew before he even told me that it was all over.

To: Maman
From Alex:
Please get Frankie off my back. She keeps making stupid, big sister remarks like "Do I know what his intentions are?" Of course I know what his intentions are.
M'enfin!
xxx Alex

CHAPTER EIGHT

It was once again that time of year when anybody who aspires to be anybody has to be seen at the Chelsea Flower Show. Why, I wondered, as I eased myself into the mid-calf floral print skirt, (mid-c. floral p. is de rigeur at the CFS), do I do this?

Well, if you are also invited to lunch, the champagne is free and flowing, of course, which is always an incentive. If, also, you are desperate to find a mechanical mole that digs up your garden leaving humps, or a life sized lost-wax reproduction of a Dartmoor pony to stick under your apple trees, or a pair of purple rubber clogs with matching plastic chrysanthemum pompom, or a wicker watering can with polythene lining to keep the water from falling out, (now WHERE is the logic in that?), or a winch to raise and lower your hanging baskets, or a matching green welligog-boot bag, then this is definitely the place to go.

Equally, if your idea of a garden consists of a minimum of flowers juxtaposed with a maximum of cerebral significance, allegory, inspirational illusion, liberally spattered with man-made acrylic panels, lumps of concrete, wire and stone effigies (your thinking man's garden gnomes), rusting water features, (yes, water RUSTS, that's what it DOES), then you will enjoy. But don't expect to find God or Divine Inspiration therein.

If, on the other hand, you actually wanted to *see* any flowers, then forget it. And I'm five foot ten and a half and can see over the top of most. It is, however, an insight into the British love of queuing. They queue for the show gardens, they queue for the food, they queue for the mineral water and the ice cream, and they queue for the toilets. They even queue for the picnic areas. Add to that the fact that my Hospitality lunch was even worse than anything that our former cook could ever have dreamed up on his bad days (and he had them all too frequently), and it can be understood why I decided that in future I would be sending the butler. Keep him away from burning coffee pots for a few hours.

I took some photos of the more spectacular arrangements, hoping to inspire him to greater efforts for our National Day party which was looming once again and niggling at my conscience.

To: Sarah
From: Manu
I'm coming to Europe. Sleeping pills didn't work. Need to visit Dignitas. You can tell that bastard if you like, but don't expect me to meet or even talk to him.
Manu

Now that's more like it. Norma is prepared to speak to Clotilde. Stay by the phone, Pollione.

To : Manu
From :Sarah
I'm here and waiting for you.
Sorry you will miss the National Day party – I know how disappointed you will be. Cook has made a thousand mini choux and tartelettes, and the rest of

them have been up since dawn breaking glasses and doing the flowers. Wish you were already here.
Don't be long, please.
And call Paolo. He needs you. We all do.
Love, Sarah

A feeling of disquiet came upon me on the exact same date every year, and had absolutely nothing do with the changing season and the resultant necessity to go out and buy a new handbag. The completely useless waste of time and money which is known throughout the diplomatic and consular corps as Our National Day goes, for the uninitiated, as follows.
A couple of months before the important date, the secretaries are kept busy fielding telephone calls from aspiring hopefuls who have suddenly remembered they hold a passport declaring them to be a citizen of your country and who have heard down the expat grapevine that the canapés are pretty good and the booze flows free and fast and in unlimited quantities. There were half a dozen old ducks in Rome, I recall, who would turn up every year regular as clockwork, dressed in silver lamé from head to toe and bearing oversized shopping bags into which they would none too discreetly slide whole platefuls of delicacies painstakingly prepared for weeks beforehand by the cook of the Italian Ambassador to the Holy See. In Russia they headed straight for the vodka without passing go or collecting 200 blinis with or without the caviar, and were invariably escorted out at the end of the festivities quoting Dostoyevsky at the tops of their stentorian voices when not bellowing forth with choice segments from Eugene Onegin. In Nigeria

they would turn up with four wives in tow and stay for the day. In a country like the U.K. where inciting folk to indulge in excessive alcohol consumption is probably already on the statute books, we will soon be needing to claim diplomatic immunity if we wish to avoid numerous hours of community service.

Apart from the freewheelers, one invites the local politicians. According to the number and calibre of whoever deigns to turn up, the success or ignominious failure of your mission is judged. Or used to be. These days most politicians have far more important things to do than queuing up on a garishly coloured stair carpet for half an hour in order to shake hands with an Excellency, grab a warm drink, be trampled on by the multitude and bombarded with dumb questions should they have the misfortune to be recognised. They can do all that in their constituencies every weekend. VIPs and notables in general get enough to eat and drink in the comfort of their or their friends' own homes anyway, so why would they bother? Ladies increasingly don't attend, unless cruising for a mate, so it is mostly the more desperate amongst them who put in an appearance.

Then there is the "eye for an eye" aspect. Ambassadors and their secretaries make mental notes of which of their not-so-chers collègues didn't bother to put in an appearance this year, and operate on a tit for tat basis next time round. Twice in my life I had escaped in undiplomatic fashion from a National Day celebration and in the end Giorgio stopped taking me, which was a satisfactory outcome for both of us, all things considered.

The most recent, in London, was the party given by a

world super power. Sorry. *The* world super power. The security was such that, despite the requisite two pieces of identification with recent recognisable photograph and despite the official chauffeur driven limo with uniformed driver and unmistakable number plate, one was obliged to queue on foot in the pouring rain for what, I later learnt, was the best part of forty minutes, just to get close enough to the Presence to shake his hand.

I burst a gasket somewhere between minutes 21 and 23.5 and was led gibbering back to look for a taxi, (the car had been whisked off to a bullet proof area and was not seen again until nightfall,) muttering obscenities fit to set both our respective nations talking about all options being on the table.

On the other memorable occasion, the Ambassador in question was a lady and had decided, without warning her guests, to make a surprise happening of the evening. There were drums, singers and acrobats mingling with the crowd, which was charming. In order to ensure that nobody missed out on the spectacle, however, she locked the doors behind them as they came in, which was not. National Day celebrations should be a quick congratulatory handshake, a couple of pertinent remarks and a hasty retreat through the back door (the best ones have a separate exit, enabling one to leave without having to go back past one's host who might conceivably be standing there with a stop watch. There seemed, on this occasion, to be no escape route and we were eventually reduced to making our way to the service area (where the waiters were fortifying themselves with the ends of the bottles) and to legging it through the kitchen window.

Doubled up for the sprint across the lawns in full view of the reception room windows, we ran head first into a security guard with dog who was roaming the grounds on the look out for interlopers bringing in drugs (it was that sort of a country) or taking out the silver (they were those sort of guests) and were ignominiously restrained and frisked in full view of said guests who by this stage were so drunk they thought it was all part of the entertainment. There were some pretty serious diplomatic bridges to repair that year I recall.

This year Giorgio had decided we would have a men only vin d'honneur at 12 noon. I was reprieved.
Had we invited wives too, there would have been 1.000 people which would have meant handbag checks right through Hyde Park.

The whole of the front hall was, however, still completely blocked with dead bottles and glasses at 11o'clock the following morning, thus impeding the entry of my charity committee who trolled up for a meeting at that hour. The place smelt like a cheap bar. After my complaints, someone went round with a room spray, after which it smelt like a tart's parlour. I realise it is considered the height of vulgarity to mention sums like this in the crunchy era, but I feel it should be made known that between waiters, food and drink, we had spent thousands and thousands of pounds in the space of two and a half hours. I have been posted to countries in my itinerant existence where they could have wiped out their national debt with what we spend on National Days, or at the very leas t could have kept a large section of the population for their entire lives in comfort and gastronomic luxury. And now, to crown it all, the Evening Standard colour supplement wished to interview me about my totally hectic life style organising non-stop receptions. I could hardly tell them I considered it to be a waste of time and money and that in any case the secret was to delegate: the boss boys might have docked Giorgio's twenty percent.

I made an effort. Neat Armani trouser suit – yes, same one - minimalist make-up. Coffee and cookies waiting. I had the journalist sent up to the private sitting room on the third floor so that the staff could carry on with clearing up the aftermath. Up there, we would also be out of the way of the Italian Minister of Defence who was due to arrive during the course of the morning with the customary trail of hangers on.

Ms. Evening Standard had prepared the usual list of politically and socially engaging topics for me to address. How long had I been in London? (Do your homework.) What was my favourite recipe? (*Recipe?* That's why I employ a cook, for heaven's sake.) Who would I like to have to a dinner party if I could choose anyone, dead or alive? I'd actually been to quite a few dinners over the years where those two categories were indistinguishable, but I refrained from mentioning it. We were into our third biscuit when Jeeves puffed back up the stairs and announced, doubtfully, that there was a gentleman trying to gain admittance saying he had an appointment with me.

"Oh," says Ms. Evening Standard Colour Supplement, "that'll be our photographer. Kev." He may have been called Kev, he may not. It is irrelevant. What *was* relevant, was that after he had heaved all his heavy equipment up to the third floor, he took one look at my crisp trouser suit elegantly draped across our admittedly shabby private sitting room armchair, and intimated that he had rather hoped I would be dressed in a full length evening gown. And would pose for him beneath the chandeliers in the ballroom.

Which was where our Defence Minister discovered me, at ten o'clock in the morning in designer gown with train, stilettoed and heavily over made-up, gazing in admiration at the only one of the floral compositions which had survived the festivities of the day before.

Beagle sulked for a week. She thought she should have been in the forefront of the picture, reclining at my feet in faithful hound mode. As if Beagle *did* reclining. More to the point, they'd finished all the cookies before she could get at them.

CHAPTER NINE

To: Sarah
From: Manu
O.K. I rang the bastard. I must say he did sound rather miserable. Not even any need for face savings, you over-estimated his masculine pride. He must have come in for a major walloping. Maybe I should be thankful to the scrubber. He even had the grace to apologise. It'll cost him dear, of course. I was thinking of maybe a cruise. What do you reckon?
He says you will be in Rome this weekend – you might put the idea into his head for me.
xxx Manu

Incorrigible, impossible, irrepressible Manuela. He must have had severely masochistic tendencies to put up with her all these years. We were, indeed, heading for Rome, as he had told her. We were to accompany Important Persons to Italy.
We left our London residence with immense dignity. Gliding effortlessly into the lead, two pairs of police motorcyclists overtook us almost apologetically and headed off to the first road junction where they held up the traffic for a mere moment until we were through without having to alter our speed for one nano second. We could have been on automatic pilot. The same regular pace was maintained from start to finish. Once the motorcade had passed, we were again overtaken with quiet confidence and the operation was repeated effortlessly at each ensuing junction until we reached the airport. I do not believe there were any hard feelings, recriminations or suppressed road rage either on the part of the halted

motorists nor on that of the bemused pedestrian spectators who, in fact, smiled and waved with enthusiasm. I have no idea who they thought we were, but I waved and smiled back as regally as I could. Such an opportunity does not come often in one's lifetime and should not be passed up, I felt.

We boarded the plane and settled back feeling perfectly relaxed.

Upon arrival at our destination, things were slightly different. Now I have done this official cortège thing before in several countries and they are frequently hairy to the extreme. You descend from your Terribly Important Aircraft and hang about drinking tea or coffee or martini cocktails or palm wine according to location as if there were no tomorrow. You exchange niceties and inane comments, and concentrate on maintaining a spontaneously casual fixed smile just to the left or right of the flashbulbs as the top bods sit side by side bonding on extremely uncomfortable and invariably highly florid armchairs. This is in order that minions Nos. 15 through 27 have time to heave the right luggage into the (invariably) wrong car. For this particular job, a university degree in art history, economics and/or political sciences is recommended. Or a close relationship with Someone in Authority if all else fails. Then, just when everyone is starting to fidget, the paparazzi are wearying of finding a new angle and the also-rans are beginning to chat amongst themselves in whispers, you suddenly find that the airport VIP lounge has emptied, you are sitting there on your own, and the entire party has hot footed it into the waiting cars. At this juncture, you panic, throw all dignity to the winds, hurl yourself at the only remaining bullet proofed door, frequently losing a shoe in the process, and cling fast to whoever happens to be inside the limo as it revs furiously and sets off at 100kph in second gear in order to catch up with the rest of them.

On this occasion, we were supposed to attach ourselves discreetly to the very end of the official cortège. The discretion was due to the fact that, once within the city walls, the Important Personnages would be heading off to a very grand demeure indeed, whilst we ourselves would be making our way to the rather anonymous bit of suburb where we maintained a bedsitter for such necessities. Scaring everybody inside and out completely witless, our driver succeeded in making up for a slow start and eventually, trailing a cloud of dust and streaks of burning tyres, we had the outriders in our sights.

Ah. Outriders.

We had, it appeared, a couple of dozen motorcycles in front of us, half a dozen to each side and another half dozen or so bringing up the rear.. The majority of the riders were standing up in their stirrups in order to wave and gesticulate more effectively at anyone idiotic enough get in their way along the designated route. No bums on seats, no hands on handlebars. Lots of flashing lights and screaming sirens. Add to this a clutch of police cars fore and aft parp parping like Mr. Toad and furiously waving those horrid baton things at anything that encroached upon their piece of highway, from horrified hedgehogs to petrified pedestrians. Meanwhile the motorbikes were executing a slalom across three lanes of traffic, infuriating the other drivers and putting everyone's life at indescribable risk. Furthermore, there was a special security chap in an armoured car who did the entire journey at 180 kph with the passenger door wide open and one leg hanging out in case immediate evacuation should have been required. Let me add that these armoured cars weigh a ton: apply the brakes hard and you might be able to get some reduction in speed half a mile further on down the road, but no way could you avoid a domino style pile up with unthinkable consequences at that speed should you need to perform an emergency halt.

Reaching, queasily, the outskirts of the city, a contemptuous flap of the police baton signified that we were on our own now, and we peeled off toward our insalubrious suburb. We had just driven through twenty-three red lights and gone the wrong way up the busiest street in town, to the complete stupefaction of even the locals who must have seen similar scenes many times in their lives, and suddenly we were supposed to adapt in a split second to obeying what rules there might still be left in this holy city.

Strangely I didn't feel much like dinner that evening.

To: Sarah
From: Manu
How did the visit go? Were you curtseying all the way up the Via Veneto?
Did you mention the cruise?
xxx Manu

To: Manu
From: Sarah
No, I didn't mention the cruise but yes, I curtseyed to everything. Not something most of the Italians managed to achieve, I noted, with the sole exception of one notable VIP groupie, of course, who skidded the width of the lecture hall, was down on her knees in one swift movement the second HRH left the podium and then raced outside to hang around by the bumper of his car, waiting in vain for another wiggle of the Royal Eyebrows. In which position she was un-royally ignored by all present.

Paolo was much more cheerful and told me you would be in London by the end of the month. Your bed is made up. Is it all right if I invite him too? It's just that there is more room in the Embassy for you to shout at each other should you wish to do so without the neighbours intervening. Chucking of china objects is, however, taboo. Some of them go back to the 16th century.

Can't wait, Sarah

*   *   *   *

Upon due consideration, I decided not to tell Giorgio I had invited Manu and Paolo to use our guest rooms whilst they settled their differences. I thought I would choose my moment. Such moments were usually on the way back from an excellent meal where he had been wined and dined wisely and well, quality over quantity and company to match. It did not take long for such an opportunity to present itself. A smattering of minor royalty, a three star chef, a gaggle of influential CEOs, an historic abode, vintage champagne, a title or three and enough highly placed politicians to provide fodder for a telegram upon the morrow. Filthy weather, but one can't have everything.

He emerged into the wind and rain socially and gastronomically sated. I seized my moment before the bloody weather could ruin everything.

He grumped of course at length about having the great Manuela/Paolo reunion under his roof. Men hate all manner of histrionics, more especially other people's, and he muttered furiously about it all being a waste of time and space in general and a pain in a certain part of the anatomy in particular.

It was not, however, this particular part of his anatomy that was troubling him at three o'clock on the morning of their scheduled arrival when he awoke with violent stomach pains after consuming a relatively innocuous dinner at a relatively innocuous Embassy. Other people's problems were pushed into the background: they would just have to sort it out by themselves. They were immensely understanding, and Paolo decided to whisk Manuela off on a cruise instead to try and patch things up. Giorgio, meanwhile, was whisked into hospital to have some tests performed.

It may not be known extensively in or around diplomatic circles, (and indeed why should it be?) that H.E. does not possess a pair of pyjamas. Of any description. When, therefore, the stomach ache was diagnosed as appendicitis by S.O.S Doctors, who are the only ones awake at that hour, we whizzed off to hospital bearing an elegant holdall containing some Taylor of Old Bond Street Lemon and Lime Shaving Cream, a Geo. Trumper of Curzon St. Super Badger Shaving Brush and a Penhaligon Cologne in a 2 litre bottle. Travelling light as is his wont. A couple of linen handkerchiefs with rolled edges hand-stitched by nuns in the hope of buying themselves eternal redemption were thrown in as an afterthought. No pyjamas.

So the ambassadorial blood tests and subsequent ultrasound were somewhat lacking in sartorial elegance. Think off-white and faded baby blue back-opening nightdress at fashionable just above the knee level, topped by shrunken dressing gown sterilised to within an inch of it's life, (both private clinic standard issue), combined with black knee socks and Todds car shoes from model's personal collection. In this season's latest upset intestine colour.

When they subsequently diagnosed a viral infection and excluded appendicitis, (viral infections were IN, that year), they stuffed him with antibiotics and painkillers and sent him back home to his pinstripes, his cook and his loving wife, and the order is significant. The remains of the day drifted by in a drug induced haze under the influence of which sundry non-specific telegrams were not very urgently dispatched until they suddenly called him back to the clinic saying they would quite like to take another look. And, say, operate this evening around 10 p.m.? If you haven't, like, got anything better to do? Sir?

I was out the door and headed for our local friendly emporium before he could open his mouth, but he caught up with me on my mobile.

The only, but ONLY, kind of pyjama he would be prepared to countenance would be a Pure Silk number.

And had I taken his inside leg measurement?

I called him back with the chilling news that pure silk pyjamas cost a hundred and twenty quid and not even bespoke.

Pure cotton you could get for thirty.

He asked where I'd put his tennis shorts and tee shirts and intimated that I could get my diplomatic hide back home forthwith and start packing them. This was what he intended to wear in the most exclusive clinic his insurance would contemplate underwriting: the one which costs the equivalent of a week in a luxury spa just to get through the swing doors before even thinking about medical attention. And, as subsequently emerged, before consuming any food either since, after one glance at the menu, all form of nourishment had to be driven over from the Embassy kitchens and smuggled into his luxury suite between hourly Nurse Patrols. In order not to offend, (we dip. wives are taught to rise to such occasions - statistically, I am sure that we consume far more eye of camel or testicle of yak than our spice-free spouses,) I spent the next three days flushing bowls of soup and purée down the expensively sanitised and fragrant toilet.

But to return to the pyjamas. I ran straight back into the local friendly emporium, patron saint of all emergency hospital admissions, and grabbed an attractive line in two-tone grey "with" cotton (whatever that means), reduced to half the price of a handmade handkerchief. Ripped off the label on my way back. Nothing wrong with THOSE, thank you.

To: Frankie
Cc: Alex
From: Maman
Papa just celebrated his last year in active service by having his appendix out. All is well and he is back home with a mild case of post-operative blues not helped by his refusing to take any painkillers in case they are fattening and by the surgeon's veto upon his frequenting the gym for at least a month. Grosvenor Square will sorely miss the sight of H.E. in pinstripes and furled umbrella with shiny black trainers and lavender hued sports bag heading for Virgin Active three times a week, but they will just have to survive it. Send him emails to cheer him up please.

To: Papa
From: Frankie
Get well soon! Everybody sends kisses!
Loooove, Frankie

To: Papa
Cc: Maman
From: Alex
I just got engaged!.
Happy?
Yeah, me too. Very.
Thought it might cheer you up.
Kisses, Alex

CHAPTER TEN

The bombshell cheered Giorgio up so considerably he was back in the gym at risk of bursting his remaining stitches within a fortnight. The fear of not fitting into his wedding outfit was keeping him awake at nights far more than the fear of encouraging a post- operative hernia from all that enforced exercise. We tried to explain the difference between a beer paunch and a bloated tummy due to all the gas they pump into you during keyhole surgery, but common sense would not prevail. Cocktail parties, on the other hand, he considered would overtax his physical resources at this delicate stage of convalescence. Which was why I found myself, a few days later, knocking back the first glass of the white and bubbly prior to greeting innumerable guests in their penguin suits whom I would once again pretend to recognise. I was dressed in a perfectly innocuous long black dress adorned with a quivering plastic lobster and one bloodshot, independently swivelling eyeball nestling where anybody else might have had a cleavage. The dress code was "Black Tie with a Surreal Element." We were celebrating the opening of an exhibition on this theme at the Victoria and Albert museum. Bowler hats, pipes and apples precariously balanced above surreal hairstyles abounded. The conversation, when analysed was pretty surreal too, though not too many people noticed, accustomed as we all were to total non-sequiturs at one's average cocktail party. "I understand His Excellency is having something removed?"

"Yes, his wife is standing in."
"Standing in what?"
"Not Jimmy Choos, that's for sure."
"Bless you."
"No no, I said Jimmy Choos."
"Sorry. Can't hear a thing over the noise. *What* did Jimmy choose?"
"Shoes."
"Sorry, can't hear you through this parsley in my ears."
And so on.

To: Maman
From: Frankie
Please do something about Alex.
She's threatening to walk down the aisle in some completely outrageous outfit she picked up at the local flea market with an organist playing reggae music in the background.
F

To: Frankie
From: Maman
She's only winding you up. Probably just nerves. Will Have a Word.
M

To: Manu
From: Sarah
Hope all is going really well for you both and that you will be back in time for the wedding because – would you believe it? Alex is getting married. And apparently to someone perfectly normal. Regulation

number of arms, legs, speaks a language we can understand. Has a good job. Doesn't partake of illegal substances - doesn't even *smoke*. There *is* a God.

Not easy planning a wedding from a distance, however. Try helping someone choose the church music over the telephone with the CD remote control in one hand, volume full blast, Alex singing along on the other end of the line and her future husband in the background going "could you ask your Mother if I really HAVE to *be* there?"

xxxxx Sarah

To: Sarah

From: Manu

I think we've made it. Just sailing round the Cape of Good Hope, which helps. Paolo being very sweet and I am behaving beautifully.

All love, Manu

CHAPTER ELEVEN

We were approaching the end of the line.

In the light of our imminent retirement, I traipsed wearily around London looking for a table.

Not just *any* table, mind you, but a table which would reflect our changed circumstances and suit our future lifestyle. One which would replace the Embassy antique number which could seat forty assorted notables with lashings of pomp and formality, Himself presiding at the far end and Herself grinning manically at the other. And Himself regularly having to send waiters sprinting up to my end to order me to make eye contact pronto because he'd run out of conversation with his neighbours and said his little speech and now wanted to get up and go for coffee prior to sending them all home. Whereas I was usually just warming up.

The rectangular item was to be replaced by a cosy little round table for eight - a number which we esteemed should not be exceeded if one wished to actually *talk* to one's guests. The main drawback to this solution, as I saw it, was that he would now get to monitor my conversation and doubtless issue Warning Glares whenever I started to get irreverent, frivolous or just plain had-it-up-to-here rude.

Oh dear - life was tough and frequently boring up at the top, but the freedom to choose one's own topics of conversation was something I would miss dearly.

To: Michael
From: Sarah

Just to say thank you for finding Manuela – seriously the most important thing you ever did for me.
We are packing up our goods and chattels and heading back to Rome for good.
Rendez-vous twice a year to catch up? Just for old times sake? I have no doubt about your ability to find us.
Best of luck in everything,
xxx Sarah

*   *   *   *

We began counting the spoons. Anything missing from the Residence was our personal responsibility We began counting the remaining vintage and garbage wines in the cellar. We began trying to remember which were our carpets and personal belongings and which belonged to the Embassy. We began trying to eradicate traces of Beagle wherever she had left her mark upon the furniture and fittings. We began saying, very reluctantly, our goodbyes. Beagle took up a strategic position under the table on a permanent basis, following the progress of the packers with an attentive eye, ear and nose. The party was over.

Thank you, staff. You were part of the family and allowed me to lead a charmed and privileged existence. Thank you, Giorgio, for your forbearance. Thank you, daughters, for surviving your vagabond upbringing and turning out to be not only normal, but even delightful, human beings. Thank you, Beagle, for staying alive and giving me the excuse I needed to don blue jeans and head out into the countryside for a breath of fresh air in between those frequently interminable receptions. On the whole, it wasn't such a bad life if you could just get your priorities sorted and keep your sense of humour.

Our successor was moving in at the front door as we moved out of the back.

His Excellency was leaving. Long live His Excellency.

My Welsh dog walker friend summed it up as she watched the removers sitting on the steps smoking themselves to an early grave.

"Hanging up your clogs, then, is it?"

I nodded.

She thought about it for a moment.

"We'll miss the Beagle," she said.